The Law Relating to Child in Conflict with Law

The Law Relating to Child in Conflict with Law

Dr. Gunjan Srivastava

First Published, 2021

Published by

Kalpaz Publications
C-30, Satyawati Nagar,
Delhi – 110052
Ph.: 011-47034999, 9811692060
www.kalpazpublications.com
E-mail: kalpaz@hotmail.com

Printed at: Gyan Press, Delhi.

Cataloging in Publication Data--DK

Courtesy: D.K. Agencies (P) Ltd. <docinfo@dkagencies.com>

Srivastava, Gunjan, author.
The law relating to child in conflict with law / Gunjan Srivastava.
pages cm
Includes bibliographical references.
ISBN 9789353243333

1. Juvenile justice, Administration of--India. 2. Juvenile delinquency--Law and legislation--India. I. Title.

LCC KNS4720.S65 2020 | DDC 364.360954 23

Dedicated to
My Loving Husband
And my Son

Contents

Justice Neeraj Tiwari JUDGE HIGH COURT AT ALLAHABAD **Dt.07.05.2021**

Foreword

The enactment of the Juvenile Justice Act, 2000 marked a watershed moment in the realm of juvenile justice whereby a rights-based legal regime was created in India. The legal regime envisaged under the Juvenile Justice Act, 2000 provided for treatment of children in conflict with law with the avowed objective of reform, rehabilitation and reintegration. However, in the aftermath of the dastardly gang-rape of a young medical student in the national capital in December, 2012 led to a rethink on the soft approach of law towards delinquent juveniles, especially those who are on the verge of majority and are accused of committing adult-like crimes such as rape and murder. The Juvenile Justice Act, 2015 is the product of this paradigm shift in state policy towards the children in the age group of 16-18.

The book entitled "The Law Relating to Child in Conflict with Law" authored by Dr Gunjan Srivastava, meticulously explores the wide ranging issues on the subject. The book has systematically encapsulated in its seven chapters, not only the history of child rights in India but its gradual development post Convention on the Rights of the Child and takes us to the present legal regime which makes it possible to treat a child as an adult in certain situations. The book contains a very lucid and exhaustive discussion on the critical issues such as age determination of children in conflict with law, the sentencing policy etc. The text is very judiciously supplemented with the leading judicial pronouncements of the High Courts and the Supreme Court of India. In my opinion the highlight of the book is the chapter in which the author has analytically presented the empirical study on the issue of juvenile delinquency. It is commendable that the book not only presents a comparative overview of child rights laws in different jurisdictions, but also what the society thinks about the treatment of delinquent children under the present juvenile justice regime in India.

JUDGE HIGH COURT AT ALLAHABAD

I congratulate Dr. Gunjan Srivastava for bringing out an excellent work at a time when greater awareness and understanding of criminality among children is required to implement the Juvenile Justice Act, 2015 in letter and spirit. The simple, lucid yet authoritative language of the book is another major highlight.

I believe that the book shall be a very useful resource for everyone to understand the legal framework for treatment of children in conflict with law. Students, lawyers, public prosecutors, police and members of judiciary shall also find it useful as a reference book.

I wish the author and the book grand success!

(Neeraj Tiwari)

Preface

The Children Act, 1960 was enacted by the parliament as the model legislation that aimed at conceptualizing a system, separate from the criminal justice under the code of Criminal Procedure, 1973, for the treatment of juvenile delinquents. However the Juvenile Justice (Care and Protection of children) Act, 2000 was enacted for the protection of children as it for the first time provided for the 'juvenile in conflict with law' and 'children in need of care and protection' to be kept separately. This segregation aims to curtail the corruption of the innocent child from the influence of the criminal juvenile. The Act was amended twice in 2006 and 2011 to mend the gaps in its implementation and the welfare of child. With the increasing number of crimes committed by children in the age group of 16-18 years in recent years it evident that the existing law under the Juvenile Justice (Care and Protection of Children) Act, 2000 were also not well equipped to tackle child delinquency of this age group. The most note-worthy feature of all enactments since 1850 has been that they were all moving in one direction of bringing an increasing number of children within the protective umbrella of juvenile justice. Nevertheless, on December 2015 a big backward step was taken by the Government by introducing the possibility of sending 16- 18 year old child to jail in exceptional circumstances under the J. J. Act, 2015[1]. Presently, since 15 January 2016, the J.J. Act, 2015 is applicable throughout India.

The new Juvenile Justice (Care and Protection of Children) Act, 2015 precisely shows that Juvenile justice system has moved from the welfare model of Juvenile Justice introduced in 2000 to crime control model (as introduced in 2015). It define child as a person who has not attained the age of 18 years, but it has authorized the courts to treat 16- 18 years old children charged with commission of heinous offences as adult and deal with them in adult criminal court.

Enforcement of this Act force the juvenile to enter into the criminal regime as transferring to the adult system breeds more criminal activities by young persons in their later lives. Treating the children between the age group of 16-18 differently also violates Article 14, 15(3) and 20(1) of Indian Constitution. Arbitrary transfer of juvenile cases to adult criminal system which may cause violation of very foundation of Constitution. The very spirit of Article 20(1) is also undermined in the existing law as the Article prohibits the infliction of greater punishment than what would have been applicable under the law of land but the provisions of new J.J.Act, 2015. This Act has given a sword in the hand of angry parents who want to restrain their children from getting into elopement, which increased number of cases of kidnapping and sexual assault against the juvenile. The enforcement of The Juvenile Justice Act, 2015 has also raised controversy regarding the Age of Consent, when read with the Protection of Children from Sexual Offences Act, 2012 (POCSO Act) and the Prohibition of Child Marriage Act (PCM Act). The POCSO Act prescribes the age of Consent is 18 years and if any offence is committed by a Juvenile under the POCSO Act then as per the section 23 of the POCSO Act it will be dealt as per the provision of Juvenile Justice Act, 2000 (Now as per the new amended Act). Precisely the PCM Act states that since the child marriages are voidable but not void in such a situation, the juvenile who are involved in love relation can marry each other and can enter in consensual sexual act. Here it is crucial to note that the consensual sexual act may attract the provision of POCSO Act and as per J.J.Act, 2015 the juvenile may be tried as adult. This book containing seven chapters, has looked at Juvenile Justice Mechanism of India with special focus on heinous crimes committed by children, as well as on common elements and responses to the serious offences by children within justice systems across the world, highlighting the positive and negative impact of approaches and practices used.

This book is an attempt made to enunciate the underlying concepts of the Juvenile Justice Law and to give brief analysis on legal mechanism along with the judicial pronouncement and judicial approach. Comprehensively while writing this book the author has deliberately focused on the international and national aspects of differential treatment of child offenders and analyzed the national and international instrument to know about the reasons why a delinquent juvenile is treated differently from an adult, though the offence committed may be similar and also examines the status of life imprisonment and death penalty awarded to juveniles for the heinous crimes committed, in various countries as well as in India and has critically analysed the differences in sentencing options in different countries and reviewed the practice of the death penalty in the international prospective. Along with this the cautious effort has been made in analysing the legislative mechanism dealing with the children who come in conflict law and the judicial responses to the age of criminal responsibility and sentencing of the child offenders. The decisions of the Supreme Court and various High Courts have been incorporated in the book at proper places.

The statistical data and the outcome of public opinion sought through empirical study on child delinquency along with table and graphs made it very comprehensive to the reader. A descriptive analysis of juvenile justice system of various countries and the international and national aspects of differential treatment of child offenders, has made it a must read book for academicians, judge, lawyers, civil society groups and functionaries of the juvenile system. The usefulness of the book is judged by those for whom it is. I shall be highly considered to have been rewarded if the book could be helpful to the students of law in appreciating the essential / special characteristics of the Juvenile Justice Act 2015.

This book is an unpretentious effort at critically analyzing and appreciating the viability of the mechanism proposed by the new measure under the Juvenile Justice Act 2015. In the present work every attempt has been made to welcome all such suggestions which were received by me as I had the privilege of valuable suggestions from my senior and learned professors from various Universities. My vocabulary fails to express my gratitude and thankfulness to my mentor and reverend teacher, Prof. Kumar Askand Pandey, RMNLU Lucknow, for his contribution in completing this book successfully. He constantly inspired me to work on this subject and has given me his valuable guidance and blessings. I owe my deep depth of gratitude to him. I am also grateful to Hon'ble Mr. Justice Neeraj Tiwari, Allahabad High Court who has given time in reading and writing a foreword for the book in spite of his busy schedule.

I wish to record my personal attachment and sense of gratitude to my loving and caring husband whose immense effort and encouragement that he made for my studies is peerless. A special mention for the time that I devoted on this book which in fact I should have spent with my five year old son. I cannot thank enough for his contribution, who happily allow me to share my time that was rightfully 'his' time.

However every possible effort have been made to present the matter in simple and comprehensibly easy language for the benefit of the readers and I believe that the book shall prove to be must read for everyone interested in understanding the present justice delivery mechanism on the care and protection of the children in India.

All the critical comments and suggestions on the book shall be highly appreciated and will be incorporated in the next edition.

— Dr. Gunjan Srivastava

List of Tables

List of Figures

- Do you think that children to be involved in crime should be punished for their crime in a similar manner as adults? 189
- Do think that a child should be punished for very serious crime in a similar manner as an adult? 190
- Do you think agree that child alleged to be in conflict with law (apprehended for committing a crime) should be placed in police lock up? 191
- Do you agree that there should be a joint proceeding of a child alleged to be in conflict with law with a person who is not a child when the child has committed crime in his association? 192
- Do you agree that when a child alleged to have committed a non-bailable offence is apprehended or detained by the police, he should be released on bail? 193
- Do you think that minor should be treated same as adult for criminal responsibility if he completes 18 years during pendency of case? 194
- Do you agree that when a child, who has been found to have committed a heinous offence, attains the age of twenty one years and is yet to complete prescribed term of stay in a place of safety, should be sent to adult prison? 195
- Do you agree that children should be sentenced to death or for life imprisonment without the possibility of release for very serious offences? 196
- Do you think that children should be given special exemption from criminal responsibility? 197
- Do you think that reducing the age of criminal responsibility can help in curing the child delinquency (child coming into conflict with law) problem? 198
- What do you think is the major cause that leads children to commit crime? 199

List of Case and Decisions

1. Abuzar Hossain alias Gulam Hossain vs State of West Bengal (2012)10 SC488, para 36 (iv)
2. Amrutlal Someshwar Joshi v. State of Mahasrastra1994 AIR 2516, 1994 SCC (6) 186
3. Arnit Das v. State of Bihar,AIR 2000 SC 2264: (2000)(2) JCC(SC)545
4. Ashwani Kumar Saxena v. State of M.P. (2012) 9 SCC 750
5. Babloo Passi v. State of Jharkhand, AIR 2009 SC 314: (2008) 13VSCC 133: (2008) 13 SCALE 137: 2009 (1) Chand Cri C170.
6. Bharat Bhushan v. State of Himachal Pradesh, AIR 2013 SC2018:CrLJ 2932: 2013 AIR SCW 2911
7. Bijendra Singh v. State of Haryana AIR 2005 SC 2262:2005 AIR SCW 2046
8. Birad Mal Singhvi v. Anand Purohit, AIR 1988 SC 1796: 1988 Supp SCC 604
9. Court on Its Own Motion v. Department of Women & Child Development [Writ Petition (Civil) 8889 of 2011]
10. Court on Its Own Motion v. Department of Women & Child Development [Writ Petition (Civil) 8889 of 2011]
11. Gaurav Jain v. Union of India, AIR 1993 SC 2178
12. Girijesh v. State of U.P, the High Court of Allahabad vide its judgment dated 15.04.2015
13. Girijesh v. State of U.P., the High Court of Allahabad
14. Gopinath Ghosh v. State of West Bengal AIR 1984 SC 237:1984 (Supp) SCC 228: 1984 Cr LJ 168

15. Graham v. Florida, 120 S Ct. 2001 (2010)
16. Hari Ram v. State of Rajasthan, Criminal Appeal No. 907 of 2009 (Arising out of S.L.P. (Cri) No. 3336 of 2006)
17. Hiralal Mallick v.State of Bihar, (1977) 4 SCC 44: 1977 SCC (Cri) 538
18. In Siddu @ Siddeshwar v. State, [Criminal Appeal No. 200465 of 2015, decision dated 23.04.2016] before the Karnataka High Court
19. Jameel v. State of Maharashtra, (2007)11SCC 420: (2007) 2 SCALE 32
20. Jitendrea Ram v. State of Jharkhand, 2006 (2)JCC 994: (2006) 9 SCC 428
21. Jyoti Prakash Rai v. State of Bihar, AIR 2008 SC 1696: 2008 (2) JCC
22. Kulai Ibrahim alias Ibrahim v. State, Rep. by the Inspector of police B- 1,Coimbatore, AIR 2014 SC 2726:2014 AIR SCW 4022:2014 CrLJ 3775
23. Lallan Singh v. State of Uttar Pradesh 2002 Cr LJ 1242
24. Lingala Vijay Kumar v. Public Prosecutor, (1978) 4 SCC 196
25. Madan Singh v. State of Bihar, 4622(2000)
26. Mahadeo s/o Kerba Maske vs. State of Maharastra and Another (2013) 14 SCC 637
27. Mahendra Singh and Others v. State of Rajasthan 2015(13) SCALE 599
28. Maneka Gandhi v. Union of India, (1978) 1 SCC 248
29. Master Abhishek (minor) Vs State: 2005 VI AD Delhi
30. Mohd. Haris alias Ayen allias Aryan v. State of Uttarakhand, 2014 CrLJ (NOC) 160 (Uttar)
31. Munna v. State of Uttar Pradesh, (1982) 1 SCC 545: AIR 1982 SC 806: 1982 Cr LJ 620
32. Parag Bharti v. State of Uttar Pradesh Criminal Appeal No.486 of 2016 (arising out of Special Leave Petition (Crl)) No.5839 of 2013 (Decided on May 12, 2016)

33. Pratap Singh v. State of Jharkhand, AIR 2005 SC2731L2005) 3SCC551:2005 SCC(Cri) 742:2005 Cr LJ 3091: 2005 Cri LR 288 (SC)
34. Rajendra Chandra v. State of Chhattisgarh & Others,(2002) 2 SCC 287
35. Ram Deo Chauhan v. State of Assam (2000) 7 SCC 455
36. Rohtas v. State of Haryana, AIR (1979), SC, 1839
37. Roper v. Simmons, 543 U.S. 551(2005)
38. Salil Bali v/s Union of India & Anr.: Writ petition (C)No. 10 of 2013 With Writ petition (C)No(S).14, 42, 85, 90 and 182 of 2013 With Writ petition (Crl)No.6 of 2013 & T.C.(C)No. 82 of 2013
39. Sheela Barse v. Union of India, (1986) 3 SCC 596: AIR 1986 SC 1773
40. State of Tamil Nadu Vs. K. Shyam Sunder, (2011) 8 SCC 737
41. Sushil Kumar v. Rakesh Kumar, (2003) 8 SCC 673
42. Umesh Chandra v. State of Rajasthan, AIR 1982 SC 1057
43. Vimal Candha v. Vikash Choudhry, (2008) 8 Scale 608
44. Vishnu v. State of Maharastra, 2006(1) JCC 78: (2006) 1 SCC 283

Abbreviations

SJPU	Special Juvenile Police Unit
(ICCPR)	International Covenant on Civil and Political Rights
CCI	Child Care Institution
CCL	The Child/ren alleged to be in conflict with law DCPU District Child Protection Unit
CICL	Child(ren) in Conflict with the Law
CINCP	Child(ren) in Need of Care and Protection
CJM	Chief Judicial Magistrate
CMM	Chief Metropolitan Magistrate
Cr.P.C	Code of Criminal Procedure, 1973
CWC	Child Welfare Committee
CWPO	Child Welfare Police Officer
DCPU	District Child Protection Unit
DLSA	District Legal Services Authority
FIR	First Information Report
ICCPR	International Covenant on Civil and Political Rights
ICP	Individual Care Plan
ICPS	Integrated Child Protection Scheme
IPC	Indian Penal Code, 1860
ITPA, 1956	Immoral Traffic Prevention Act, 1956
JJ Act, 2000	Juvenile Justice (Care and Protection of Children) Act, 2000

JJ Act, 2015	Juvenile Justice (Care and Protection of Children) Act, 2015
JJ MR, 2016	Juvenile Justice (Care and Protection of Children) Model Rules, 2016
JJB	Juvenile Justice Board
JJWA	The Juvenile Justice and Welfare Act
JMFC	Judicial Magistrate of First Class
LSWDO	Local Social Welfare and Development Officer
NGO	Non-governmental Organisation
NHRC	National Human Rights Commission
NLSIU	Centre for Child and the Law, National Law School of India University, Bangalore
NLSA	National Legal Services Authority
OH	Observation Home
PJU	Police Juvenile Unit
PO	Probation Officer
POCSO Act	Protection of Children from Sexual Offences Act
RCACHR	Rights of the Child, and the American Convention on Human Rights
SBR	Social Background Report
SCH	Secure Children's Home
SHRC	State Human Rights Commission
SIR	Social Investigation Report
SJPU	Special Juvenile Police Unit
SLSA	State Legal Services Authority
SLSA	State Legal Services Authority
UNC	U.N. Convention
UNCRC	United Nations Convention on the Rights of the Child

UNCRPD	United Nations Convention on the Rights of Persons with Disabilities
YOI	Young Offender Institution or Secure Training Centre
PSC	Parliamentary Standing Committee
UN	United Nations

1

Introduction

1.1. Introduction

> "*Part of being a child is getting into mischief. Mischievous activities of children are expected and accepted as well, by the society. However it depends on how far the mischievous activity is tolerable.*"

The treatment of juvenile delinquents has been a much-debated issue in India as the society prepares itself to come to terms with the rising graph in juvenile delinquency. While there is no denying the fact that delinquent juveniles lack mental maturity and are often driven by their passion. Developing a just, effective juvenile justice system has been proven a herculean task. Policymakers were struggling with the challenge of balancing two opposing themes—the welfare of child offenders and public safety. Since the past century, juvenile justice policy has swung like a pendulum from one theme to the other. Finally, on Dec 22, 2015 the Juvenile Justice (Care and Protection of Children) Act, 2015 (here in after referred as J. J. Act, 2015) received parliamentary approval. The government justified the law as a measure that would have a deterrent effect on potential juvenile offenders. However, the opponents argue that the law would defeat the objective of having the separate juvenile justice system, and would not serve the goal of deterrence. This study has evaluated the potency of the counter-claim which proposes that the existing law be better implemented, and thereby examine the necessity for the introduction of a new approach governing juvenile policy in India.

Children constitute about 41 percent of India's total population. Over 2462 children, mostly between the age group of 16 to 18 years, have been apprehended for crimes like rape and murder across the country in 2016, the highest in last decade. As many as 44171 such cases were registered in 2016 as compared to 21088 cases in 2006. According to NCRB data, 44171 of the total of juveniles apprehended in 2016, 32577 were in the 16-18 age group, 10957 were in the age group of 12-16 and 637 were between the age group 7-12. Whereas, 27963 such youngsters below 18 years of age were held in 2012, 31725 in 2013, 33526 in 2014, 31396 during 2015, 3041 in 2017 and 28677 in 2018. Data reveals that the number of juvenile crimes shows a slight downfall in 2015. The data shows increasing cases of rape by juveniles between the age group of 16 to 18. It is pertinent to mention here two highly gruesome gang rape cases that shook the public conscience. One occurred in Delhi on 12 December 2012 and another happened in South Mumbai in July 2013. On conviction, the court awarded the death penalty and life imprisonment to the adult offenders as per the magnitude of their role in the crime. However, the maximum penalty available to the Juvenile Justice Board for the minors involved in the crimes was three years in juvenile homes. The cases of murder by juveniles have also shown a surge in the last ten years. As many as 605 youngsters below the age of 18 years were apprehended for murder in 2006 as against 901 arrests in 2016. NCRB data, states that 8464 juveniles were apprehended in Madhya Pradesh, 7712 in Maharashtra, 2,943 in Rajasthan, 2,394 in Chhattisgarh and 2,085 in Gujarat in 2016. In the same year, 1,229 adolescents were apprehended in Andhra Pradesh, 2,810 in Tamil Nadu, 1,587 in Uttar Pradesh and 2,626 in Bihar, the data said. The maximum numbers of cases against juveniles were reported in Madhya Pradesh 20.6 percent (7,369 cases) and Maharashtra with 18.4 percent (6,606 cases) is on second number. Delhi is on third number with 7.0 percent (2,499 cases) during 2016. Most of the juveniles apprehended for crimes were in the age group of 16 to 18 years (73.8 percent), (32,577 out of 44,171) during 2016. This study has looked at Juvenile Justice Mechanism of India with special focus on heinous crimes committed by children, as well as on common elements and responses to the serious offences by children within justice systems across the world, highlighting the positive and negative impact of the approaches/ practices used. It has then reviewed the practices from a number of specific countries and analysed their strengths and weaknesses in order to identify effective responses to the serious offences by children. This study has aimed at critically analysing the viability of the mechanism proposed by the new measure under the Juvenile Justice Act 2015.

1.2. Rationale for differential sentencing to child offender

In order to understand the need for differential treatment of child offender, it is significant to appreciate the rationale for such differentiation, more so today when there is a sentiment intensified to exclude children from the ambit of juvenile justice protection, which the legislature, to some extent, has succeeded. Generally, the heinousness of crime is co-related with the maturity of the juvenile. The Transfer System for the Research and Development Psychology proves to the contrary, that the seriousness of the crime cannot be counted as determining factor of the maturity of the child, signifying that the determination of maturity is based on a flawed parameter.[1] According to the psychologists, the brain of the human being is divided into two parts, the first one is cognitive abilities and second one is social psychological capability. Neuroscience findings show that while the cognitive capacity of a child above the age of sixteen is similar to that of an adult, while the psychological maturity is not.[2] The development of cognitive abilities makes the child gradually capable of multidimensional, cautious and hypothetical thinking, improving his ability to understand decisions.[3] Through the development of their cognitive faculties, children often know right from wrong; six years old may know that it is wrong to kill, but he is not sure about what killing is, or why it is wrong.[4] However, maturity of judgment involves the exercise of both cognitive abilities and psychological capabilities.[5] While psychological exhalations suggest that children lack emotional and social capabilities that are better developed in adults.[6] For the convenience of understanding the mental status of the child it is significant to discuss second part of brain of individual first, as the juveniles above the age of 16 shows the former, the latter is absent. The psychosocial capabilities control socio-emotional part, which, is related to emotions and is controlled by punishments or rewards.[7] This part of brain enables a person to control his impulse, with reason to guide his behaviour, the long-term consequences of his acts being factored in. The research also steadily proves that the children have a greater tendency than adults to make decisions based primarily on emotions such as fear, anger, rather than driven by logic or reason.[8] Due to this precise inducement, the youth tend to commit such acts, which involve high risk, and no or very little incentive.[9] The research signifies that youth while making decisions, are unable to look forward more than a few days in future[10] and thereby they focus on the short-term payback rather than on long-term impacts. Further, the studies established that stressful situations only intensify the risk that emotion, rather than rational thought, will lead the choice children make.[11] The research shows that this part of brain undergoes a massive turbulences and changes during childhood and therefore children tend to commit certain acts that give them a high and feeling of sensation. In order to feel the sensation, youth in their ages of 16-18 have a high tendency to take risk without appraising the pros and cons of the same.[12] The role played by the emotion is intensified only in stressful situation. Consequently, lack of proper development of the psychosocial maturity make children unable to apply their cognitive skills effectively, and are persuaded by emotional and social variables.[13]

The studies of Neuroscience impute such difference in maturity between a child and an adult to the difference in growth of the prefrontal cortex in children. The prefrontal cortex play leading role in performance of importance of functions such as planning, reasoning, judgment and impulse control and mood regulation. Therefore, the prefrontal cortex is main responsible factor in controlling the propensity of a person towards impulsive activities. The prefrontal cortex is in developing stage during adolescence. The scientific research, proven that because of the absence of a well-functioning prefrontal cortex, adolescent tend to use a part of the brain that referred to as amygdala during decision making. The amygdala played pivotal role for impulsive and aggressive behaviour. However, in case of adults, the prefrontal cortex maintains a balance to the emotions and impulses originating from the amygdala. Adolescence, is the time when because of the dominance of the amygdala over the prefrontal cortex, children often react in line with gut instinct and unable to balance their instincts against rational and reasoned responses. Consequently, adolescents, even at the age of sixteen are more prone to be influenced than adults. They are also less likely to evaluate the repercussion of their acts and future outcomes before acting and therefore are likely to over emphasise the rewards without fully analysing the risk involved. Consequently, they are also unable to understand and appreciate the future consequences of their current actions. The scientific research strongly reinstate that maturity measured through risk appraisal abilities, is linked to the growth of the brain, which is gradually developed as the age of the individual advances. This suggests that all children of a given age have the same level of maturity, since the growth of the prefrontal cortex remains the same at a particular age. Therefore, the commission of a serious offence by a juvenile is not a sign of maturity of the child, as maturity remains incessant. Instead commission of such crimes by children is bound to occur in circumstances of neglect, exploitation and abuse (…) the child having been socialised in a way where his/her decision making goes awry, rather than in a context of premeditation and criminality.[14]

Further, it is acknowledged that there exists no scientifically precise method to determine the maturity of an individual.[15] Such determination would exceed the limits of science, the result being fraught with errors and arbitrariness.[16] Since such a case-by-case analysis of maturity to determine culpability is scientifically impossible, a presumption of maturity exists beyond the age of eighteen. The first part of the brain is cognitive part and it is helpful in long-term planning, evaluation of pros and cons, and in controlling excitements and emotions. The interrelation between these two parts of the brain gets matured towards the last phase of juvenility or around the age of twenty years. Most of the juvenile learn to control their impulsive behaviour at this age and maturity in their behaviour becomes visible. All these changes in the brain take place between sixteen to twenty years and therefore, the age group of sixteen to eighteen is most prone to criminality. This is the reason why in order to decide a threshold, eighteen years is globally accepted as the age of juvenility and the same is the reason why juveniles should be treated differently in the criminal justice system as against their adult counterparts. These psychological and scientific facts and principles justify the purely reformatory approaches towards delinquent juveniles. The age group of sixteen to eighteen is that period of juvenility when the child is passing through the most crucial phase of his physical, emotional and psychological development. This is the most critical period of transition in his/her life and cannot be viewed in isolation or in separation from the childhood. We have in our country the age of eighteen years as the minimum age for taking many an important decision or even for conferring certain rights.[17]

Although by age sixteen, adolescent reach at level of intellectual maturity; psychological maturity continuous to develop into early adulthood. According to Ruban C. ...the biological age of majority is close to 22 years and the pertinent parts that govern impulsivity, judgment, planning for the future, foresight of consequences, and other characteristics that make people morally culpable, develops after attaining the age of maturity.[18] Adolescents do not put fact together and draw conclusion the way adults do.[19]

PSYCHOSOCIAL MATURITY AND INTELLECTUAL ABILITY

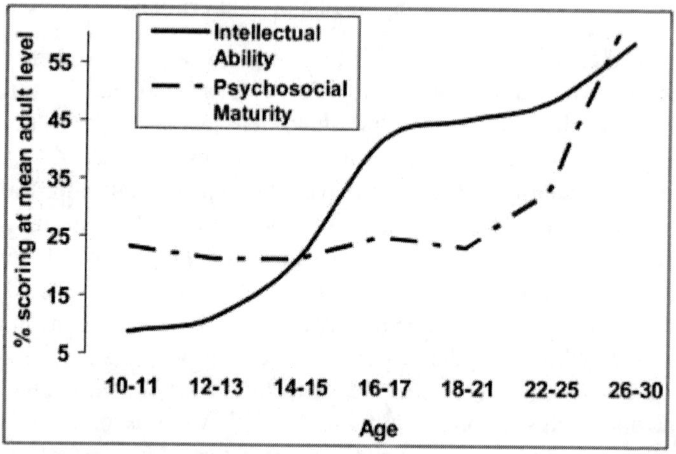

(*Source:* http://www.dhs.state.illus/page.aspx?item=64924)

Those who claim that the juveniles in the age group of sixteen to eighteen should be treated as adults for their criminality, argue that in the present era of information explosion, children mature early and know everything even before they turn sixteen. Therefore, when they commit crimes, they know the consequences of their conduct; therefore, they must be answerable to the criminal justice system like adults. This argument is fallacious as that there is a sea-gap between mental maturity and having information. Children may have a lot of information today about everything but that does not suggest in any way that they are mature also.[20] However, the maturity of judgment, the evidence from developmental neuroscience, suggests the ability to think rationally and to differentiate between good and evil does not complete before the person is in early twenties. Maturing of the brain continues until the early 20s in those relevant parts that govern impulsivity, judgment, planning for the future, foresight of consequences, and other characteristics that make people morally culpable.[21] If the children of today are using the information that they have for doing acts without understanding consequences thereof, it only shows their mental immaturity. Brain development is hardly complete at the age of eighteen years. Instead, brain development continues into adulthood and sometimes is not complete until the age of twenty-five years.[22] It has been discovered by many neuropsychologist that *adolescent brains are far less developed than previously believed."*[23] As a result, although today's teens mature physically at younger age than their parents do, and although they take on many of the behavioural trappings of adulthood, *that does not mean that they understand the full implications of their behaviour."*[24] According to Maharukh Adenwala, *The Juvenile Justice (Care and Protection of Children) Act, 2015 has reversed the well founded principle of juvenile justice by allowing Juvenile Justice Boards to waive the right of children above the age 16 years who have committed a heinous offence into the criminal justice system, this means the treatment of a juvenile will depend upon the type of offence committed instead of his situation."*[25]

It has been acknowledged by the United States Supreme Court that teenagers don't have fully developed brains and that youths are less mature and not fully developed, and thus are less culpable.[26] The United States Supreme Court observed, Developments in psychology and brain science continue to show fundamental difference between juvenile and adults minds. In this respect, to punish a juvenile, like an adult would result in excess punishment.

This is the reason why it is now widely recognised that a child offender requires a different approach from that which would be adopted in relation to an adult criminal[27] and underlines the need to have a differential sentencing policy for person below the age of 18 years whose cognitive faculties do not reach complete state of development even in the early twenties. The principal aim of differential sentencing of child offender is to prevent them from reoffending. Sentencing needs to show that the conduct of the child offender is not acceptable and should address any other factors that may lead to reoffending in future. At the same time, the dispositional order passed on a child offender should also demonstrate the efficacy of criminal law and must restore the confidence of the society in rule of law.

1.3. Period of adolescence and delinquency

The phases of human development and growth can be categorised into three groups i.e. the childhood, the adolescence and the adulthood. Usually psychologists[28] have classified the persons in the age group of 0-18 years into *Children or Pre-Adolescents* and *Adolescent*. Further, the Adolescent are divided into three sub-groups: *Early-Adolescence* (12-14 years), *Middle-Adolescence* (15-18) and *later-Adolescence* (18-21) years based on their brain and psychosocial development.[29] The first category that is the person in the age group of 0-11 years comes within the periphery of childhood period in which brain development is least but there is physical development of the body parts. Later sub-groups are part of the period of adolescence period.

(i) Primary changes versus secondary changes: text and contexts

Adolescence period is the period of transition from the period of childhood to adulthood. This is the period, which makes a person to accept the role of the adulthood. This is time when an adolescent is entering into the adult life. This period demonstrates the number of changes in the child with respect to their biological, psychological and social physiognomies. Grayason N.Holmbeck[30] has tried to view this period as a period of storm and furry and characterised by the conflict-personality. Generally, this approach is perceived as the observations of the clinical psychologists who are treating the children with adolescent problems. Although, the public perception and public policy formulation are based on this approach. This perception is also being augmented when the writers use it while working for the media outlets who described this period as rebellious, frustration-oriented and conflict derive which needs instantaneous rectification. This perspective is in charge in the juvenile policy of various countries, which are moving towards the crime control model of criminal justice where the primary concern is the security of the society and application of the law and order approach. But there is another approach[31] regarding adolescence, that is, the pragmatic approach, which views adolescence not as the period of storm and fury but as period of primary changes which occur in the biology, psychology and social role of children which have an impact on the contexts (family and peer relationship, school and work environment). These primary changes in the adolescent in the light of contexts go on to produce the secondary changes of identity formation, achievement orientation, sexuality, intimacy, autonomy and attachment. The conclusion of all these changes in the life of the adolescent defines the type of adolescent when child is exposed to others in the society.[32] J.P. Hill,[33] has elaborated these developmental changes,[34] which is shown in the following table:

The Developmental Changes

Primary Changes	Impact Upon	Contexts	To Produce	Secondary Changes
Biological/Puberty		Family Relationship		Identity Formation
Psychological/cognitive		Peer Relationship		Achievement
Social Redefinition	School environment			Sexuality
	Work environment			Intimacy
				Autonomy
				Attachment

Source: Jean Paiget, The Construction of reality in the Child (Basic books, New York, 1954).

Generally, the primary changes occur in three domains: physiological, psychological and social roles. As far as the physiological changes are concerned, there are changes in the physiology of the person like development of the bodily organs and the primary and secondary sexual characteristics. The psychological changes begin from the birth of human being. As per the theory of Jean Piaget,[35] It is stage-based: *sensorimotor stage* (since birth to two years of age) where there develops in the child the conscience of the world around her by the reflex and touching; *pre-operational stage* (2-7 years of age) where the child begins to think of the things symbolically where one thing may symbolise or stand for other than itself. At this stage, the thinking of the child is still egocentric and the child cannot express any standpoint so he just regards other people. *Concrete-operational stage* (7-11 years of age) in the children is the turning point in respect of their socio-psychological development as there is beginning of logical and operational thought in the child and the process of conversation starts whereby the child begins to remember the number, weight and mass without taking into account the shape or symbol of the thing. *Formal-operational stage* begins approximately at eleven years of age and last until the adulthood and in this stage the child begins to talk about the abstract concept and test the hypothetical question.

As far as the social changes are concerned, the social status of the child goes under tremendous changes. In case of non-industrial societies, on the completion of puberty, there are certain rituals, which take place like the rite de passage.[36] The purpose of these rituals is to make the person aware of the responsibilities, which he/she has to undertake on the onset of the adulthood. However, in the case of industrial society, there are no such rituals but the changes take place parallel to their social status.[37] These changes occur in different arenas: political (e.g. voting rights), economic (e.g. adolescents can work without restriction), interpersonal (e.g. changes in power relations within the family) and legal (e.g. adolescents in their later phase can be tried in mainstream adult courts).[38]

All changes that occur in the adolescence period have an impact on the interaction of that adolescent with the society. If any change occur in environment such as the broken family or the parents have separated, the primary changes, which take place in the changed environment, will have an impact on the secondary changes such as identity formation of the adolescent and he/she may emerge as the degenerate or delinquent adolescent.

1.4. The determination of age for criminal responsibility

Generally, the persons below the age limit are immune from any criminal responsibility. However, the question arises that, is the age group (age group 0-18 years) taken as a whole be considered under the definition of the child', or is there any gradations within the group itself? This perception of gradation makes difference between the juvenile below 12 years and above 16 years as they took the view that the person above the age of 16 years were mature enough to know the consequences of their actions and they should be treated as an adult for the crime committed. Thus, the juvenile justice systems in various countries began to move from traditional welfare –ism to the crime control and began to punish the children guilty of heinous crimes in the same manner as the adult. By invoking the misguided rhetoric of *adult time for adult crime",* there was a continuous trend to extend the jurisdiction of the criminal courts by reducing the age of the child.[39] Under the Indian law, children between 7-12 years of age having sufficient maturity and between 12-18 years who have committed an offence are responsible for their criminal acts. Nevertheless, such children are not to be dealt in the same manner as the adults, the focus should not be on punishment but on rehabilitation and reformation, which is necessary for the positive youth development.

1.5. Definition of child

In India, there is no one definition of a child. The child has been defined differently for different purposes under various laws. The Census of India, 2011 defines children as persons under the age of 14 years. The Constitution of India in Article 23 and Article 45 refers to children, as persons that are below the age of 14 years. Most Government programmes are targeted at children below the age of 14 years. In India the age of majority is 18 years for girls and 21 years for boys. Indian Penal Code, 1860, Section 82 says that

- Nothing is an offence which is done by a child under the age of 7. Under Section 83, Nothing is an offence which is done by a child above seven years of age and under twelve, who has not attained sufficient maturity of understanding to judge of the nature and consequences of his conduct on that occasion. The age of criminal responsibility is raised to 12 years if the child has not attained the ability to understand the nature and consequences of his or her act. Child Marriage Restraint Act, 2006 says, child means a person who if a male, has not

Age of Child Under Various Legislation/Laws[45]

S. No.	Legislation/Laws	Age specified (in years)
1.	Arms Act 1959	16
2.	Apprentices Act 1850 (Rep)	10-15
3.	Articles 24, 45 of Constitution of India	14
4.	Articles 15, 39(e) and (f) of Constitution of India	Not specified
5	Plantation Labor Act 1951	14
6.	Employment of Children Act 1938	14
7.	Factories Act 1948	14
8.	Child Marriage Restraint Act 2006	18 for girls, 21 for boys
9.	Option of puberty under Muslim law	15-18
10.	Children Act 1960	16 for boys, 18 for girls
11.	Guardians and Wards Act 1890	18/21
12.	Hindu Minority and Guardianship Act 1956	18
13.	Code of Criminal Procedure 1973 Section 125	18
14.	Hindu Adoption and Maintenance Act 1956	15
15.	Indian Contract Act 1872	18
16.	Indian Majority Act 1875	18
17.	Section 82 of Indian Penal Code	Below 7
18.	Section 83 of Indian Penal Code	7-12
19.	Section 361 of Indian Penal Code	16 for boys, 18 for girls

completed 21 years of age and if a female has not completed 18 years of age. During 1986, under the Juvenile Justice Act, the age limit for the juvenile was lowered to 16. In the year 2000, amendments were made and the age limit is raised to 18 but Section 15 of Juvenile Justice Act, 2015, treats all the children below 18 years equally, except that those in the age group of 16-18 can be tried as adults if they commit a heinous crime. However, intellectuals are demanding that for all protective purposes the age of the child should be uniformly up to 18 years. The protection should also be extended to the age for employment, which means any person employing the child under 18 shall be subjected penal and civil consequences for the crime and the civil wrong of employing child labour, which shall be totally prohibited.

1.6. Definition of child/juvenile

According to Section 2(12) of Juvenile Justice (Care and Protection of Children) Act 2015, Child means a person who has not completed eighteen years of age. Section (35) defines juvenile as a child below the age of eighteen years. The word juvenile 'is defined the first time in the Act, 2015 whereas section 15(1) Assumes 16 years as the age of criminal responsibility for heinous crimes.[40] As per Section 2(42) orphan 'means A child who has no any biological parents or a guardian or an adoptive parent or a judicial guardian. Under Section 2 (60) surrendered child' means A child who is relinquished by a biological parent or a guardian or adoptive parents due to physical, mental or other disabilities or social factor which cannot be controlled by them and Child Welfare Committee is declared as surrendered child. Section 2 (13) says that child in conflict with the law 'means, a child who is alleged or found to have committed an offence and who has not completed eighteen years of age on the date of commission of such offence.

As per Section 2 (14) child in need of care and protection means a child who are destitute, downtrodden, deprived or oppressed in one way or the other. In *Robert Heitkamp v. Bal Anand World Children Welfare Trust, Mumbai, India,*[41] the Supreme Court of India held that judicial pronouncement can add to the definition any other type of children such as mentally ill or stunted children.

The Juvenile can be termed, defined and referred to as a child who has not attained a certain age at which he, like an adult person under the law of the land, can be held liable for his criminal acts. Juvenile and minor in legal terms are used in different context. Juvenile is used when reference is made to a young offender and minor relates to legal capacity or majority.[42] For a more clear meaning resort can profitably be made to some other sources. Unlike an adult person, a Juvenile, having not attained prescribed age, cannot be held liable for his criminal act. The age criteria for being a juvenile vary from country to country and state to state.

1.7. Definition of delinquency

The eschatological meaning of the word Delinquency 'is wrong doing.' Any act or conduct of a juvenile, which is socially undesirable, can be defined as an act of Delinquency. Juvenile delinquency generally means the failure of children to meet certain obligations expected of them by the society. The sociological thinkers give a liberal interpretation to the term delinquency. This view is well expressed by the definition given by Clyde B. Vedder who says, juvenile delinquency refers to the anti-social acts of children and of young people underage. Such acts are either specifically forbidden by law or may be lawfully interpreted as constituting delinquency, or as requiring some form of official action.[43] Whether a particular act or conduct of the child would be deviant or not will depend on various factors and vary in different States, Cities and time. Delinquency is a Legal term that was first defined in 1889 when Illinois passed the first law on Juvenile Delinquency: Since then each state has passed delinquency laws. In U.S., the laws were passed for changing the concepts of Delinquency, which have led to changes in some of states. The Definition of delinquency includes conduct, which violates the law only when committed by children e.g. truancy, ungovernable behaviour and running away.[44] A child is delinquent only when so adjudged by a juvenile court, following a formal complaint. This viewpoint is based on the Classical theory of crime, which stresses the rigid application of law to all offenders, as a safeguard against arbitrary and tyrannical exercise of powers by political and administrative authorities.

1.8. Brief legislative background

In India the legislative contextual of juvenile justice, mechanism began during the British rule and was directly imported from the Western ideas and advancement in the field of prison reforms and juvenile justice. The first legislation dealing with children in conflict with law was passed in 1850 i.e the Apprentices Act, 1850 that was binding over the children under the age of 15 years found to have committed petty offences as apprentices. The Act[45] required that children between the ages of 10-15 years convicted in courts to be provided vocational training as part of their rehabilitation process. This Apprentices Act 1850 was the harbinger of much other legislation to follow, laying down special provisions in relation to children. The Indian Penal Code 1860 declared children below 7 years of age as *doli incapax,* while the presumption of *mens rea* could be rebutted in case of children in the 7-12 age groups[46]. Thereafter this Act[47] another legislation named the Reformatory Schools Act, 1876 provided that the child offenders up to 15 years of age sentenced to imprisonment or transportation were sent to reformative schools instead of ordinary prisons. Reformatory Schools Act, 1876 was repealed and replaced by Reformatory Schools Act, 1897, that empowered the local governing bodies to effect the reformation in a more organised manner. The Reformatory Schools Act, 1897 is a milestone in field of youth legislation in India. The Act proved fundamental in the field of children's law applicable to those states where no Children's law or any other special laws have been enacted dealing with the juvenile offenders. Just after a year, The Code of Criminal Procedure 1898 came into force and authorised magistrates to send juvenile offenders to reformatories instead of prisons in the specified circumstances along with provisions relating to grant probation and trial of children by the juvenile court.[48] The report of the Indian Jails Committee, 1889, reiterated the need for segregation and classification of offenders according to their age and duration of sentence.[49] Preparation for a Children Act was underway in Madras since 1917 and it was passed in June 1920[50]. Madras Act started the era of segregation of juveniles from adult offenders[51] and established a separate juvenile court and the residential institutions under it in 1920, which was followed by many other States.

Children Act in Bengal and Bombay were enacted in quick succession in 1922 and 1924 respectively. More States followed suit in the years to follow; the Delhi Children Act, 1941, The Mysore Children Act 1943, The Travancore Children Act, 1945, The Cochin Children Act, 1946, and The East – Punjab Children Act 1949. These different State Child legislations encompassed the children of two categories i.e. (i) delinquent children and (ii) destitute and neglected children. The juvenile courts handled these children with the full consideration of welfare of the children of both categories. The child welfare Board handled neglected children and the Children's Court deal with the delinquent children.[52] This statute was predecessor of J.J. Act, 1986.[53] Till 1960 there were some States which had not enacted any legislation regarding the juvenile delinquency namely, Nagaland, Orissa, Sikkim, Tripura, Andaman and Nicobar Islands, Arunachal Pradesh, Chandigarh, Dadra and Nagar Haveli, Lakshadweep and Mizoram. In *Hiralal Mallick v.State of Bihar,* law in various States. However the States had their own separate Children's Act, the provision contained in each State's Children Act were not uniform. Even the definition of the term 'child' and 'neglected children' varied from State to State. Even so the States laid down different cut-off ages for deciding the criminal responsibility.[54] In 1960 the first central legislation, The Children Act, 1960 was enacted by the parliament as the model legislation that aimed at conceptualising a system, separate from the criminal justice under the code of Criminal Procedure, 1973, for the treatment of juvenile delinquents. The Children Act, 1960 introduced a sex-discriminatory definition of child it defined a child to be a boy who has not attained the age of sixteen years or a girl who has not attained the age of eighteen years.[55] However, during this period, States were allowed to frame their own laws on the subject as the 1960 Act extended only to the Union Territories.[56] Nevertheless, this resulted in similar cases of juvenile delinquency being dealt with differently by courts of each States that lead to discrepancy in judicial practice.[57] This discrepancy promoted the Supreme Court to observe that a parliamentary legislation on the subject of juvenile justice was desirable.[58] The Children Act, 1960 established two distinct adjudicatory bodies to deal with children in conflict with law[59] and children in need of care.[60]

The lack of uniformity in the legislative enactment of the various State encouraged the Hon'ble Supreme Court to observe in *Sheela Barse vs. Union of India*[61] That We would suggest that instead of each of the State having its own Children's Act, different in procedure and content from the Children's Act in other States, it would be desirable if the Central Government initiates Parliamentary legislation on the subject, so that there is complete uniformity in regard to the various provisions relating to children in the entire territory of the country. The Children's Act which may be enacted by Parliament should contain not only provisions for investigation and trial of offences against children below the age of 16 years but should also contain mandatory provisions for ensuring social, economic and psychological rehabilitation of the children who are either accused of offences or are abandoned or destitute or lost. Moreover, it is not enough merely to have legislation on the subject, but it is equally, if not more, important to ensure that such legislation is implemented in all earnestness and mere lip sympathy is not paid to such legislation and justification for non-implementation is not pleaded on the ground of lack of finances on the part of the State. The greatest recompense which the State can get for expenditure on children is the building up of powerful human resources ready to take its place in the forward march of the nation.

In 1985, the General Assembly adopted the United Nations Standard Minimum Rules for the Administration of Juvenile Justice, also known as the Beijing Rules. With the advent of the Beijing Rules, Nations introduced separate legislations for juvenile offenders and children requiring care and protection and for first time the word juvenile was used in international law, and the term juvenile justice was coined. This change in terminology was then reflected in domestic law with the passing of the Juvenile Justice Act 1986. In 1986, Parliamentary passed the Juvenile Justice Act for the whole country. The Act was enforced throughout the territory of India except the State of Jammu and Kashmir on October 2, 1987, bringing in a uniform system of juvenile justice throughout the country. However, the Juvenile Justice Act 1986 retained the principal features of the Children Act 1960. It continued the same sex-discriminatory definition of child. It provided two separate authorities renamed as Juvenile Court and Juvenile Welfare Board to deal with the two categories of delinquent and neglected children.[62] Pending their inquiries before their respective competent authorities, both these categories of children were kept in the Observation Home. However, the Act has presented numerous un-avoidable interpretational problems due to ambiguities about its relationship with other special legislation due to the manner of its drafting. Dr. Ved Kumari,[63] in her research paper has examined the scheme, scope and operation of the Juvenile Justice Act, 1986 and found that the legislation suffer from certain inherent lacunae as well as from implementation difficulties.[64] However, the Juvenile Justice Act, 1986 is repealed by the Juvenile Justice (Care and Protection) Act, 2000 (Refer section 69(1) of Act, 2000).

However the Juvenile Justice (Care and Protection of Children) Act, 2000 was enacted for the protection of children as it for the first time provided for the juvenile in conflict with law and children in need of care and protection to be kept separately. This segregation aims to curtail the corruption of the innocent child from the influence of the criminal juvenile.[65] The Act was amended twice in 2006 and in 2011 to mend the gaps in its implementation and the welfare of child.[66] With the increasing number of crimes committed by children in the age group of 16-18 years in recent years it evident that the existing law under the Juvenile Justice (Care and Protection of Children) Act, 2000 were also not well equipped to tackle child delinquency of this age group. The most note-worthy feature of all enactments since 1850 has been that they were all moving in one direction of bringing an increasing number of children within the protective umbrella of juvenile justice. Nevertheless, on December 2015 a big backward step was taken by the Government by introducing the possibility of sending 16-18 year old child to jail in exceptional circumstances under the J. J. Act, 2015[67]. Presently, since 15 January 2016, the J.J. Act, 2015 is applicable throughout India.

REFERENCES

1. Maharukh Aden Walla, Swagata Raha et. al., Handbook for Advocates working with Child in Conflict with law in India, Centre for Child and the Law (CCL) National Law School of India University (NLSIU), Bangalore, 2018.

2. Laurence Steinberg, Adolescent Development and Juvenile Justice, 16(3), The Development of Clinical Psychology 55 (2008).
3. *Ibid.* 56.
4. Human Rights Watch, The difference between youth and Adults October, 2005, available at https//www.hrw.org/reports/2005/us1005/6.htm (last visited on April 15, 2017).
5. Steinberg, supra note 32, 56.
6. Dr. K. A. Pandey, Brain Science, Juvenile Justice (Care and Protection of Children) Act, 2015: A Critique, 7 7 RMLNLU J (2015) 54, See. Elizabeth Kauffman and Laurence Steinberg, (Im) maturity of Judgment in adolescence: Why Adolescent May Be Less Culpable than Adults.
7. Behavioural Science and Law, Vol. 18 (2000), pp. 742-43.
8. Steinberg, *Supra* note 25.
9. Dr. K.A. Pandey, Brain Science, Juvenile Justice(Care and Protection of Children) Act, 2015: A Critique, 7 RMLNLU J 2015) 54.
10. Catherine, C. Lewis, How Adolescents approach Decisions: Changes over Grades Seven to twelve and policy implications 52 Child Development 538, 541-42(1981) (This study examined how only twenty five percent of students in standard X (whose approximate age is sixteen) consider the long term impacts of their decisions, in comparison to forty two percent of students in class XII (whose approximate age is eighteen).
11. Dr. K. A. Pandey, E-Pathshala Available at http://epgp.inflibnet.ac.in/index.php (Visited on Jan 12, 2018).
12. Dr. K. A. Pandey, E-Pathshala Available at http://epgp.inflibnet.ac.in/index.php (Visited on Jan 12, 2018).
13. Steinberg, supra note 23, 56.
14. 18. Center for Child and the Law, National Law School of India University, Submission on Clauses14. 17 (3) and 19 of the Juvenile Justice (Care and Protection of Children Bill, 2014, available at https://www.google.co.in/url?sa=t&rct=j&q=&erc=s&source=web&cd=2/7cad=rja&uac= 8&ved=0ahUKEwjGxIDXgITQA hUBLY 8KHZdIDGc QFggkMAE&url=https percent 3a percent 2F percent 2Fwww.nls.ac.in percent 2 FccI percent 2Fjjdocuments percent 2FMWCDNLSIUNIMHANS.docx&usg=AF QjCNdiRozNjsp QXVS Y9DRsUJgencWNG&sig2=L_ xk6Y0AAgCs8WtMHetRew (visited on Feb12 2014)

15. A study released by Elizabeth Scott and Laurence Steinberg, former members of the Jhon and Catherine T. Mac Arther Foundation Research Network on Adolescent and Juvenile crime states. The problem with individualised assessments of immaturity is that practitioners lack diagnostic tools to evaluate psychological maturity and identity formation on an individualised basis. Recently, courts in some areas have begun to use a psychopathy checklist, a variation of an instrument of an instrument developed for adults, in an effort to identify adolescent psychopaths for transfer or sentencing purposes. This practice, however, is fraught with the potential for error; it is simply not yet possible to distinguish incipient psychopaths from youths whose crimes reflect transient immaturity. For this reason, the American Psychiatric Association restricts the diagnosis of psychopathy to individuals aged eighteen and older. Evaluating antisocial traits and conduct in adolescence is just too uncertain.
16. Richard J. Bonnie &Elizabeth S. Scott, The Teenage Brain: Adolescent Brain Research and the Law, 22(2) Current Directions In Psychological Science 161(2013); Rakshit, supra note 22; supra note 11, p. 10.5.
17. Minimum age for being eligible to exercise the right to vote is eighteen years .even to enter into a valid civil contract, the minimum age is eighteen years.
18. American Bar Association, Ruban C. Gur, Declaration of Ruben C. Gur, P.H.D. 15 (2016).
19. Foundation Research Network on Adolescent Development and juvenile justice, MacArther. (2006, September) Network overview: A century of change in juvenile justice (p. 2) Philadelphia.
20. Dr. K. A. Pandey, Brain Science, Juvenile Justice(Care and Protection of Children) Act, 2015: A Critique, 7 RMLNLU J (2015).
21. Dr. K.A. Pandey, E-Pathshala Available at http://epgp.inflibnet.ac.in/index.php (Visited on Jan 12, 2018) See also Paus. Thomas, Jay Gield, et, al., Steinberg Maturation of Neural Pathways in Children and Adolescent: In Vivo Study. Science, 283(1999).
22. Paus. Thomas, jay Gield, et, al., Steinberg Maturation of Neural Pathways in Children and Adolescent: In Vivo Study Science, 283 (1999).
23. Hybrid Medical Animation, Cruel and Unusual Punishment: The Juvenile Death Penalty, American Bar Association 1 (2004).

24. Beyer, Recognising the child in the Delinquent, Kentucky Children's Right Journal, Vol. VII, No. 1, Spring 1999, 45, 55.
25. Mahrukh Adenwala, A dislocation of the juvenile justice system, The Wire (The Wire May 23, 2015).
26. Graham v. Florida, 120 S Ct. 2001 (2010); Roper v. Simmons, 543 U.S. 551(2005).
27. Dr. K.A. Pandey, E-Pathshala Available at http://epgp.inflibnet.ac.in/index.php (Visited on Jan. 12, 2018).
28. Lawrence Steinberg, Deborah Lowe Vandell, et. al., Development: Infancy Through Adolescence 5-9 (Engage Learning, Belmont, CA, 2011) Eva.
29. Laurence Steinberg, Adolescence 263-265 (Mc Graw-Hill Inc. New York, 5th ed. 1999).
30. Grayson, N. Holmbeck, Adolescenc, in V.S Ramachandran (ed.), I Encyclopedia of Human Behaviour 17 (Academic Press, San Diego, 1994).
31. *Ibid.*, at 17-28.
32. Muzaffar Hussain Mir, Age of Criminal Responsibility and The Child Criminal Justice: Imperatives of Developmental Model of Juvenile Justice For India, Vol. 2., Jamia Law Journal, 2017.
33. J.P. Hill, Understanding Early Adolescence: A Framework (Centre for Early Adolescence, Carrboro, N.C., 1980).
34. Supra note 50 at 18-24.
35. Jean Paiget, The Construction of reality in the Child (Basic Books New York, 1954).
36. William Damon (ed), Handbook of Child Psychology 217-220, John Wiley & Sons, New York, Fifth Edition.
37. Douglas Davies, Introduction: Raising the Issues, in Jean Holm and Jhon Bowker (eds.), Rites of Passage 1-9(printer Publishers, London, 1st edition, 1994).
38. Vincent Tinto, Stages of Student Departure: Reflections on the longitudinal Character of Student Leaving 59 THE 438(1988).
39. Supra note 50 at 20.
40. Kevin Hile, Trail of Juvenile as Adults: Point – Center point 26-35 (Chelsea House Publishers, Philadelphia, 2003).
41. Ved Kumari, The juvenile justice system in India from welfare to rights, Oxford University Press, New Delhi, First Published, 2004.

42. Juvenile Justice (Care and Protection of Children) Act, 2015 Section 15(1) – in case of a heinous offences alleged to have been committed by a child, who has completed or is above to his mental and physical capacity to commit such offence, ability to understand the offence, and may pass an order in accordance with the provisions of sub-section (3) of section 18.
43. AIR 2008 (NOC) 1024 (Bom.).
44. See the Black Dictionary of Law.
45. Clyde, B. Vedder and Dora B. Somerville, The Delinquent Girl, USA, Charles C. Thomas, 154 pp, 1973 and 1975.
46. Ruth Shonle Cavan Theodore N. Ferdinand, Juvenile Delinquency (III Edition): 27.
47. The apprentice Act 1850.
48. Ved Kumari, The Juvenile Justice System in India From Welfare to Rights, Oxford University Press, New Delhi, First Published 2004.
49. The Apprentices Act 1850.
50. Sections 29 B, 399 and 562, CrPC. 1898.
51. Report of the Indian Jail Committee 1889, April 1889, p. 20.
52. Fort St-George Gazette For Statement of Objects and Reasons Part iv, 18 December 1917, pp. 1156-58. For Report of Selection Committee, See *Ibid.*, 26 December 1919, pp. 1213-16. For proceedings in Council, See *Ibid.*, 23 December 1919, p. 1367, and *Ibid.*, 8 June 1920, pp. 690-704.
53. Juvenile Justice Act 1986.
54. Ms. Maharukh Andenwalla, Child Protection and Juvenile Justice System for Juvenile in Conflict with Law, Childline India Foundation.
55. Juvenile Justice Act 1986.
56. (1977) 4 SCC 44: 1977 SCC (Cri) 538.
57. For example, the Madras Children's Act defined child as persons below the age of 14 years but applied it to young offenders till the age of 18 years. The Bombay Children Act includes children till the age of 16 years and West Bengal Children Act included children up to the age of 17 years.
58. The Children Act, 1960, section 2(e). 63. *Ibid.*, 1(2).
59. Sheela Barse v. Union of India, (1986) 3 SCC 596: AIR 1986 SC 1773 (per Bhagwati J: (….) we would suggest that instead of each State having its own Children's Act in other States, it would be desirable

if the Central Government initiates Parliamentary Legislation on subject so that there is complete uniformity in regard to the various provisions relating to children in the entire territory of the country).

60. Childline India, Child protection and Juvenile Justice System, 14, available at http:// childlineindia.org.in/pdf/ CP-JJ-JCL.pdf (Last visited on March 10, 2017)
61. The Children's Court.
62. The Child Welfare Board.
63. (1986) 3 SCC 596: AIR 1986 SC 1773.
64. Ved Kumari, The Juvenile Justice System in India From Welfare to Rights, Oxford University Press, New Delhi. First Published 2004.
65. Dean, Faculty of Law, University of Delhi.
66. Suman Nalwa and Hari Dev Kohli, Commentary on The Juvenile Justice Act, Second edition, Universal Publication, New Delhi.
67. Mahrukh Andenwalla, Child Protection and Juvenile System for juvenile in conflict with law, (1st edition, 2006, Childline India Foundation, Mumbai).
68. Suman Nalwa &Hari Dev Kohli, Commentary on The Juvenile Justice Act, Second edition, Universal Publication, New Delhi.

2

International Instruments Relating to Special Treatment of Juvenile

2.1 Introduction

In this chapter, the author focuses on the international and national aspects of differential treatment of child offenders. For the candid understanding, it is imperative that the national and international instrument should be analysed to know about the reasons why a delinquent juvenile is treated differently from an adult, though the offence committed may be similar.

2.2 Philosophy of differential treatment on international platform

There were mainly two different rationales in varied parts of the world for the establishment of a separate system for juveniles: (i) the principle of seclusion of children from adult offenders; and (ii) the principle of parens patriae, i.e, the state is responsible for all juveniles requiring care and protection.[1] Gradually, the welfare approach [parens patriac] shifted to the rights approach, which respects the Constitutional and procedural rights of a juvenile. Since juvenile justice has been acknowledged as part of the human rights discourse. A child in conflict with the law, should "be treated in a manner consistent with the promotion of the child's sense of dignity and worth, and which reinforces the child's respect for the human rights and fundamental freedoms of others and which takes into account the child's age and the desirability of promoting the child's reintegration and the child's assuming a constructive role in society."[2]

2.3 The third international congress for the welfare and protection of children (1902)[3]

The Third International Congress for the Welfare and Protection of Children (1902)[4] was concerned on the issues of neglected children and the possibilities of their developing criminal propensities if proper care and upbringing not provided.[5] Therefore, the Congress focuses on the care of neglected juveniles to protect them from tuning into delinquent juvenile.

2.4 Norms for differential treatment of juvenile

(i) The Geneva Declaration of The Rights of the Child, 1924[6]

The Geneva declaration of the rights of the Child, 1924 is the first crucial document that comprehended and acknowledged the existence of specific rights to children and the accountability of adults towards children. It declares, "The mankind owes to the child, the best it has to give." The document advocated the theory that child offenders should be transformed, and not penalised. It imposes a duty on humankind – "The delinquent child must be reclaimed." This declaration focuses on the social and economic entitlement of the children and it laid the foundation for the setting up of future International standards in the fields of children's rights. The declaration emphasised on the welfare of children and recognised their right to protection, development, support and relief.[7]

The fundamental needs of children were précised in five aspects. They are as follows:

(i) The child must be provided the standard conditions for its proper development, both physically and spiritually.

(ii) The child, who is hungry, must be fed, the sick must be nursed, the backward must be helped, the delinquent must be reclaimed, and the orphan and the waif must be sheltered and scoured.

(iii) The child must be the first to receive relief in times of distress.

(iv) The child must be put in a position to earn livelihood and must be protected against every form of exploitation.

(v) The child must be brought up in the consciousness that its talent must be developed to the service of its fellow men.

(ii) Universal Declaration of Human Rights, 1948[8]

The Article 16 of this Declaration is very crucial which relates to reintegration and social rehabilitation of juvenile delinquents. Under this Article the emphasis is on protection and care of family because "The family is the natural and fundamental unit of society and is should look after by society and the State". If family is taken care of, the children will automatically be looked after. Moreover, if children are protected and taken care of and family is left impoverished, all child-care steps and measures are defeated. Therefore, it is mandatory to secure the human rights of the parents first; the human rights of their children will be secured automatically.

(iii) The International Covenant on Civil and Political Rights (1966)[9]

Article 6 mandates The State Parties not to make legislations that award death punishment for the offence committed by juvenile who is below eighteen years of age.

Article 7 of covenant prohibiting to punish in inhuman or degrading manner states as- The juvenile offender shall not be punished in an inhuman or degrading manner. They should not be subject to any torture or cruelty during the custody or detention.

Article 10 prescribing the provision for segregation from adult offenders, states as, The juvenile alleged as accused of any offence shall be kept separated from adults and brought as speedily as possible for adjudication. Juvenile offenders shall be separated from adults offenders and be provided the treatment suitable to their age and legal status.

(iv) The United Nations Standard Minimum Rules for the Administration of Juvenile Justice, 1985

Under the *The Beijing Rules*[10] 'juveniles' is defined as a child or young person who, under the respective legal systems, may be dealt with for an offence in a manner which is different from an adult.[11] It obligates the adjudicating authority to conduct proceedings in a manner that is conducive to the best interests of the juvenile and shall be conducted in an atmosphere of understanding, which shall allow the juvenile to participate therein and to express herself or himself freely.[12]

Rule 3: No Distinction between Status Offender and Juvenile Offender

Rule 3 does not make any differentiation between the juvenile offender and status offender. It provides that the Rules 3 - Shall be applicable to both the juvenile offenders and to juveniles who may be proceeded against for any specific conduct that would not be punishable if committed by an adult. In other words, the juvenile offenders and status offenders (non-delinquent) both should be treated equally. The Rule 3 could not be warranted in the present era of legal system. Here the Rule 3 is deemed a weak rule.

Rule 4: Minimum Age of Criminal Responsibility

Rule 4 Provides that The minimum age for criminal responsibility shall not be fixed at too low age level, bearing in mind the facts of emotional, mental and intellectual maturity.

Rule 5 provides that The juvenile justice system shall emphasise the well-being of the juvenile and shall ensure that any reaction to juvenile offenders shall always be in proportion to the circumstances of both the offenders and the offence. The second interpretation of the directives under Rule 5 precisely allows the punishing of juvenile offenders but with certain limitation.

Rule 6 recognising the vulnerability of juveniles allows the scope of discretion at all stage administration of justice, states as Appropriate scope for discretion shall be allowed at all stages of proceedings and at the different levels of juvenile justice administration, including investigation, prosecution, adjudication and the follow-up of dispositions. Moreover, Rule 6(2) ensures that The exercising of official control over the juvenile offenders shall be made accountable at all stages.

Rule 7: Procedural Safeguards

Rule 7 providing to a juvenile the basic procedural safeguards, states as, The procedural safeguards assured to an adult – such as the presumption of innocence, the right to counsel, the right to be informed of the charges, the right to the presence of a parent or guardian, the right to remain silent, the right to confront and cross-examine witnesses and the right to appeal to a higher authority shall be guaranteed at all stages of proceedings.[13]

Rule 8: Right to Privacy

Rule 8 directives for the protection of the right to privacy of juvenile– The juvenile's right to privacy shall be respected at all stages in order to avoid harm being caused to her or him by undue publicity or by the process of labeling. Rule 8(2) states– In principle, no information that may lead to the identification of a juvenile offender shall be published.

Rule 10: Early Notification

Under **Rule 10** directives are provided, regarding the initial notification to the guardian of the juvenile offenders, Upon the apprehension of a juvenile, his or her parents or guardian shall be immediately informed of such apprehension and where such immediate notification is not possible, the parents or guardian shall be notified within the shortest possible time thereafter. Rule 10(2) A judge or other competent official or body shall, without delay, consider the issue of release.

Diversion/s

As per the Rule 11, Consideration shall be given, wherever required, to deal with juvenile offenders without resorting to formal trial by the competent authority. Rule 11(3) Any diversion involving referral to appropriate community or other services shall require the consent of the juvenile, or his or her parents or guardian, provided that such decision to refer a case shall be subject to review by a competent authority, upon application. Rule 11(4) In order to facilitate the discretionary disposition of juvenile cases, efforts shall be made to provide for community programmes, such as temporary supervision and guidance, restitution, and compensation of victims.

Special Police Unit

As per **Rule 12**, The police officers who frequently or exclusively deal with juveniles or who are primarily engaged in the prevention of juvenile crime shall be specially instructed and trained. In large cities, special police units should be established for that purpose.

Directives for Pending Trial

Rule 13 ensures directives, as Detention pending trial shall be used only as a measure of last resort and for the shortest possible period of time Rule 13(4) – Juveniles under detention pending trial shall be kept separate from adults and shall be detained in a separate institution or in a separate part of an institution also holding adults." Rule 13(5) "While in custody, juveniles shall receive care, protection and all necessary individual assistance including social, educational, vocational, psychological, medical and physical that they may require in view of their age, sex and personality.

Competent Authority for Adjudication

Rule 14(1) ensures competency of adjudicating authority - Where the case of a juvenile offender has not been diverted (under rule 11), she or he shall be dealt with by the competent authority (court, tribunal, board, council, etc.) according to the principles of a fair and just trial.

Rule 14(2) states as- The proceedings shall be conducive to the best interests of the juvenile and shall be conducted in an atmosphere of understanding, which shall allow the juvenile to participate therein and to express herself or himself freely.

Right to be Represented

Rule 15(1) ensures the right to be representation properly and states as, Throughout the proceedings the juvenile shall have the right to be represented by a legal adviser or to apply for free legal aid where there is provision for such aid in the country.

Social Inquiry Reports

Rule 16(1) declares as In all cases except those involving minor offences, before the competent authority renders a final disposition prior to sentencing, the background and circumstances in which the juvenile is living or the conditions under which the offence has been committed shall be properly investigated so as to facilitate judicious adjudication of the case by the competent authority.

Directive Principles for Adjudication and Disposition

Rule 17(1)(a) postulates the infliction of punishment in proportion, as 'The reaction taken shall always be in proportion not only to the circumstances and the gravity of the offence but also to the circumstances and the needs of the juvenile as well as to the needs of the society'. The rule postulates the principle of individualisation of punishment.

Rule 17(1) (b) guides as- 'The restrictions on the personal liberty of the juvenile shall be imposed only after careful consideration and shall be limited to the possible minimum'.

Rule 17(1) (c) instructs as - 'Deprivation of personal liberty shall not be imposed unless the juvenile is adjudicated of a serious act involving violence against another person or of persistence in committing other serious offences and unless there is no other appropriate responses'.

Rule 17(1) (d) ensures the well-being of the juvenile shall be the guiding factor in the consideration of her or his case.

Rule 17(2) proscribes death sentence to juvenile offenders.

Rule 17(3) proscribes corporal punishment to juveniles.

Diverse Disposition Methods

Rule 18(1) prescribes numerous alternatives or diversified programmes to replace the institutional method of treatment:-

a. Care, guidance and supervision orders;

b. Probation;

c. Community service orders;

d. Financial penalties, compensation and restitution;

e. Intermediate treatment and other treatment orders;

f. Orders to participate in group counseling and similar activities;

g. Orders concerning foster care, living communities or other educational settings;

h. Other relevant orders.

Minimum Use of Institutionalisation

Rule 19(1) provides mandate for minimum use of institutionalisation or incarceration of the juvenile- The placement of a juvenile in an institution shall always be a disposition of last resort.

Avoidance of Delay in Disposal of Cases

Rule 20(1) ensures for Expeditious disposal of cases of juvenile offenders.

Records

Rule 21(1) proscribes the disclosing of the records of juvenile offenders shall be kept strictly confidential and closed to third parties. Access to such records shall be limited to persons directly concerned with the disposition of the case at hand or other duly authorised persons.

Rule 21(2) states, as the records of juvenile offenders shall not be used in adult proceedings in subsequent cases involving the same offender.

Fair Representation

Rule 22(2) ensures the fair representation - 'The Juvenile justice personnel shall reflect the diversity of juveniles who come into contact with the juvenile justice system. Efforts shall be made to ensure the fair representation of women and minorities in juvenile justice agencies'.

Rule 23 postulates the effective implementation of dispositional directions passed by the competent adjudicatory authorities.

Rule 23(2) ensuring the proper implementation of orders of adjudicating authority, states, Suitable provisions shall be made for the implementation of orders of the competent authority, as referred to in rule 14(1) above, by that authority itself or by some other authority as circumstances may require.

Rule 23(2) assures Provisions should also be made to include the power to modify the orders as the competent authority may deem necessary from time to time, provided that such modification shall be determined in accordance with the principles contained in these Rules.

Provision of Required Assistance

Rule 24(1) commands the States To make efforts to provide juveniles, at all stages of the proceedings, with necessary assistance such as lodging, education or vocational training, employment or any other assistance, helpful and practical, in order to facilitate the rehabilitative process.

Involvement of Volunteers and Community Resources

Rule 25(1) obliges for involvement of volunteers, local institutions voluntary organisations, and other community resources to contribute effectively to the rehabilitation of the juvenile in a community setting and, as far as possible, within the family unit.

Objectives of Institutional Treatment

Rule 26(1) refers the objectives of training and treatment of juveniles placed in institutions is to provide care, protection, education and vocational skills.

Rule 26(2) ensures - The juveniles in institutions shall receive care, protection and all necessary assistance.

Rule 26(3) protect the juvenile from being exploit by the hardened adult criminal- 'The juveniles in institutions shall be kept separate from adults and shall be detained in a separate institution or in a separate part of an institution'.

Rule 26(5) ensures the right of access- 'In the interest and well-being of the institutionalised juvenile, the parents or guardians shall have a right of access'.

Application of the Standard Minimum Rules for the Treatment of Prisoners Adopted by the United Nations

Rule 27(1) prescribes- The Standard Minimum Rules for the Treatment of Prisoners and related recommendations shall be applicable as far as relevant to the treatment of juvenile offenders in institutions, including those in detention pending adjudication.

Rule 27(2) lays down- Efforts shall be made to implement the relevant principles laid down in the Standard Minimum Rules for the Treatment of Prisoners to the largest possible extent so as to meet the varying needs of juveniles specific to their age, sex and personality.

Frequent and Early Recourse to Conditional Release

Rule 28(1) prescribes- The conditional release from an institution shall be used by the appropriate authority to the greatest possible extent, and shall be granted at the earliest possible time.

Rule 28(2) prescribes- The juveniles released conditionally from an institution shall be assisted and supervised by an appropriate authority and shall receive full support by the community.

Semi-Institutional Arrangements

Rule 29(1) proposed for proper reintegration- Efforts shall be made to provide semi-institutional arrangements, such as half-way houses, educational homes, day timing training centers and other such appropriate arrangements that may assist juveniles in their proper reintegration into society.

Promotion of Research for Planning, Policy Formulation and Evaluation

Rule 30(3) Directs Efforts shall be made to establish a regular evaluative research mechanism built into the system of juvenile justice administration.

Rule 30(4) Directs The delivery of services in juvenile justice administration shall be systematically planned and implemented as an integral part of national development efforts.

(v) The United Nations Convention on the Rights of the Child (1989)[14]

Article 1 prescribes the definition of a child as– A child means every human being below the age of eighteen years unless, under the law applicable to the child, majority is attained earlier.

Article 37 prohibits the imposition of capital or life imprisonment,- States Parties shall ensure that: no child shall be subjected to torture or other cruel, inhuman or degrading treatment or punishment. Neither capital punishment nor life imprisonment without possibility of release shall be imposed for offences committed by persons below eighteen years of age.

Article 37(b) prohibits the arbitrary deprivation of liberty- No child shall be deprived of his or her liberty unlawfully or arbitrarily. The arrest, detention or imprisonment of a child shall be in conformity with the law and shall be used only as a measure of last resort and for the shortest appropriate period of time.

Article 37(c) prohibits the inhuman treatment- Every child deprived of liberty shall be treated with humanity and respect for the inherent dignity of the human person, and in a manner which takes into account the needs of persons of his or her age. In particular, every child deprived of liberty shall be separated from adults unless it is considered in the child's best interest not to do so and shall have the right to maintain contact with his or her family through correspondence and visits, save in exceptional circumstances.

Article 37(d) ensures the right to speediest access to legal and other suitable assistance- Every child deprived of his or her liberty shall have the right to prompt access to legal and other appropriate assistance, as well as the right to challenge the legality of the deprivation of his or her liberty before a court or other competent, independent and impartial authority, and to a prompt decision on any such action.

Article 40 (1) provide mandates to States Parties recognise the right of every child alleged as, accused of, or recognised as having infringed the penal law to be treated in a manner consistent with the promotion of the child's sense of dignity and worth, which reinforces the child's respect for the human rights and fundamental freedoms of others and which takes into account the child's age and the desirability of promoting the child's reintegration and the child's assuming a constructive role in a society.

Article 40(2)(a) Prohibits- No child shall be alleged as, be accused of, or recognised as having infringed the penal law by reason of acts or omissions that were not prohibited by national or international law at the time they were committed.

Article 40(2) (b) (i) provides the 'Principle of innocence'.

Article 40(2) (b) (ii) Prescribes The principle of reasonable opportunity to be heard. It directs as- The charges against him or her to be informed promptly and directly through his or her parents or legal guardians, and be provided with legal or other appropriate assistance in the preparation and presentation of his or her defence.

Article 40(2) (b) (iii) Directs for fair hearing- The accused child shall have a right to have the matter determined without delay by a competent, independent and impartial authority or judicial body in a fair manner, according to law, in the presence of legal or other appropriate assistance and, unless it is considered not to be in the best interest of the child, in particular, taking into account his or her age or situation, his or her parents or legal guardians.

Article 40(2) (b) (iv) prohibits for self-incriminatory testimonial, 'No accused child shall be compelled to become a witness against himself or herself'.

Article 40(2) (b) (v) confers right to appeal as- To go for appeal or revision against the order of the subordinate authority before the higher competent authority.

Article 40(2) (b) (vii) confers- The child right to privacy at all stages of the proceedings.

Article 40(3) directs the States Parties- To seek to promote the establishment of laws, procedures, authorities and institutions specifically applicable to children alleged as, accused of, or recognised as having infringed the penal laws.

Article 40(3) (a) instruct the State to fix the minimum age of criminal responsibility below which children shall be presumed not to have the capacity to infringe the penal law.

Article 40(3) (b) says- Whenever appropriate and desirable, measures for dealing with such children without resorting to judicial proceedings, providing that human rights and legal safeguards are fully respected.

Article 40(4) prescribes- The variety of dispositions, such as care, guidance and supervision orders, counseling, probation, foster care, education and vocational training programmes and other alternatives to institutional care shall be available to ensure that children are dealt with in a manner appropriate to their well-being and proportionate both to their circumstances and the offence.

(vi) The United Nations Rules for the Protection of Juveniles Deprived of their Liberty (1990)[15]

In 1990, The United Nations General Assembly adopted two international instruments regarding juvenile justice were[16]- "*the United Nations Rules for the Protection of Juveniles Deprived of their Liberty" [the Havana Rules] and "the United Nations Guidelines for the Prevention of Juvenile Delinquency"* [*the Riyadh Guidelines*].

The Havana Rules is the first international instrument that defines, juvenile in terms of age– A juvenile is every person under the age of 18.[17] The aim of the juvenile justice system as reflected under the Havana Rules is to uphold the rights and safety and promote the physical and mental well-being of juveniles.[18] Furthermore, the

Havana Rules are proposed for the establishment of minimum standards recommended by the United Nations for The protection of juveniles deprived of their liberty in all forms, consistent with human rights and fundamental freedoms, and with a view to counteracting the detrimental effects of all types of detention and to foster the integration in society.[19]

The Havana Rules also criticise pre-trial detention – Detention before trial shall be avoided to the extent possible and limited to exceptional circumstances[20], as also post-trial incarceration –

"Deprivation of the liberty of a juvenile should be a disposition of last resort and for the minimum necessary period and should be limited to exceptional cases. The length of the sanction should be determined by the judicial authority, without precluding the possibility of his or her early release."[21]

(vii) Havana Rules, 1990

Rule 1 provides- The imprisonment should be used as a last resort. It has second meaning that a delinquent juvenile for very heinous crime, may be sentenced to imprisonment.

Rule 2 provides that if a juvenile is depriving of the liberty, the Beijing Rules set forth shall be followed.

Rule 11(a) states, A juvenile is a person who is under the age of 18. It provides further that deprivation of liberty shall be according to law.

Rule 11(b) prohibits the deprivation of liberty. - Deprivation of liberty means any form of detention or imprisonment or the placement of a person in a public or private custodial setting, from which this person is not permitted to leave at, will, by order of any judicial, administrative or other public authority.

Rule 12 ensures, juveniles detained in facilities should be guaranteed the benefit of meaningful activities and programmes which would serve to promote and sustain their health and self-respect, to foster their sense of responsibility and encourage those attitudes and skills that will assist them in developing their potential as members of society.

Rule 14 confers the right to appeal, 'The juveniles shall be provided right to challenge the legality of the execution of the detention.

Juveniles Under Arrest or Awaiting Trial

Rule 17 lays down the 'Principles of fair trial' to an accused person. It States- The juveniles who are detained under arrest or waiting trial are presumed to be innocent and shall be treated as such until their guilt is proved beyond reasonable doubt.

Rule 18(a) prescribes the principle of fair trial. It ensures, that the juveniles should have the right of legal counsel and be enabled to apply for free legal aid, where such aid is available, and to communicate regularly with their legal advisers. Privacy and confidentiality shall be ensured for such communications.

The Management of Juvenile Facilities

Rule 19 prescribes the provisions regarding the removal of stigma attached with juvenile delinquency. It says– Records of the juvenile delinquent should be placed confidential and third party should be allowed to have access as per the procedure made therein. After discharge of the juvenile delinquent from the institutions, the record should be destroyed at the appropriate time.

Rule 22 directs that the parents, guardians or close relative of the juvenile should be informed without delay about admission, place, transfer and release.

Rule 23 directs to managing authority, that as soon as possible after reception, full reports and relevant information on the personal situation and circumstances of each juvenile should be prepared and reported to the administration.

Rule 30 prescribes for 'Open detention facilities for juveniles.

Suitable Environment and Accommodation

Rule 31 ensures that Juveniles deprived of their liberty have the right to facilities and services that meet all the requirements of health and human dignity.

Rule 37 ensures, that every detention facility shall ensure that every juvenile receives food that is suitably prepared and presented at normal meal times and of a quality and quantity to satisfy the standards of dietetics, hygiene and health.

Education, Vocational Training and Work

Rule 39 confers the right to education- The juveniles above compulsory school age who wish to continue their education should be permitted and encouraged to do so, and every effort should be made to provide them with access to appropriate educational programmes.

Rule 41 ensures, that every detention facility should provide access to a library that is adequately stocked with both instructional and recreational books and periodicals suitable for the juveniles, who should be encouraged and enabled to make full use of it.

Rule 42 provides that every juvenile should have the right to receive vocational training in occupations likely to prepare him or her for future employment.

Rule 44 provides that all protective national and international standards applicable to child labour and young workers should apply to juveniles deprived of their liberty.

Rule 46 confers the right to remuneration, - Every juvenile who performs work should have the right to an equitable remuneration.

Rule 49 ensures the right to medical care, - Every juvenile shall receive adequate medical care, both preventive and remedial, including dental, ophthalmological and mental health care, care, as well as pharmaceutical products and special diets as medically indicated.

Rule 50 confers- Every juvenile a right to be examined by a physician immediately upon admission to a detention facility, for the purpose of recording any evidence of prior ill-treatment and identifying any physical or mental condition requiring medical attention.

Rule 59 postulates the principles of social reintegration of juveniles into community after his or her discharge from the detention

Center. It states as, - Every juvenile should have the opportunity of adequate communication with the outside world, which is an integral part of the right to fair and humane treatment and is essential to the preparation of juveniles for their return to society.

Rule 60 prescribes provisions similar to parole and licence while undergoing institutional treatment. It states, Every juvenile should have the right to receive regular and frequent visits, in principle once a week and not less than once a month, in circumstances that respect the need of the juvenile for privacy, contact and unrestricted communication with the family and the defence counsel.

Rule 61 prescribes the provision - Every juvenile should have the right to communicate in writing or by telephone at least twice a week with the person of his or her choice, unless legally restricted, and should be assisted as necessary in order effectively to enjoy this right. Every juvenile should have the right to receive correspondence.

Rule 63 prohibits, "Recourse to instruments of restraint and to force for any purpose should be prohibited."

Rule 64 point out the exception to the above Rule 63. States as, Instruments of restraint and force can only be used in exceptional cases, where all other control methods have been exhausted and failed, and only as explicitly authorised and specified by law and regulation.

Disciplinary Procedures

Rule 67 prohibits cruel, inhuman or degrading treatment in disciplinary matter. States as- All disciplinary measures constituting cruel, in human or degrading treatment shall be strictly prohibited, including corporal punishment, placement in a dark cell, closed or solitary confinement or any other punishment that may compromise the physical or of mental health of the juvenile concerned.

Rule 68 prescribes guidelines - In the matter of legislation or regulations adopted by the competent administrative authority. It directs the authority to establish norms taking full account of the fundamental characteristics, needs and rights of juveniles.

Rule 75 confers right to every juvenile - To have the opportunity of making requests or complaints to the director of the detention facility and to his or her authorised representative.

Rule 76 confers - Right to every juvenile to make a request or complaint, without censorship as to substance, to the central administration, the judicial authority or other proper authorities through approved channels, and to be informed of the response immediately.

Rule 77 recommends for establishing an independent office (ombudsman) to receive and investigate complaints made by juveniles deprived of their liberty and to assist in the achievement of equitable settlements.

Rule 78 confers - Right to every juvenile to request assistance from family members, legal counselors, humanitarian groups or others where possible, in order to make a complaint.

Rule 80 recommends, that Competent authorities should provide or ensure services to assist juveniles in re-establishing themselves in society and to lessen prejudice against such juveniles.

Rule 82 provides that the administration should provide for the careful selection and recruitment of every grade and type of personnel. Since the proper management of detention facilities depends on their integrity, humanity, ability and professional capacity to deal with juveniles, as well as personal suitability for the work.

Rule 87(b) suggests that all personnel should rigorously oppose and combat any act of corruption, reporting it without delay to the competent authorities.

(viii) The United Nations Guidelines for the Prevention of Juvenile Delinquency, "The Riyadh Guidelines" (1990)[22]

Guideline 56 investigates about status offences and status offenders. It expresses that, law should be made to prevent further criminalisation victimisation and stigmatisation, of juveniles, accordingly to ensure that any act which is not considered an offence and not punished if committed by an adult is not considered an offence and not punished if committed by a juvenile.

This provision of the Guidelines clearly speaks of removal of status offender from the jurisdiction of administration of juvenile justice. It asserts the proposition that justice to delinquent juvenile is different from the justice to the neglected or other juveniles. The removal of status offenders which includes many categories of children in the present definition of children in need of care and protection establishes the fact that juvenile justice system generally begin with taking into custody of children which results into deprivation of liberty of children. That is the reason, the Guidelines suggests removal of status offenders from the administration of juvenile justice. Considering this guidelines, the children in need of care and protection should be also taken out from the jurisdiction of administration of juvenile justice, which essentially envisages custodial treatment.

Guideline 58 provides for diversionary programmes for juvenile delinquents outside the juvenile justice system. It clearly suggests that to the best possible extent the juvenile delinquent accused of non-serious offences should be dealt with under various rehabilitator schemes and programmes outside the jurisdiction of juvenile justice administration. It clearly establishes the fact that juvenile justice essentially relates to administration of juvenile justice and that cannot be done without depriving the liberty of the juvenile delinquent. It further suggest that the custody and liberty is the main issue involved in the juvenile justice system and for that reason the international documents binding or non-binding provide for diversionary programmes in the justice system.

To achieve the task of diversion is a mirage because it involves participation of the community and the community cannot be forced to involve in the rehabilitative processes of juvenile delinquents.

2.5 Conclusion

In the conclusion, it has been observed that from the global perspective the term juvenile justice includes, civil and political as well as economic, social and cultural justice. By implication, it refers to both, after onset of delinquency and before the onset of delinquency. To be more precise, the first one refers to the administration of juvenile justice by applying internationally accepted standards and norms and second refers to schemes and policies of the government to prevent the first incident of crime.

However, the proper functioning of justice administration and welfare administration from one platform at the municipal level appears to be debatable. At the municipal level, implementation of the binding international covenant is confronted with the problem of coordination, monitoring etc. apart from the constitutional limitation created by the principles of federalism.

REFERENCES

1. Ved Kumari, The Juvenile Justice System in India – From Welfare to Rights, p. 47, Oxford University Press, 2004.
2. UNCRC, 1989, Article 40(1).
3. The Third International Congress for the Welfare and Protection of Children was held in London from 15th to 18th July 1902, under the patronage of His Majesty King Edward VII.
4. The Third International Congress for the Welfare and Protection of Children was held in London from 15th to 18th July 1902, under the patronage of His Majesty King Edward VII.
5. Report of the Proceeding of Third International Congress, 1902, cited in Juvenile Delinquency: A Comparative Study by A.D. Attar, Chap. II (Popular Prakashan, Bombay, 1964)].
6. Adopted by the League of Nations on 26th September 1924.
7. Geneva Declaration of the Rights of the Child, 1924, available at http://www.humanium.org/en/childrens.(visited on July 23, 2017).
10. Adopted by UNO General Assembly Resolution 40/33, dated 29.11.1985 cited in Law Relating to Juvenile Justice in India by R.N. Choudhry, pp. 1235-1243, Orient Publishing Company, 3 edn, 2009.
11. Beijing Rules, 1985, Rule 2.2(a).
12. Beijing Rules, 1985, Rule 14.2.
13. Beijing Rules, 1985, Rule 7.1.
14. Adopted and opened for signature, ratification and accession by General Assembly Resolution 44/25 dated 20-11-1989, and came into force on 2-9-1990, in accordance with Article 49.8.
15. Ian Brownlie and Guy S. Goodwin-Gill, Basic Documents on Human Rights, Oxford University Press, 2nd edn., 1981].

16. Both on 14th December 1990.
17. Havana Rules, 1990, Rule 11(a).
18. Havana Rules, 1990, Rule 1.
19. Havana Rules, 1990, Rule 3.
20. Havana Rules, 1990, Rule 17.
21. Havana Rules, 1990, Rule 2.
22. Adopted by General Assembly Resolution 45/112, dated 14.12.1990 cited in Law Relating to Juvenile Justice in India by R. N. Choudhry, pp. 1225-1234 (Orient Publishing Company, 3rd edn., 2009).

3

Global Prospective on Juvenile Justice

3.1 Introduction

This chapter is focused on descriptive analysis of juvenile justice system of various countries. The author found that there is a plethora of information available on specific juvenile justice systems and comparative analysis of juvenile justice systems but the diverse nature of the various juvenile justice systems precludes one from presenting a concise illustration of the similarities and differences between the various juvenile systems. There are discrepancies in specific issues across regions, despite that some general observations can be made about the administration of juvenile justice. However, the majority of the countries have committed in principle to a comprehensive juvenile justice system, and many having specific legislation for child offenders, but in practice there is a lack of full implementation.

Considering the limitation of this chapter the emphasis is only on country's approaches to define delinquency, and processing those who are officially labelled as delinquent with the charge of heinous crimes. Further, in this chapter, the author examines the status of life imprisonment and death penalty awarded to juveniles for the heinous crimes committed, in various countries as well as in India and critically analyses the differences in sentencing options in different countries and reviews the practice of the death penalty in the international prospective.

3.2 Juvenile Justice in the United Kingdom

In England, there is Youth Justice System, which is aimed to prevent crime by children and young people who are under 18 years. The Youth Justice Board has power to place juveniles in custody and usually those aged less than 15 years of age, are sent to Secure Children's Home. Those who are older than 15 years are to be held in either a Young Offender Institution or Secure Training Centre (STC). Whereas, 17 years old female young people are normally placed in YOI.

(i) Age of criminal responsibility

Section 50 of the Children and Young Person Act 1933 states: It shall be conclusively presumed that no child under the age of ten years can be guilty of any offence.[1]

(ii) Definition of "children" and "young people"

Under the criminal justice system a child is defined as a person under the age of 14; and young person as a person who has attained the age of 14 and is under the age of 18.[2]

(iii) The Court System

The following guidelines regulate the judgment of the juvenile justice system for juveniles:

1. When the child is under the age of ten, criminal proceedings cannot be brought, however, the police may initiate care proceedings if other evidence is available to show that the child requires care or control;
2. When the child is between the ages of ten to fourteen years, criminal proceedings may be brought if there is evidence to rebut doli in capas; and
3. When the child is between the ages of fourteen and sixteen years, there are no specific legal restraints, which constrain criminal proceedings.

A child between the ages of 12 and 17 may be shifted to criminal court. When the juvenile is accused jointly along an adult person the case is heard by the adult Court. In the case where the juvenile found guilty, the criminal court sent the juvenile to court for disposition. The juvenile is not discharged or fined by the criminal court.[3]

When the juvenile denies accepting the charges against him, then the safeguards of criminal trial as to the admissibility of evidence and the burden of proof are retained. Thus, in a contested case, there are two stages. The first is conducted as if it were a criminal trial. The second is civil in nature with civil rules of evidence and proof.

The Juvenile court proceedings are conducted before one to three magistrates drawn from a panel. The following dispositions are available for criminal cases in the juvenile court:

(1) Fines up to $ 125;

(2) Compensation to the victim;

(3) Required attendance at an attendance centre;

(4) Up to 6 months in a detention centre;

(5) Commitment to Borstal training;

(6) Conditional discharge; and

(7) Unconditional discharge.

(iv) Sentences for serious offences

Rebutting the presumption - children should be tried summarily in a youth court, sentencing Guidelines prescribes that the children who are, charged with homicide, subject to a minimum statutory sentence. Charged together with an adult offender who sent to the Crown Court and it has been determined that the cases should be kept together, or charged with a grave crime and a youth court have convicted them, to be presented before the Crown Court for trial and sentence.

Where children aged 10-17 years have been convicted of serious crimes in the Crown Court, can be punished with number of long-term sentences.

(v) During her Majesty's Pleasure under Section 90 of the PCC(S) Act, 2000

Section 90 of the Criminal Courts (Sentencing) Act 2000[4] it is provided that a person below the age of 18 when the offence was committed, is convicted of murder shall be detained at Her Majesty's pleasure.

When a child is convicted, or pleads guilty to murder, will be awarded life sentenced. Under the Schedule 21 of the Criminal Justice Act 2003, the minimum term of life sentence awarded is 12 years for a person under 18 years of age. For discretionary life sentence the release and recall provisions are the same.

(vi) A determinate sentence under section 91 of the powers of Criminal Courts (sentencing) under PCC(S) Act, 2000

This grave crimes, provision, empowered the court to sentence a child as an adult. The provisions under the Section 91[5] prescribes that children and youth who are convicted of certain stipulated serious offences other than murder for which the prescribed punishment is imprisonment for 14 years or more, may be sentenced up to maximum sentence for the offence, which may be for life. The child who is convicted of a serious offence or for many other offences including sexual offences could attract a sentence of 14 years or more (even where the maximum sentence is less than 14 years or more) or several offences relating to firearms.

The children sentenced under Section 90 or under 91 are liable, under Section 92[6], to be detained in such place and under such conditions as the Secretary of State may direct or arrange with any person.[7]

The objective of sentence passed under Section 90/91 is to achieve the objective of separate juvenile justice system. These sections are to create deterrent effect and to some extent, they are retributive in essence as well as focused on the needs of special attention to given to the rehabilitation of the juvenile offenders. Significantly, such sentences vary in terms of their length as well as in terms of how and where the offenders are put into custody. The young person who, sentenced to no more than a few months' detention, due to his/ her age or vulnerability will spend rest of sentence in secure accommodation in a SCH. But the juvenile offenders who are charged with murder or some other grave crime, after spending custodial periods first in a SCH or STC and then in a Prison Service under 18 establishment, will consequently move to, the adult prison system to complete the remaining part of their custodial sentence.

Under section 91 offenders may, in most of the cases automatically released on licence before the completion of their sentence. Normally Home detention curfew will be applied. The licence period will continue until the completion of sentence.[8]

The procedures provided for the release of those juvenile offenders who, are sentenced to imprisonment at her Majesty's pleasure or a life sentence are same as adult who are sentenced for life and includes consideration by the Parole Board.

Section 226 of the Criminal Justice Act, 2003 provides, young people convicted of a specific sexual or violent offences which carry a maximum punishment of 10 years imprisonment, or more, and, who are deemed threatening for society, will be sentenced for imprisonment for 10 years unless the court takes into account that sentence of imprisonment for life is justified under section 91 or an prolonged Sentence under section 228 would be adequate in terms of public protection.

Sentence under s.226 explain, that the young person must remain in custody until the custodial part (the tariff) set by the Court has been served, after serving the custodial part offender will be eligible for parole. Release from custody is subject to the consideration of the Parole Board. If the board is satisfied that it is safe for them to be released, i.e. when a full risk assessment denotes that they no longer risk to the public. The provision of Home Detention Curfew unlikely section 91 is not available. The juvenile offender once released, may remain on license for indefinite period, but in case of life licenses, they have to get their license renewed at the 10 years point by the Parole Board and every year subsequently. The Parole Board have power to terminate the license if deems fit.

Section 228 provides, Young people who have been convicted of sexual or violent offences (including if they have been convicted of an offence carrying a maximum penalty of 10 years or more) and if court considered them to be dangerous, will be sentenced to an Extended Sentence which extends the period on license and prevent them from early release except on parole.

3.3 Juvenile Justice in United States of America (USA)

It is a difficult task to present a description of Juvenile Justice in the United States; the reason is that the United States includes fifty-one political jurisdictions (50 states and the District of Columbia) which have legal authority to define delinquency.[9] Yet juvenile justice in United States is characterised by complex political jurisdictions, there are some common factors to juvenile justice in U.S. focussing on commonalities, the author attempts to portray the juvenile justice system of U.S.[10]

(i) Apprehension and transfer and police procedure

The juvenile offender may be apprehended by a community agency,[11] but in most of the cases, the juvenile offender will be apprehended by the local police. Apprehended juvenile may be transferred to a social agency for treatment. He may be unconditionally released, or released on certain conditions.

The apprehended juvenile may be reprimanded and released, or the police officer may serve as a problem resolver between the complaining party and the juvenile and / or his parents.

Many police departments have Police Juvenile Units. If the juvenile is apprehended and brought to the Police Juvenile Unit of the police department, the Police Juvenile Unit may attempt to resolve the conflict between the complaining party and the juvenile and/ or his parents. However, non-judicial resolution is given more importance.

The juvenile is assigned to a juvenile officer of Police Juvenile Unit. The juvenile officer disposes off the cases by selecting one of the following options:

1. The child offender may release to parents with official reprimand;
2. May release with official report of field interrogation;
3. May released to some other juvenile agency;
4. May refer to juvenile court without detention; or
5. May refer to juvenile court with detention.

(ii) Definition

In most of States, the juvenile can be held in detention for up to forty-eight hours without a court order. If a juvenile is to be detained beyond forty-eight hours, a detention hearing takes place within this period.[12]

(iii) The judicial process

If the counselor and judge decide further legal proceedings are necessary, the district or county attorney is notified and a charge sheet is drawn up. A recommendation from the police department or a complainant's petition is required before a juvenile appears in juvenile court. When a petition is filled with the juvenile court, a probation officer is assigned, but he cannot be involved with the juvenile unless the juvenile is detained prior to adjudication (Kansas Criminal Justice Standards and Goals, 1975). The pre-trial procedural steps in the juvenile court are as follows:

(1) Complaints go to the clerk of the court;

(2) A probation officer is assigned;

(3) The probation officer interviews parents;

(4) The probation officer inquire into circumstances of the alleged problem Arraignment;

(5) The probation officer presents the complaint; and

(6) A public defender is appointed.

Most of the states have four separate hearings for juvenile;

1. **The detention hearing** is the hearing to decide whether or not the juvenile should be held in custody pendency the plea hearing;

2. **The plea hearing** is that hearing where the juvenile admits or denies involvement in the alleged misbehaviour (i.e., arraignment);

3. **The adjudicatory hearing** is hearing to decide whether or not the juvenile committed the alleged delinquent act; and

4. **The dispositional hearing** is the hearing to determine that disposition which is best for the child and the community.

However, in some states the judge conducts the plea hearing, the adjudicatory hearing, and the disposition hearing at the same time.

The adjudicatory hearing must be scheduled within two weeks of the detention. This hearing must engage a prosecuting attorney, a defence counsel, and the juvenile court judge. The guardian ad litem[13] plays a crucial role in safeguarding the rights of the juvenile and his or her family.[14] Under the adjudicatory hearing, the juvenile may be dismissed with a warning to both the juvenile and his parents or the judge may include that the juvenile did not commit the alleged act. If the court concludes that the juvenile did commit the alleged act, the judge will then schedule a dispositional hearing. If the judge conducts the adjudication and the disposition in the same hearing, he will have information about the alleged offence and the social history of the child and his family at the hearing.

In rare cases, the juvenile may be shifted to adult court. Prior to transfer of jurisdiction, a waiver hearing must be held.[15] If he is tried, and found guilty in an adult court, he may be sentenced to an adult prison.

Prior to the disposition hearing, the juvenile court judge reviews the social history of the juvenile which is prepared by a probation officer, the social history includes information regarding prior offences, current offences, family relationships, school records, prior contact with the police, and the probation officer's recommendations. At the dispositional hearing, the judge will make a decision in the best interests of the child and the community. The traditional alternatives include the following: probation, a state juvenile institution (youth centre), foster care, a private agency, or a community-based facility.

3.4 Juvenile Justice in Canada

In Canada the youth offender between the ages of 12 and 18 are governed by The Youth Criminal Justice Act. The criminal and correctional law will be applicable to the youth above the 12 and below 18 years of age at the time of when the crime was committed. Under certain conditions, Youth between the ages of 14 and 17 may be treated as adults. The Youth Criminal Justice Act will try all the case of offences committed by youth but exception to this, for specific offences and in specific circumstances a youth may be sentenced an adult sentence.[16]

3.5 Juvenile Justice in Italy

Article 98 (1) of Italian Penal Code states, A person who has reached the age of 14 but not 18 at the time of committing a crime and who is *capable of understanding and willing* must be punished but the punishment may be reduced. Whether the youth offenders (between the ages of 14 and 18) are capable to understand and to form mental intent, must be precisely determined by presiding officer. The youth offenders may be sentenced same as the adult but with considerable punitive and reductions. The orders and sentences applicable to adults may also be applied to minors. If the court observed that the youth is at the risk of re-offending, the court may send him to judicial reformatory.[17]

3.6 Juvenile Justice in Germany

In Germany, the minimum punishment for juvenile delinquency is imprisonment for six months and the maximum 5 years for the juvenile aged between 14 -17 years. In Germany unsuspended youth penalty means high security prisons for duration of 6 months up to 5, or in exceptional cases, 10 years. For the very serious offences the maximum length of youth imprisonment is ten years same as adult. In the case of 18-20 year-old young offenders, the maximum penalty is ten years. The pre-conditions for youth imprisonment are either the dangerous tendencies of the youth offender that are to avoid community sanctions as inappropriate, or the gravity of guilt, serious crimes (like murder, aggravated robbery etc).[18]

3.7 Juvenile Justice in Pakistan

The Pakistan Penal Code of 1860, the Code of Criminal Procedure of 1898 and the statutes which are awarding punishment for criminal offences are applicable generally to all in the four provinces of Pakistan, excluding the tribal areas. According to the Pakistan Penal code, "nothing is an offence which is done by a child under seven years of age"[19]; further, under section 83, "nothing is an offence which is done by a child above seven years of age and under twelve, who has not attained sufficient maturity of understanding to judge of the nature and consequences of his conduct on that occasion". The criterion for attainment of maturity denotes that a child having sufficient understanding to form a criminal intent at the time of commission of the offence. The Pakistan Penal Code states if a child above the age of 12 or between the ages of 7-12 has attained sufficient maturity of understanding can be convicted and sentenced to all the relevant punishments provided under penal code, including the capital punishment. Pakistan penal code provides a child under the age of 15 years is apprehended or detained for an offence, which is punishable with imprisonment of less than 10 years, shall be treated as if he was accused of commission of a bailable offence. No child under the age of 15 years shall be arrested under any of the laws dealing with preventive detention or under the provisions of Chapter VIII of the Criminal Procedure Code. Exception to this law the Court may refuse to grant bail to a child aged 15 years, if there are reasonable grounds to ascertain that such child is engaged in an offence which in its opinion is heinous, serious, gruesome, brutal, sensational in character or shocking to public morality or he has earlier conviction of an offence punishable with death or imprisonment for life.

Pakistan's penal laws do not provide a minimum age limit for imposing capital punishment that doesn't differentiate between the minimum age of criminal responsibility and the age below which death penalty may not be imposed. Minors are considered to be legally responsible at the same level as adults. Although, Qisas and Diyat Ordinance provides that the death sentence may not be imposed below the age of 18 for murder or any other offence. This Ordinance has amended the laws relating to offences of causing injury, murder and homicide and replace respective sections of the Pakistan Penal Code, The Hudood laws of 1979 which relate to the offences of theft, armed robbery, rape, drinking and using drug fornication, false accusation of fornication, and which replace Pakistan: Death penalty for juveniles. The relevant sections of the Pakistan Penal Code, apply, without exception, to all parts of Pakistan and override all other legislation, including legislation relating to children.[20] The Hudood Laws provided Hadd or fixed punishment for the offences, provided certain strict evidential requirements are fulfilled. The punishments awarded as Hadd punishments include stoning to death for fornication, and armed robbery, judicial amputation for theft and flogging for consumption of intoxicants. Though Hudood Laws are pertinent to offenders irrespective of age but the Hadd punishments may not be imposed on children.

However, the definition of a child under the Hudood laws differs from that of other laws in Pakistan: A child is a person who has not attained puberty. The Hudood law relating to fornication differentiates between the genders of the offenders, for a male the age of criminal responsibility is 18 years while for a female it is 16 years or at attainment of puberty. Thus, a girl of 12 years who has attained puberty is legally adult and could be sentenced to the Hadd punishments. But in practice no child has so far been sentenced to stoning to death, or to public flogging, to judicial amputation yet the laws provided on the statute book can be imposed. The legal position of children in Pakistan is no very clear, as there are several laws at the federal and provincial level which partly contradict or supersede each other and which are interpreted differently in the legal practice of different courts. Provincial laws contain different provisions in respect of children and the age of criminal responsibility. The relevant law enforced in Sindh, the Sindh Children Act of 1955, states under section 68(1) a youthful offender, a person below 16 years of age, shall not be sentenced to death or life imprisonment. While The Punjab Youthful Offenders Ordinance of 1983 in section 45(1) states no offender below the age of 15 years at the time of the occurrence of offence may be sentenced to death or life imprisonment. The special laws related to children in Sindh and Punjab override the provisions of the Pakistan Penal Code. There are no special laws regulating penalties for children in Baluchistan and the North-West Frontier Province.[21]

3.8 Juvenile Justice in Northern Ireland

In Northern Ireland the Juvenile Justice System is based on the principle of restorative justice, construed as mainstreamed, statutory-based with youth conferencing system under the Justice (Northern Ireland) Act 2002.

On the recommendation of a review of the criminal justice system in 2000, The Juvenile Justice Board was substituted by an Executive Agency that paves the path of institution of the Youth Justice Agency and The Youth Conference Service has worked throughout Northern Ireland until the end of 2006. It is applicable on persons who are under the age of 18 years for both all type of offences; except offences which attract a life sentence.[22]

The juvenile justice system depends upon the service of youth conferences. The offender and offender's supporters with the victim and victim's supporters/representative are brought together with the offender in an arranged meeting that is assisted by professionals. Both the parties are given an opportunity to put their part at the meeting through conference, in order to discuss the offence and its repercussions, and to agree on an action plan for the offender. There are two types of conference: diversionary and court-ordered. In diversionary conference the juvenile offender is referred by the prosecution service as a substitute to alternative to prosecution. In court-ordered conference a young person is referred post-conviction. In the case of court-ordered conferences, the action plan agreed by the participants must be approved by the court. For referring a child to youth conference service the admittance of the guilt and consent for participation in conference is mandatory.

Following the conviction of the child offender the court is required to send a child to youth conferencing, in all cases except those which carry a mandatory life sentence, are try-able on arraignment only in the case of an adult, or for specific terrorism offences. However youth conferencing is used for a broad variety of offences including serious offences such as assault and sexual offences. In case of serious offences, the process is supervised by a Priority Youth Offender Team. Through the approach known as circles of support and accountability, the child is intensively supervised, up to seven days a week, and helped to complete their recuperative plans.

3.9 Juvenile Justice in South Africa

According to The Child Justice Act of South Africa, a child who is fourteen years or above at the time of commission of offence can be treated as adult and sentenced to imprisonment for any offence. Under The Child Justice Act, a separate and distinct procedure for delinquent children, has been established which encapsulated numerous protection measure to check the exposure of children to the possible harmful effects of prosecution and detention. This provision is taken from the Constitution of South Africa (section 28(1)(g)), which provides mandates.... For every child the right not to be detained, in cases where children are detained, this must be for the shortest appropriate period of time and it is used as a measure of last resort.

Section 69 of the Child Justice Act, provides The sentencing of children which is aimed at encouraging the child to understand the repercussion of their offence committed and be accountable for it; providing individualised responses which strikes a balance between the circumstances of the child, the nature of the offence and the interests of society; promoting reintegration of the child into the family and community, including any necessary supervision, guidance, treatment or services; and should use imprisonment only for the shortest appropriate period of time and only as a measure of last resort.

Section 53 of the Child Justice Act enumerates listing of diversified measures which can be imposed subject to the gravity of the crimes... (Such as, common assault without bodily harm, defamation, contempt of court, trespass and blasphemy). These measures can include oral or written apologies, supervision and guidance orders, formal cautions, family time orders, compulsory school attendance, peer association orders, good behaviour orders and referral to counseling or therapy. In case of heinous offences (including kidnapping or abduction, murder, human trafficking, arson and sexual offences) multifarious orders include: (i) Compulsory attendance at a specified Centre or place for a specified vocational, educational or therapeutic purpose, which may include a period or periods of temporary residence; (ii) Referral to intensive therapy to treat or manage problems that have been identified as a cause of the child coming into conflict with the law, which may include a period or periods of temporary residence; and (iii) Placement under the supervision of a probation officer on conditions which may include restriction of movement...without the prior written approval of the probation officer.[23]

For imposing a sentence to imprisonment to a child, justice courts are required to take following consideration into account- (i) The seriousness of the offence, with due regard to the quantum of harm done or risked through the offence and the culpability of the child in this regard; protection of the community; (ii) The severity of the impact of the offence on the victim; (iii) Previous failure of the child to respond to non-residential alternatives; and (iv) The desirability of keeping the child out of prison.[24]

In 2009, the Constitutional Court observed that the Criminal Law Amendment Act 105 of 1997, which made certain sentences (including life imprisonment) applicable to the child of 16 and 17 year olds, constituted an unjustifiable infringement of children's constitutional rights, particularly their rights to imprisonment as a last resort and for the shortest period of time.

3.10 Juvenile Justice in Philippines

The Juvenile Justice Welfare Act in Philippines is based on a juvenile justice and welfare system that significantly incorporate the Principles of restorative justice, rehabilitation and reintegration. The Juvenile Justice and Welfare Act (JJWA), was enacted in consonance of the provisions of Article 40 of the CRC whereby ...children in conflict with the law must be treated in a manner consistent with the promotion of the child's sense of dignity and worth, taking into account the child's age and desirability of promoting his/her reintegration.

Under the JJWA, Children below fifteen years old are not held liable for any offence but are, instead referred to a Local Social Welfare and Development Officer (LSWDO) for mediation. Children between 15 and 18 years of age deemed not to be mature enough to form a criminal intent. When children of 15 – 18 years who are thought to be mature enough to form criminal intent will be referred either to a law enforcement officer (regarding offences with an imposable penalty of six years or less) or to a prosecutor or judge (penalty is more than six years).

The JJWA incorporated numerous rights of delinquent children, as a safeguard. It includes not to be sentenced to capital punishment, life imprisonment without the possibility of release penalty or life imprisonment and the right to bail, diversion and probation as alternatives to custody. It also include the right to an automatic suspension of sentence, but can be imprisoned, especially on reaching the age of 18, if they are convicted of committing a heinous crime at the age of 15 or above. Senator Francis Pangilinan, author of the JJWA, says that, children who commit serious offences might, in special case, be placed in the custody of the Department of Social Welfare and Development.[25]

3.11 Juvenile Justice in Finland

According to Finland penal law the age of criminal responsibility is fifteen and the offenders below 15 are dealt with by the child protection authorities. In Finland the child conviction is welfare based rather than described as custody or imprisonment as they would be in England and Wales. The crime in Finland is viewed as a symptom of extensive social problems and reflection of person's emotional or behavioural issues. Hence Finland is able to successfully avoid criminalising and their youth, instead taking a rehabilitation- and treatment-based approach to offending by young people. Conceivably, Finland removes a significant number of children from their homes, and places them in a broad range of facilities, such as special psychiatric units, youth detox clinics, shelters, reformatories and foster care.[26]

Instinctively in Finland, crime rates are low and have a low rate of incarceration but a high degree of involvement in the lives of young people.

3.12 Juvenile Justice in Iran

The Iranian Penal Code differentiate between the minimum age of criminal responsibility and the age at which children are regarded to be legally responsible at the same level as adults. Therefore according to Iranian law, a fifteen year-old boy and a nine year-old girl are tried same as adults and can be sentenced the capital punishment. As per the Iranian law, child attains adulthood at puberty (*bulugh*), as stipulated by its interpretation of Shari'a and as specified in Iran's 1991 Civil Code as 15 lunar years (14 years and 5 months) for boys and 9 lunar years (8 years and 8 months) for girls. Furthermore article 82 of the Iranian Penal Code establishes capital punishment as the penalty for adultery crimes (*hodud*), "irrespective of the age or marital status of the offender." Therefore, *hodud* crimes are deemed as crimes against God, the Supreme Leader of Iran has no power to grant pardons in such cases. Punishment is stipulated by the Quran and Sunna, and, cannot be altered by any authority.

Iranian law imposes "*qesas*" punishment for the offence of murder, which provides that the family of the victim has the sole power to determine whether the accused should be executed. Iranian jurisprudence considers *qesas* a personal right of the victim's family that neither the judge nor any other authority can overrule; regardless of that the perpetrator is a juvenile. A death sentence is also prescribed for the extended list of crimes, including: adultery, same-sex relations, apostasy, and certain drug-related offenses.

Unfortunately, Iran leads in the execution of juvenile offenders and hence in 2016, it had the maximum number of the executions of juvenile offenders. A report by Amnesty International, the country has registered 73 executions of minors between 2005 and 2015, including at least 4 in 2015.[27] Iran executed at least one juvenile offender in 2010, and five in 2009. Unfortunately, this figure is an underestimate of the true number of executions, taking into account, because Iranian government refused to disclose data on these executions, which it considers confidential.

During its Universal Periodic Review before the United Nations Human Rights Council, Iran negated the requests from member states to eradicate the juvenile death penalty. Regardless of absolute ban on capital punishment to persons below the age of 18 years, government officials continuously insist that Iran complies with international norms because it does not execute juvenile offenders until they turn 18. Iran is considered as the world's second-most prolific executioner.

3.13 Juvenile Justice in Saudi Arabia

Saudi Arabia doesn't have a codified penal law, specifying the acts which constituting criminal offenses or a published official interpretation of Sharia law, which established the foundation for all laws. Though, judges are empowered with broad discretion to interpret and apply Sharia principles in criminal cases. Saudi courts have imposed the death penalty for wide array of offenses, which include drug trafficking, adultery, corruption, sabotage, political rebellion, apostasy and murder. The courts are empowered to sentence the death penalty as a discretionary punishment (ta'zir) for any other acts it deems to be criminal. Under interpretations of Shari'a law prevailing in Saudi Arabia, murder and manslaughter are considered to be primarily offenses against a private right (qisas). In the qisas cases, the deceased's family has rights to choose the execution of the offender, have monetary compensation, or a pardon. On November 24, 2008, the Shura Council, an appointed advisory body having certain parliament functions as well, passed a measure to raise the age of majority from 15 to 18, despite the opposition of the Council's Islamic Affairs, Judiciary, and Human Rights Committee. On October 4, 2010, the Council again debated on the age of majority in the context of a drafted law on protecting children from violence and neglect. The Saudi Cabinet has not passed any of measure into law and their applicability to capital punishment, leaving the capital punishment in vague. Children have been tried as adults and sentenced to death for crimes committed at age of 13 years. The Human Rights Organisation, Reprieve, reports, Saudi Arabia executed at least four juveniles in January 2016 during a mass execution of 47 people.[28] According to Reprieve, One of the four, Ali al-Ribh, had been arrested in school, tortured and forced to a falsely confess for involvement in anti-government protests, and executed.[29] Reprieve also reports, three other Saudi juveniles—Ali al-Nimr, Dawoud al-Marhoon, and Abdullah al-Zaher—who were arrested following pro-democracy protests in 2012 face execution after having been tortured into signing false confessions, which were used in a secretive counter-terrorism court to convict them, and sentence them to death."[30]

3.14 Juvenile Justice in Sudan

In Sudan no separate definition of child is provided under criminal law. Definition of a child is drawn from the definition of "adult" provided in the Criminal Act, which is as "adult means any person whose puberty has been established by definite natural features and who has completed 15 years of age, and whoever attains 18 years of age shall be deemed an adult even if the features of puberty do not appear."[31]

3.15 Juvenile Justice in Nigeria

Nigeria defines the age of adulthood nationally as 17, and 12 in states, in northern Nigeria which are governed under Shari'a laws, some of which define the age of criminal responsibility at the age of 17.

3.16 Egypt and Sri Lanka also sentence under-18s to death

In Egypt there were more than 500 people sentenced to death in 2014.

Some of those were under 18.[32]

In Sri Lanka there are more than 60 people sentenced to death in 2014.

Some of those were under than 18.[33]

3.17 International standards for age determination of criminal responsibility

The **UNCRC** did not prescribe any specific minimum age of criminal responsibility but the United Nation Committee explained that, The minimum age of criminal responsibility differs widely owing to history and culture. The modern approach would be to consider whether a child can live up to the moral and psychological components of criminal responsibility; that it, whether a child, by virtue of her or his individual discernment and undertaking, can be held responsible for essentially anti-social behaviour. If the age of criminal responsibility is fixed too low or if there is no age limit at all, the notion of responsibility would become meaningless.[34]

In international regime, the cut off limit for the end of 'childhood' is 18 unless under the law applicable to the child, majority is attained earlier.[35] A person attain his or her 18 years of age, are deemed to be fully responsible for their actions and the repercussion there of. Although by age eighteen, adolescent reach level of intellectual maturity; psychological maturity continues to develop into early adulthood. According to Ruban C, The biological age of majority is close to 22 years and the pertinent parts that govern impulsivity, judgment, planning for the future, foresight of consequences, and other characteristics that make people morally culpable, develops after attaining the age of maturity.[36] Further it is acknowledge that there exists no scientifically precise method to determine the maturity of an individual.[37] Such determination would exceed the limits of science, the result being fraught with error and arbitrariness.[38] The age at which children reach the status of adulthood, the age of 'maturity', is not of course an objective or measurable concept. Since such a case by case analysis of maturity to determine culpability is scientifically impossible, a presumption of maturity exists beyond the age of eighteen. There is evidence to suggest that significant brain development continues until the early 20s. However, the main objective of setting an age of majority is to create uniformity for administrative purposes. Therefore it is required to set uniform age of majority worldwide.

In the international standards, the underlying premise for treating children and young people differently when they come into conflict with the law is that they are more susceptible to positive influence and more amenable in changing their behaviour as compared to adults. The UN Committee on the Rights of the Child stated authoritatively in General Comment No. 10 that ..... in order to protect the best interests of the child, traditional objectives of criminal justice, such as repression/ retribution, must give way to rehabilitation and restorative justice, and that this can be done in consonance with attention to effective public security and safety.

Age of Criminal Responsibility Chart

Jurisdiction	**No criminal responsibility**	**Presumption against criminal responsibility**	**Treatment as child/ juvenile**
1	2	3	4
COMMON WEALTH	Under 10 years Crimes Act, 1914, S 4m Criminal Code Act, 1995, S.7.1	10 years to less than 14 years S.4N Criminal Code Act Abolished by Statute Crime and Disorder Act, 1988, S. 34, 1995, S. 7.2	Not specified
AUSTRALIAN CAPITAL TERRITORY	Under 10 years (Since 10 May, 2000) Children and Young People Act, 1999, S. 71(1)	10 to less 14 years Children and Young People Act, 1999, S. 8	Under 18 years children and Young People Act, 1999, S.8 (—young person)
NORTHERN TERRITORY	Under 10 years Criminal Code S. 38(1)	10 to less than 14 years Criminal Code S. 38(1)	Under 18 years (since 1 June, 200) Juvenile Justice Act. S. 3 —juvenile)

contd...

contd...

Jurisdiction	No criminal responsibility	Presumption against criminal responsibility	Treatment as child/ juvenile
1	2	3	4
NEW SOUTH WALES	Under 10 years Children (Criminal Proceedings Act, 1987 S. 5	10 to less than 14 years Common law *doli incapax*	Under 18 years Children (Criminal Proceedings) Act, 1987, S. 3 (–adult)
VICTORIA	Under 10 years Children and Young Persons Act, 1989, S. 127	10 to less than 14 years Common law *doli incapax*	Under 17 years Children and Young Person Act, 1989. S. 3 (–child)
SOUTH AUSTRALIA	Under 10 years Young Offenders Act 1993, S. 5	10 to less than 14 years Common law *doli incapax*	Under 18 years Young Offenders Act, 1993, S.4 (-Youth)
WESTERN AUSTRALIA	Under 10 years Criminal Code Act Compilation Act, 1913, S. 29	10 to less than 14 years Criminal Code Act Compilation Act, 1913, S. 29	Under 18 years Young Offenders Act, 1994, S. 3 (Young Person)
QUEENSLAND	Under 10 years Criminal Code Act, 1899, S. 29(1)	10 to less than 14 Years (since 1 August, 1997) Criminal Code Act, 1899, S. 29(2)	Under 17 years Juvenile Justice Act 1992 Ss. 5.6 (–Child)
TASMANIA	Under 10 years (since 1 February, 2000) Criminal Code, S. 18(1)	10 to less than 14 years Criminal Code, S. 18(2)	Under 18 years (since 1 February 2000) Youth Justice Act, 1997, S. 3 (–young)

The Criminal / Penal Code of many countries prescribed higher minimum ages of criminal ages of criminal responsibility

Canada, Greece, Netherlands	12 years
France, Israel, New Zealand	13 years slaughter years (except where the for age murder/man limit is 10)
Australia, Germany, Italy and many Eastern European Countries	14 years
Sweden	15 years
Japan, Portugal, Spain	16 years
Belgium, Luxembourg	18 years

However, the important point about setting an age of majority is that it creates uniformity. It would be unjust for different countries to have different ages and 18 years is commonly held to be the age of majority worldwide.

3.18 The countries which award death punishment and life-imprisonment to juvenile for capital cases

Around the world, 58 countries practice harsher punishment and even death punishment for heinous crimes.[39] This practice is absolutely banned by International Human Rights law as declared in the International Covenant on Civil and Political Rights (ICCPR),[40] the U.N. Convention on the Rights of the Child, and the American Convention on Human Rights. The ICCPR was adopted by the United Nations General Assembly, and was ratified on March 23, 1976. Article 6(5) of the treaty states: "Sentence of death shall not be imposed for crimes committed by persons below eighteen years of age." The ICCPR has 172 parties and six more signatories without ratification. Parties to the treaty, including the U.S., ratified the Covenant in 1992, but with certain reservations. The U.S. was one of three countries, which took substantive reservations to Article 6[41] the others were Norway and Ireland. However those reservations became silent, when death penalty was abolished by the Norway and Ireland. Subsequently, the U.S. Supreme Court declared the execution of juvenile offenders to be unconstitutional. In Roper v. Simmons in 2005 The United States Supreme Court observed that sentencing the death penalty on offenders who were below the age of 18 at the time of the murder for which they were charged, violates the Eighth Amendment. It is a violation of international law to sentence a person to death for a crime they committed before they turned 18. The acknowledgement of this ban is so universal that it is broadly recognised as a peremptory norm of customary international law. "The death penalty for juvenile offenders appears to have been abandoned by nations everywhere in large part due to the express provisions of the United Nations Convention on the Rights of the Child and of several other international treaties and agreements.[42] Since 1990, juvenile offenders are known to have been executed in only eight countries: China, Democratic Republic of Congo, Iran, Pakistan, Yemen, Nigeria, Saudi Arabia, and the United States.

The incident of first juvenile execution was in 1642 of Thomas Graunger in Plymouth Colony, Massachesetts. Since 1608 a total of approximately 365 persons have been executed for juvenile crimes, constituting 1.8 percent of roughly 20,000 confirmed American executions. Since the restoration of the death penalty in 1976, there has been 22 persons of these executions are for juvenile crimes. These 22 recent executions of juvenile offenders make up about two percent of the total executions since 1976. Before 2005, there were 38 U.S. states that allow capital punishment:

There were 71 juvenile offenders awaiting execution on death row at the time of the *Roper v. Simmons* decision,: thirteen in Alabama; five in Mississippi; four in Arizona; four in North Carolina; four in Louisiana; three in Florida; two in Georgia; one in Nevada; two in Pennsylvania; three in South Carolina; twenty nine in Texas; and one in Virginia. A United Nations report in August 2014 revealed that more than 160 juvenile offenders had been awarded death sentenced and were grieving on death row awaiting their sad executions. In 2015, Iranian authorities executed at least 830 people and four of them were reportedly below 18 years of age.

In August 2015 Report on the United Nations' Secretary-General on human rights in Iran expressed persisting concern "at the frequency of executions, especially for drug-related offences and of juvenile offenders." The U.N. report expressed that, however authentically no official data were available, 160 children below age of 18 were allegedly awarded death punishment in the country as at

2014.[45] Amnesty International reported that purportedly Iran has executed 73 juvenile offenders between January 2005 and November 2015, and believes “the real number is likely to be much higher as many death penalty cases are believed to go unreported. As reported by Amnesty, the Iranian government has not officially announced any of the juvenile executions.[46] Amnesty International reports that along with Iran, military tribunals in Somalia’s semi-autonomous Puntland region continue to carry out executions of children. Five children, all between ages 14 and 17, were hanged on April 8, 2017 for the charge of killing of three senior government officials and their alleged involvement in the armed group Al-Shabaab’s. Michelle Kagari. Amnesty International’s Deputy Regional Director for East Africa, the Horn and the Great Lakes, states These five boys were executed following a fundamentally flawed process during which they were tortured to confess, denied access to a lawyer and additional protections accorded to juveniles, and tried in a military tribunal.” Amnesty asked to Puntland authorities to exonerate the lives of two other boys, named Muhamed Yasin Abdi, 17, and Daud Saied Sahal, 15, who were on death row by military execution.[47] The British Foreign and Commonwealth Office express that Puntland state authorities had more than 50 juveniles in custody whom the European Union believes had been forced to participate in fighting by Al Shabaab. The children were apprehended during a successful government operation against Al Shabaab in March 2016.

In January 2016, The Human Rights Organisation, Reprieve, reports Saudi Arabia has executed at least four people below 18 during a mass execution of 47 people. Reprieve, reported that one of the four, Ali al-Ribh, had been arrested in school, tortured forced to confess his involvement in anti-government protests, and executed.[48] Reprieve reports that three other Saudi juveniles—Ali al-Nimr, Dawoud al-Marhoon, and Abdullah al-Zaher—who were arrested following pro-democracy protests in 2012 faced execution after having been tortured into signing false confessions, which were used in a secretive counter-terrorism court to convict them, and sentence them to death.[49]

Reported Executions of Juvenile Offenders in Other Countries Since 1990

Country	Name of the prisoner	Age at crime (c), Trial (t), sentence(s) or executed In(e)	Year of death	Notes
CHINA	Zhao Lin	16 (C), 18 (E)	2003	China revised a law in 1997
	Gao Pan	16 or 17 (C)	2004	forbidding the execution of defendants under age 18 at the time of the crime, but juveniles continue to be executed due to insufficient care in determining the age of defendants.
DEMOCRATIC REPUBLIC	Kasongo 14 (C)	14 (C)	2000	In 2001, the death sentences of five children were commuted. At the time of writing there was a moratorium on executions in effect.
IRAN	Kazeem Shirafkan	17 (E)	1990	In December 1993, a bill to raise the minimum age to 18 was approved by the parliament, but must still receive the approval of the highest governing body in Iran, the Guardian Council, to become law.

contd...

contd...

Country	Name of the prisoner	Age at crime(c), Trial(t), sentence(s) or executed In(e)	Year of death	Notes
	Male (name unknown)	16 (E)	1992	
	Male (name unknown)	17 (E)	1992	
	Ebrahim Qorbanzadeh	17 (E)	1999	
	Jasem Abrahimi		2000	
	Mehrdad Youssefi	17 (E)	2001	
	Mohammad Mohammadz-adeh	17 (C), 21 (E)	2004	
	Atefeh Rajabi Sahaaleh	16 (E)	2004	
	Salman	17 (C)	2004	
	Iman Farrokhi	17 (C)	2005	
	Ali Safarpour Rajabi	16 or 17(C)	2005	
	Mohmoud Asghari	15 or 16(C)	2005	
	Ayaz Marhoni	16 or 17(C)	2005	
	Farshid Farighi	14 or 16(C)	2005	
	Name unknown	17 (E)	2005	
	Name unknown	17 (C)		
	Rostam Tajik	16 (C)	2005	
	Majid Segound (Sagvand)	17 (C)	2006	
	Sattar	17 (C)	2006	

contd...

contd...

Country	Name of the prisoner	Age at crime(c), Trial(t), sentence(s) or executed In(e)	Year of death	Notes
	Morteza M	16 (C)	2006	
	Naser Batmani	Under 18 (C)	2006	
	Mohammad Mousawi	16 (C)	2006	
	Said Qanabar	17 (E)	2006	
	Mohammad Pezhman (Pejman)	Under 18 (C)	2007	
	Amir Asgari	Under 18 (C)	2007	
	Hossein Gharabaghloo	16 (C)	2007	
	Babak Rahimi		2007	
	Name Unknow	Under 18 (C)	2007	
	Name unknown	Under 18 (C)	2007	
	Mohamad Reza Tork	16 (C)	2007	
	Makwan Moloudza deh	13 (C)	2007	
	Amir Hoshang Fazollahza deh	Under 18 (C)	2007	
	Mohammad Hassanza deh		2008	
	Hasan Mozafari	Under 18 (C)	2008	
	Rahman Shahidi	Under 18 (C)	2008	
	Reza Hejazi	15 (C)	2008	
	Behnam Zare	15 (C)	2008	
	Ghlamreza H	17 (C)	2008	
	Ahmad Zare	17 (C)	2008	

contd...

contd...

Country	Name of the prisoner	Age at crime(c), Trial(t), sentence(s) or executed In(e)	Year of death	Notes
	Mola Gol Hassan	17 (C)	2009	
	Delara Darabi	17 (C)	2009	
	Ali Jafari	17 (C)	2009	
	Bahnoud Shojaee	17 (C)	2009	
	Mosleh Zamani	17 (C)	2009	
	Mohammad A.	17 (C)	2010	
	A.N.	17 (C)	2011	
	H.B.	17 (C)	2011	
	Ali Reza Molla Soltani	17 (E)	2011	
	Mohammad Norouzi	17 (C)	2011	
	Vahid Moselemi	17 (C)	2011	
	Ehsan	17 (C)	2011	
	Amir Shirmohammadi	17 (C)	2011	
	Amir A.	14 (C)	2012	
	Shahruz	17 (C)	2012	
	Samad	16 (C)	2012	
	Bahra Ahmadi	17 (C)	2012	
	Said Afshar	17 (C)	2013	
	Abdolhamid Sekhavatian	17 (C)	2013	
	Arman Mohammadi	12 (C)	2013	
	Name Unknown	14 (C)	2013	
	Name Unknown	Under 18 (C)	2013	

contd...

contd...

Country	Name of the prisoner	Age at crime(c), Trial(t), sentence(s) or executed In(e)	Year of death	Notes
	Ahmad Seif Panahi	16 (C)	2013	
	Ahmad Jenkhoo	15 (C)	2013	
	Abdolaziz Rajs	17 (C)	2013	
	Iraj Nasiri	15 (C)	2013	
	Mehras Rezaei	17 (C)	2014	
	Hassan Zolfaqari	17 (C)	2014	
	Reza Ganjlu	17 (C)	2014	
	Janat Mir	Under 18 (C)	2014	
	Ahmad Rahimi	17 (C)	2014	
	Ali Fouladi	16 (C)	2014	
	Ebrahim Hajati	16 (C)	2014	
	Amir Sardahai	17 (C)	2014	
	Hadi Veysi	15(C)	2014	
	Fardin Ja'Farian	14 (C)	2014	
	Rahim Norallahzadeh	14 (C)	2014	
	Javed Saberi	17 (C)	2015	
	Fatemeh Salbehi	17 (C)	2015	
	Samad Zahabi	17 (C)	2015	
	Vazir Amroddin	16 (C)	2015	
NIGERIA	Chiebore Onuoha	15 (C)	1997	
	Name Unknown	17 (E)	1992	In July 2000, the Juvenile Justice System

contd...

contd...

Country	Name of the prisoner	Age at crime(c), Trial(t), sentence(s) or executed In(e)	Year of death	Notes
	Shamun Masih	14 (C)	1997	
	Ali Sher	13 (C)	2001	
	Mutabar Khan	16 (C)	2006	
PAKISTAN	Aftab Bahadur	15 (C)	2015	Ordinance was promul-gated, abolishing the death penalty for anyone under 18 at the time of the crime. in July 2002 it was announce that 74 young offenders had been taken off death row.
	Shafqat Hussain	14 (T)	2015	
	Ansar Iqbal	15 (A)	2015	
	Faisal Mehmood	Under 18 (C)	2015	
	Muhammad Afzal	16 (S)	2015	
SAUDI ARABIA	Moeid bin Hussein Hakami	17 (C)	1992	
	Dhahian Rakan al- Sibail	17 (C)	2007	

contd...

contd...

Country	Name of the prisoner	Age at crime(c), Trial(t), sentence(s) or executed In(e)	Year of death	Notes
	Sadeq Mal-Allah	17 (C)	2007	
	Issa Bin Muhammad Umar Mohammad	17 (C)	2009	
	Sultan Bin	17 (C)	2009	
	Sulayman Bin Muslim al-Muwallad			
	Rizana Nafeek	17 (C)	2013	
	Sa'id Bin Nasser Bin Muhammad al- Shahrani	17 (C)	2013	
	Ali Bin Muhammad Bin Hazam al- Shihri	17 (C)	2013	
SUDAN	Imad Ali Abdullah	17 (C)	2005	
	Mohammed Jama Gesmallah	16 (C)	2005	
	Abdulrahman Zakaria Mohammed		2009	
YEMEN	Nasser Munir Nasser I Kirbi	13(E)	1993	In 1994 Yemen abolished the death penalty for people under 18 at the time of the crime.

contd...

contd...

Country	Name of the prisoner	Age at crime(c), Trial(t), sentence(s) or executed In(e)	Year of death	Notes
	Adil Muhammad Saif al-Maamari	16(C)	2007	
	Fuad Ahmed Ali Abdulla	Under 18 (C)	2012	

(*Source:* Amnesty International "Indecent and Internationally Illegal: The Death Penalty Against Child Offenders" September 2002, with updated information from Amnesty International: Execution of Child Offenders - Updated Summary of Cases, Executions of Juveniles Since 1990 (Latest version: April 2016)).

3.19 Conclusion

The International Covenant on Civil and Political Rights also formally prohibits the death penalty in its Article 6, stating that Sentence of death shall not be imposed for crimes committed by persons below eighteen years of age; Each country have their own laws and jurisdiction, therefore juvenile laws are also vary country to country. Each country is authorised to go its own way. Therefore the justifications for this practice among these countries are expected to vary. However, there are some common points that forced these countries to impose capital punishment for heinous crimes.

1. Violent crime committed by children, especially homicide, is regarded much worse in the United States and internationally in most other countries.
2. Rate of Juvenile homicide increased significantly till the mid- to late-1990s. Although they have dropped intensely after that there is still a great public fear of juvenile homicide.
3. Juvenile murderers seem to be particularly brutal and impassive to civilized entreaties to stop the killing;
4. Most political leader strongly support for tougher punishments for violent juvenile crime; and

5. Improving the societal environment, which inculcates violent juvenile crime, is daunting task, which is nearly an impossible one to attain, significantly seems to be a huge task nearly impossible to achieve in any significant measure.

On the ground of above-mentioned grounds, some countries are in favour of imposing death penalty on children for heinous crimes. However most of the countries are opposing the death penalty to juvenile and they have also their own grounds to oppose the death penalty to the juvenile for heinous crimes. Arguments against the juvenile death penalty typically concentrate on a similarly wide spectrum of concerns:

1. Almost all of these young offenders had terrible childhoods. Due to their youth age, such teenagers did not get a chance to be mature and grow out of the terrible effects of their terrible childhoods.
2. Medical research, during the past decade indicates that significant brain development continues until the early 20s the adolescent brain does not mature organically until the late teens or early twenties, with impulse control being the last to fully develop.
3. The threat of capital punishment does not deter young offenders who do not understand death well enough and consider themselves as immortal.
4. The retributive desire to visit extremely harsh punishment upon egregious offenders is blunted at least somewhat if that offender is a child.
5. Severe punishments for violent juvenile crimes are only short term solutions, with the only effective long-term solutions would be cleaning up the neighbourhoods, schools, and societal arrangement that continue to produce such violent teenagers.

REFERENCES

1. John A. Winterdk, Juvenile Justice International Perspectives, Model, and Trends, CRC Press, UK 2015.

2. See, for example, section 117 of the Crime and Disorder Act 1998'. However, for the purpose of the Children Acts 1989 and 2004, a child is anyone who has not reached their eighteen birthdays. Although the phrase juvenile is still widely used to describe young people under 18 in English it carries connotations of childish and immature behaviour.
3. John A. Winterdk, Juvenile Justice International Perspectives, Model, and Trends, CRC Press, UK 2015.
4. Formerly Section 53(1) of the Children and Young Persons Act 1933
5. Formerly Sections 53(2) and 53(3) of The Children and Young Persons Act 1933.
6. Formerly part of Section 53(3) of The Children and Young Persons 1933 Act.
7. John A. Winterdk, Juvenile Justice International Perspectives, Model, and Trends, CRC Press, UK 2015.
8. John A. Winterdk, Juvenile Justice International Perspectives, Model, and Trends, CRC Press, UK 2015.
9. The age of majority varies from state to state. Most states defines age 18 as the age majority. Three states use age 21 as the age of majority, while four states use age 19 as the age of majority.
10. John A.Winterdk, Juvenile Justice International Perspectives, Model, and Trends, CRC Press, UK 2015.
11. For example, school authority.
12. John A. Winterdk, Juvenile Justice International Perspectives, Model, and Trends, CRC Press, UK 2015.
13. The court appointed representative of the juvenile.
14. The In Re Gault U.S. Supreme Court decision of 1967 established that a juvenile is entitled to the following rights: (1) right to representation by counsel: (2) right to confront and cross-examine witnesses; (3) privilege against self-incrimination; (4) right to remain silent; and (5) right to notification of specific charges and an opportunity to refute them. This decision did not guarantee the right to a trial by jury.
15. The criteria for transfer to adult court are specified in the Kent decision.
16. John A.Winterdk, Juvenile Justice International Perspectives, Model, and Trends, CRC Press, UK 2015.

17. *Ibid.*
18. John A.Winterdk, Juvenile Justice International Perspectives, Model, and Trends, CRC Press, UK 2015.
19. Section 82 of the Pakistan Penal Code.
20. Amnesty International March 1995 AI Index: ASA 33/07/95.
21. Availablehttps://www.amnesty.org/download/Documents/172000/asa330071995en.pdf Pakistan: Death penalty for juveniles Amnesty International March 1995 AI Index: ASA 33/07/95.(visited on February 18,2016
22. John A. Winterdk, Juvenile Justice International Perspectives, Model, and Trends, CRC Press, UK 2015.
23. Section 53 of the Child Justice Act of South Africa.
24. Section 53 of the Child Justice Act of South Africa.
25. C. Trinidad and B. Torre, Seeds of Hope: Learning from Programmes for CICL of Cordaid Pertner Organisations (Cordaid, 2011).
26. Reprieve, "Global executions in 2016," December 29, 2016, Available at https://reprive.org.uk/press/globe-execution-2016 visited on 22/5/17
27. Reprieve, "Global executions in 2016," December 29, 2016, Available at https://reprive.org.uk/press/globle-execution-2016 visited on 22/5/17
28. Reprieve, "Global executions in 2016," December 29, 2016, Available at https://reprive.org.uk/press/globle-execution-2016 visited on 22/5/17
29. Available at https://reprive.org.uk/press/globle-execution-2016 visited on 22/5/2018
30. Reprieve, "Trump in Saudi Arabia as juveniles face execution," May 15, 2017.
31. available at www.org/news/2010/10/08/iran-saudi-arabia(visited on February 18, 2018)
32. United Kingdom Foreign and Commonwealth Office, "Human Rights Priority Country status report: January to June 2016," updated February 8, 2017. Egypt and Sri Lanka also sentence under-18s to death
33. *Ibid.*
34. Suman Nalwa and Hri Dev Khohli, Comentary on The Juvenile Justice Act, Universal Law publication, second edition, 2016.

35. United Nations Convention on the Rights of the Child (CRC), Article 1.
36. Ruban C. Gur, American Bar Association, Declaration of Ruben C. Gur, P.H.D.15 (2016).
37. A study released by Elizabeth Scott and Laurence Steinberg, former members of the Jhon and Catherine T. MacArthur Foundation Research Network on Adolescent and Juvenile crime states. the problem with individualised assessments of immaturity is that practitioners lack diagnostic tools to evaluate psychological maturity and identity formation on an individualised basis. Recently, courts in some areas have begun to use a psychopathy checklist, a variation of an instrument of an instrument developed for adults, in an effort to identify adolescent psychopaths for transfer or sentencing purposes. This practice, however, is fraught with the potential for error; it is simply not yet possible to distinguish incipient psychopaths from youths whose crimes reflect transient immaturity. For this reason, the American psychiatric Association restricts the diagnosis of psychopathy to individuals aged eighteen and older. Evaluating antisocial traits and conduct in adolescence is just too uncertain.
38. Richard J. Bonnie and Elizabeth S. Scott, The Teenage Brain: Adolescent Brain Research and the Law, 22(2) Current Directions In Psychological Science 161 (2013); Rakshit, supra note 22; supra note 11, p. 10.5.
39. Available at https://reprive.org.uk/press/globle-execution-2016 visited on 22/5/2018
40. Part 111 of ICCPR Article 6
    1. Every human being has the inherent right to life. This right shall be protected by law. No one shall be arbitrarily deprived of his life.
    2. In countries which have not abolished the death penalty, sentence of death may be imposed only for the most serious crimes in accordance with the law in force at the time of the commission of the crime and not contrary to the provisions of the present Covenant and to the Convention on the Prevention and Punishment of the Crime of Genocide. This penalty can only be carried out pursuant to a final judgment rendered by a competent court.
    3. When deprivation of life constitutes the crime of genocide, it is understood that nothing in this article shall authorise

any State Party to the present Covenant to derogate in any way from any obligation assumed under the provisions of the Convention on the Prevention and Punishment of the Crime of Genocide.

4. Anyone sentenced to death shall have the right to seek pardon or commutation of the sentence. Amnesty, pardon or commutation of the sentence of death may be granted in all cases.
5. Sentence of death shall not be imposed for crimes committed by persons below eighteen years of age and shall not be carried out on pregnant women.
6. Nothing in this article shall be invoked to delay or to prevent the abolition of capital punishment by any State Party to the present Covenant.

41 Article 37 (a) of the United Nations Convention on the Rights of the Child provides that "Neither capital punishment nor life imprisonment without possibility of release shall be imposed for offences committed by persons below eighteen years of age."

42 Daddu.net/5worst-capital-punishment-countrie.

45. UN Secretary-General, Report to the General Assembly, Situation of human rights in the Islamic Republic of Iran, A/70/352, p. 30 (August 31, 2015).

46. Amnesty International, Growing Up on Death Row: The Death Penalty and Juvenile Offenders in Iran, p. 28 (2016).

47. Amnesty International, "Somalia: Halt execution spree of children in Puntland," April 28, 2017.

48. 39.Https://reprieve.org.uk/press/global-executions-2016.

49. Reprieve, "Trump in Saudi Arabia as juveniles face execution," May 15, 2017 Available at https://reprive.org.uk/press/trump-saudi-arabia-juvenile-face-execution/ visited on 4/5/2018.

4

Legislative Framework of Juvenile Justice Mechanism with Special Reference to Heinous Crime and Judicial Responses

4.1 Introduction

This has been recognised all over the world that child offenders should be treated differently from adults. That is why a different parallel legislation has been made, and that resulted in the creation of a separate system, specifically meant for juvenile, namely, the juvenile justice system, to deal with children alleged or found to have committed offences. This chapter has been divided into two parts; In the first part the author has analysed the legislative mechanism dealing with the children who come in conflict with law and in the second half, the research has tried to analyse the judicial responses to the age of criminal responsibility and sentencing of the child offenders.

4.2 Analysis of laws in India on juvenile in conflict with law

A distinct system for children alleged or found to have committed an offence has been in existence in provinces / States since the Children Acts.[1] The Courts established under these systems (Acts) were empowered to try all cases in which a child is charged with the commission of an offence.[2] Under the Children Act 1960,[3] Children's Courts were set-up "for exercising the powers and discharging the duties conferred or imposed on such court in relation to delinquent children under this Act,"[4] and were empowered "to deal exclusively with all proceedings under this Act relating to...delinquent children."[5]

Provisions of the Children Act, 1960 were incorporated under the J.J. Act, 1986. Juvenile Courts were established "for exercising the powers and discharging the duties conferred or imposed on such court in relation to juvenile delinquents under this Act",[6] and such Juvenile Courts were given the "power to deal exclusively with all proceedings under this Act relating to...delinquent juveniles."[7] Similar powers were given to JJBs under the J.J. Act 2000 -"power to deal exclusively with all proceedings under this Act relating to juvenile in conflict with law."[8] Provisions for exclusive dealing of juvenile cases by the Juvenile Justice System was strengthened with the insertion of sub-Section (4) to Section 1 of the J.J. Act, 2000.[9] However the J.J. Act 2000 was enacted for the protection of children this Act was amended twice in 2006 and again in 2011 to address gaps in its implementation and make the law more child friendly. Whereas, the increasing cases of crimes committed by the children between the age group of 16-18 years in recent years make it apparent that the existing provisions and system under the Juvenile Justice (Care and Protection of Children) Act, 2000 are not well equipped to tackle child offenders in this age group. The data provided by the national Crime Records Bureau shows that crimes by children between the age group of 16-18 years been augmented, especially in particular categories of serious and heinous offences. Therefore, numerous changes were required in the J.J. Act, 2000 to tackle the aforementioned issues and as consequence of that a comprehensive legislation came into force that is "Juvenile Justice (Care and Protection of children) Act 2015" herein after referred as J.J. Act, 2015.

4.3 The Juvenile Justice (Care and Protection of Children) Act 2015

In all above mentioned Acts there was no categorisation of offences committed by the juveniles. In India as well as on International platform the right of every child is well recognised and advocated as that child offenders should be dealt differently from adults. "The right of the child alleged as, accused of, or recognised as recognised as having infringed the penal law must be treated in accordance with the provisions of article 40 of CRC."[10]

Therefore it is apparently clear that every person who is under the age of 18 years when the offence was committed must be treated as per the provisions of juvenile justice.[11] This well-entrenched practice of child offenders without exception being dealt with under the Juvenile Justice System, has been overturned by the J.J. Act, 2015, which allows the Juvenile Justice Board discretion to exclude from the juvenile justice system, children above 16 years who have allegedly committed heinous offences.[12]

The Juvenile Justice Act 2015 legitimises the transfer of the juveniles who are above the age of 16 to adult courts, if the Juvenile Justice Board inferred that the juvenile is mature enough to judge the consequence of his actions and his level of maturity indicates that he has committed the heinous crimes as an adult.[13]

For the first time the J.J. Act, 2015 introduced the classification of offences. By such classification treatment of a child in conflict with the law depends upon the offence the child is alleged to have committed. The Act[14] classifies offences into three categories: (i) petty offences;[15] (ii) serious offences;[16] (iii) heinous offence.[17] Hence, ascertaining the category of offence is crucial, more particularly regarding heinous offences as such children in conflict with the law may be tried as adults.

4.4 Provisions of juvenile justice act 2015, relating to child in conflict with law

The provisions of The J.J. Act, 2015 regarding the child in conflict with law are as follows:-

(i) Powers of juvenile justice board

The Juvenile Justice Board (here in after used as JJB) has the power to exclusively deal with proceedings under the J.J. Act, 2015 related to children in conflict with the law, in their jurisdiction except as otherwise provided in the Act.[18] The provision conferring such power upon the JJB is a non-obstante clause and will thus override any other law in force.

The powers conferred upon the JJB can also be exercised by the High Court and the Children's Court under Section 19, or while hearing appeals, revision, or otherwise.[19]

The JJBs power should be read together with Section 1(4)(i) of the J.J. Act, 2015, which pertains to the application of the Act. It states:

> "Notwithstanding anything contained in any other law for the time being in force, the provisions of this Act shall apply to all matters concerning ….children in conflict with law, including – apprehension, detention, prosecution, penalty or imprisonment, rehabilitation and social re-integration of children in conflict with law."

The proceedings could relate to bail, detention, and preliminary assessment, inquiry into the child's involvement in the offence, prosecution, rehabilitation and social reintegration of children in conflict with the law or amendment of any order passed.[20]

Functioning as a Bench, the JJB has the powers available to a Metropolitan Magistrate or Judicial Magistrate of First Class under the Code of Criminal Procedure.[21]

(ii) Inquiry by juvenile justice board

In cases of *Petty* offences, as per Section 14(5)d "it shall be disposed of by the Board through summary proceedings, as per the procedure prescribed under the Code of Criminal Procedure, 1973."[22] The final report in petty or serious offences shall be filed before the JJB within two months from the time the police receive information, except in cases in which it was not clear that the person involved was a child.[23]

"*Inquiry of serious offences* and of heinous offences for children under sixteen years of age at the time of offence alleged to be committed shall be disposed of by the Board, by following the procedure for trial in summons cases under the Code of Criminal Procedure, 1973.[24] Preliminary assessment should be carried out only for children above 16 years alleged who have the aggregation of a heinous offence."[25]

Inquiry of Serious Offences

Offence	Nature of proceedings before JJB	Final report from police	Time limit for disposal
Petty	Summary	Within 2 month from the time police receives information. Extension in cases in which it was not	4 months from date of production + maximum of 2 months
		reasonably known that the person involved in the offence was a child.	extension; termination thereafter
Serious	Trial in summons Case		4 months from date of production + 2 months extension +further granted by CMM/CJM or reasons in writing
Heinous	Preliminary Assessment (16-18 years)	Statements of witnesses and other documents prepared during investigation to be produced within 1 month.	3 months
	Trial in Summons Case (Children above 7 years; children above 16 and below 18 years who are not transferred after preliminary assessment	Not specified	4 months from date of production = 2 months extension granted by CMM/CJM for reasons in writing.

(iii) Time limitation

"An inquiry should be completed within 4 months from the date of first production of the child before the JJB, unless the period is extended.[26] The period can be extended for a maximum period of two more months based on the circumstances of the case and after recording the reasons for the extension."[27] Further, in case of serious and heinous offences, the Chief Judicial Magistrate or the Chief Metropolitan Magistrate can grant further extension of time for reasons given in writing.[28] If the inquiry for petty offences remains inconclusive even after six months (four months of the stipulated period plus two months of the extended period), the proceedings will stand terminated.[29]

(iv) Nature of inquiry

While examining witnesses and conducting the inquiry, the JJB should ensure that the proceedings are not conducted strictly "adversarial." They must use the power available to judges under Section 165 of the Indian Evidence Act to put any question to any person at any time or order any document to be produced[30]. The proceedings have to be child-friendly.

(v) Presence of the child during inquiry

The JJB may allow the child to be not present during the inquiry, if it feels that the child is not needed to be present for the inquiry.[31] If child's presence is required it may be limited only to the recording of the statement and can continue the inquiry even in the absence of the child[32]. The JJB should however, bear in mind the fundamental principles of participation and natural justice and ensure that the child's right to be heard is not compromised.[33] If the child is required to attend the proceedings before the JJB, the child will be eligible to refund of travel expenses for self and one escort according to actual expenditure incurred.[34] The payment can be made by the JJB or DCPU, as the case may be. For instance, if a CICL is released on bail and returns to his home in a different city, the JJB should reimburse the travel expenses incurred by the child and his guardian for all the hearings that they have to attend.

(vi) Presence of a parent or guardian during inquiry

The JJB may require a parent or guardian who has the actual custody of the child to be present at any proceeding in respect of the child if it thinks fit.[35] However, persons in whose presence the child feels comfortable should be allowed to attend the sitting.[36]

(vii) Prohibition on joint proceedings

The JJB cannot jointly hold proceedings of a child with a person who is not a child, even if they are co-accused in the same case.[37] Further, if during inquiry, a person alleged to be CICL is found to be an adult after age determination, he cannot be dealt with along with a child.[38]

4.6 Establishment of children's court

A Children's Court has been defined under two legislations -i.e. courts established under the Commissions for Protection of Child Rights Act, 2005 and a Special Court under the Protection of Children from Sexual Offences Act, 2012, where they exist.[39] Where they do not exist, the Sessions Court having jurisdiction to try offences under the J.J. Act would come within the ambit of a Children's Court.

The responsibility for establishing a Children's Court under the Commission for Protection of Child Rights Act, 2005, (CPCR Act) is with the State Government. The State Government must in concurrence with the Chief Justice of the High Court notify at least a court in the State or specify, for each district, a Court of Session to be a Children's Court to try offences against children or violation of child rights.[40] Under the Protection of Children from Sexual Offences Act, 2012, (POCSO Act), the State Government should designate for each district a Sessions Court to be a Special Court in consultation with the Chief Justice of the High Court. If a Sessions Court has been notified as a Children's Court under the CPCR Act, or a Special Court has been designated for related purposes under any other law for the time being in force, then, such court will be deemed to be a Special Court.

4.7 Responsibility of the children's court after child is Transferred b JJB

The Children's Court is required to decide whether there is a need for trial of the child as an adult as per provisions of the Cr.P.C.[41] If it decides that there is no need for trial as an adult, it can conduct the inquiry as a JJB and pass orders under Section 18(1).[42] The Children's Court should record its reasons while arriving at a conclusion as to whether the child should be treated as a child or an adult.[43] The Act and the Model Rules do not explain the procedure that needs to be followed by the Children's Court to arrive at this decision.

4.8 Age appeal

The Children's Court should decide the appeal, if filed against the JJBs order declaring the age of the child, before proceeding with the case.[44] For instance, if a child is declared to be 16 years and is transferred to the Children's Court for trial by the JJB, the Children's Court should consider the appeal, if it is filed; contesting the age that has been declared by the JJB, before it decides whether there is need for trial of the child as an adult.

4.9 Conflict with the Act regarding appeal against Preliminary Assessment

The JJ MR 2016 states that if an appeal against the order of the JJB passed after the preliminary assessment is filed, it should be disposed by the Children's Court first before it proceeds with the case.[45] This provision, however, is in conflict with Section 101(2) of the J.J. Act 2015 which requires appeals against the order of a JJB passed after preliminary assessment to be filed before a Sessions Court and not Children's Court.

4.10 Procedures to be followed if child is tried as an adult

The Children's Court should follow the procedure for trial by sessions under the Cr.P.C. if it decides to try the child like an adult.[46]

(i) Prohibition on joint trials

The Children's Court should ensure that a child alleged to be in conflict with the law is not jointly tried with a person who is not a child.[47]

4.11 Considerations

The Children's Court should consider the special needs of the child, the tenets of fair trial and maintain a child friendly atmosphere while trying a child as an adult.[48]

4.12 Orders that cannot be passed

Children's Court cannot impose death penalty or life imprisonment without the possibility of release for any offence.[49]

ICP: An Individual Care Plan prepared by the Probation Officer, CWO or recognised voluntary organisation based on interactions with the child and family wherever possible, should form part of the final order passed by the Children's Court.[50]

4.13 Placement and reformative services

If the child is found to be involved in the offence, the child could be sent to the Place of Safety till the child attains 21 years.[51] Reformative services comprising of educational services, skill development, alternative therapy such as counseling, behaviour modification therapy, and psychiatric support should be provided to the child during the period of stay in the place of safety.[52]

4.14 Tracking of progress and reformation assessment

- The progress of the child should be evaluated by the Probation Officer, DCPU or social worker on a yearly basis and a report should be submitted to the Children's Court for review.[53]
- The purpose of the tracking is also to ensure that no ill-treatment is meted out to the child.[54]
- The psycho-social progress of the child will have to be assessed with the help of psycho-social experts.[55]

- The Children's Court can also direct the periodical production of the child and at least once every three months to assess the progress made and the facilities provided by the institution for implementation of the individual care plan.[56]
- When the child attains the age of 21 years, the Children's Court will have to provide for a follow up by the Probation Officer, DCPU or a social worker or by itself, to evaluate if the child has undergone reformative changes and if the child can be a contributing member of the society.[57]
- The Children's Court should also interact with the child to assess whether the child has undergone reformative changes and if the child can be a contributing member of society.[58]
- The periodic reports of progress of the child and evaluation of relevant experts should be taken into consideration and based on this the Children's Court could decide whether the child should be released or whether the child should complete the remainder of the term in jail.[59]
- Based on the progress reports, the Children's Court could direct that the institutional mechanism be strengthened if it is found to be inadequate.[60]

4.15 Decisions following reformation assessment

Based on the assessment, as per Rule 13(8)(vi)(c) the Children's Court can:

(c)(a) Release the child forthwith

(c)(b) Release the child on execution of a personal bond with or without sureties for good behaviour.

(c)(c) Release the child and issue directions regarding education, vocational training, apprenticeship, employment, counseling and other therapeutic interventions with a view to promoting adaptive and positive behaviour, etc.

(c)(d) "Release the child and appoint a monitoring authority for the remainder of the prescribed term of stay. The monitoring authority, where appointed shall maintain a Rehabilitation Card for the child in Form 14 or, as per Section 20(2)(ii) direct the child to complete the remainder of the term in jail.

4.16 Monitoring authority (MA)

The Children's Court can appoint a Probation Officer, Case Worker, Child Welfare Officer, or fit person as a monitoring authority.[61]

(i) Monitoring process

- In the first quarter, the child should meet the MA on a fortnightly basis or at such intervals as may be directed by the Children's Court. Time and venue of the meeting will be fixed by the MA in consultation with the child.[62]
- MA should forward its observations on the child's progress on a monthly basis to the Children's Court.[63]
- Recommendations for further follow up should be made by the MA at 117 the end of the first quarter.[64]
- After release, if the child is found to be indulging in criminal activities or associating with people with criminal antecedents, the child should be brought before the Children's Court for further orders.
- After the first quarter, the child should meet the MA at such intervals as may be directed by the Children's Court based on the recommendations made by the MA at the end of the first quarter and the MA should forward its report to the Children's Court which should review it every quarter.[65]
- If it is found that the child no longer requires to be monitored, the MA should place the detailed report with recommendations before the Children's Court which should issue further directions either terminating the monitoring or for its continuation. Monitoring Authority (MA):

4.17 Appellate function of sessions courts and children's court

The J.J. Act states that appeals from orders of the JJB will lay before the Children's Court while that passed after the preliminary assessment will lie before the Sessions Court.[66] The Sessions Court can take the assistance of experienced psychologists and medical specialists while deciding the appeal against a JJBs order passed after the preliminary assessment.[67] To ensure fairness however, the experts engaged by the Sessions Court have to be different from those the JJB had engaged to conduct the preliminary assessment.[68]

While Children's Court may be designated Sessions Court, all Sessions Courts are not Children's Courts. This distinction should be borne in mind in the context of appeals from orders passed after the preliminary assessment. A Children's Court cannot hear the appeal against a transfer order passed by the JJB as that would vitiate the fairness of the trial against the child by the same court, if the appeal fails.

4.18 Procedure to followed by children's court after child is transferred by JJB

(i) Apprehension and production of child in conflict with law

Children are not 'arrested' because they are not to be treated as criminals, but they can be 'apprehended'. The J.J. Act 2015 does not use word 'arrest' anywhere, instead words 'apprehension' or 'apprehended' have been used in Section 1(4)(i), Section 6(1), Section 8 (3) (b), Section 10(1), Section 12(1), Section 12(2) and in Section 13(1). Further 'Principle of non-stigmatising semantics' under Section 3(viii) of the J.J. Act 2015 prohibits use of accusatory words in the processes pertaining to a child.

The State, in its parens patriae role, does not arrest children, but whenever there is a need, it does take care of them and restricts their liberties in their best interest. For this purpose, the J.J. Act, 2015 uses the word apprehension instead of arrest. Power to apprehend is to be exercised in the interest of child.

The proviso to Rule 8(1), JJ Model Rules, 2016, states: Provided that power to apprehend shall only be exercised with regard to heinous offences, unless it is in the best interest of the child. For all other cases involving petty and serious offences and cases where apprehending the child is not necessary in the interest of the child, the police or the Special Juvenile Police Unit or Child Welfare Police Officer shall forward the information regarding the nature of offence alleged to be committed by the child along with his social background report in Form 1 to the Board and intimate the parents or guardian of the child as to when the child is to be produced for hearing before the Board.

Apprehension for Offences

Categories of offences	Petty	Serious	Heinous
Status of power of police to apprehend (first approach)	Apprehension possible only if it is the interest of child	Apprehension possible only if it is in the interest of the child	Apprehension Must
Status of power of Police to apprehended (second approach)	No Apprehension	No apprehension	Apprehension police only if it is in the interest of child

(ii) Production of child before board in cases where apprehension has been made

Relevant provisions in the J.J. Act in this regard is provided in Section 10 (1) and Section 13 (1) of the J.J. Act, 2015 which are as below:

Section 10(1) As soon as a child alleged to be in conflict with law is apprehended by the police, such child shall be placed under the charge of the special juvenile police unit or the designated child welfare police officer, who shall produce the child before the Board without any loss of time but within a period of twenty four hours of apprehending the child excluding the time necessary for the journey, from the place where such child was apprehended:

Section 13(1) Where a child alleged to be in conflict with law is apprehended, the officer designated as Child Welfare Police Officer of the police station, or the special juvenile police unit to which such child is brought, shall, as soon as possible after apprehending the child, inform -

I. the parent or guardian of such child, if they can be found, and direct them to be present at the Board before which the child is produced; and

II. the probation officer, or if no probation officer is available, a Child Welfare Officer, for preparation and submission within two weeks to the Board, a social investigation report containing information regarding the antecedents and family background of the child and other material circumstances likely to be of assistance to the Board for making the inquiry. Further relevant provisions in this regard are provided in following Rules in the JJ MR, 2016.

Rule 8 (2) When a child alleged to be in conflict with law is apprehended by the police, the police officer concerned shall place the child under the charge of the Special Juvenile Police Unit or the Child Welfare Police Officer, who shall immediately inform:

(i) the parents or guardian of the child that the child has been apprehended along with the address of the Board where the child will be produced and the date and time when the parents or guardian need to be present before the Board;

(ii) the Probation Officer concerned, that the child has been apprehended so as to enable him to obtain information regarding social background of the child and other material circumstances likely to be of assistance to the Board for conducting the inquiry; and

(iii) a Child Welfare Officer or a Case Worker, to accompany the Special Juvenile Police Unit or Child Welfare Police Officer while producing the child before the Board within twenty-four hours of his apprehension.

Rule 9: Production of the child alleged to be in conflict with law before the board.

When the child alleged to be in conflict with law is apprehended, he shall be produced before the Board within twenty-four hours of his being apprehended, along with a report explaining the reasons for the child being apprehended by the police. A perusal of above-said provisions makes it abundantly clear that the power to apprehend has to be justified before through a report.

Rule 10. Post-production processes by the Board:-

On production of the child before the Board, the report containing the social background of the child, circumstances of apprehending the child and offence alleged to have been committed by the child as provided by the officers, individuals, agencies producing the child shall be reviewed by the Board…

Whenever a child alleged to be in conflict with law is apprehended, it is necessary for the police to justify before the JJB, as to why such power of apprehension has been exercised. Rule 8(1) requires the police to provide the circumstances under which child was apprehended. Rule 9(1) confirms this requirement in more emphatic terms:

When the child alleged to be in conflict with law is apprehended, he shall be produced before the Board within twenty-four hours of his being apprehended, along with a report explaining the reasons for the child being apprehended by the Police. It is thus clear that it is for police to first provide reasons for apprehending a child.

It must be kept in mind that the question of seeking bail comes only after the JJB is satisfied that the police have exercised its power of apprehension, keeping in view best interest of child. On production of the apprehended child, the JJB is mandated to review such report of the police under Rule 10(1) and then proceed to pass orders listed further.

(iii) Procedure to be adopted in cases where child is not apprehended

In this Section, the procedure which needs to be adopted in cases where a child is not apprehended by the police is dealt with. The proviso to Rule 8(1) states: … For all other cases involving petty and serious offences and cases where apprehending the child is not necessary in the interest of the child, the police or the Special Juvenile Police Unit or Child Welfare Police Officer shall forward the information regarding the nature of offence alleged to be committed by the child along with his social background report in Form 1 to the Board and intimate the parents or guardian of the child as to when the child is to be produced for hearing before the Board.

This above-said rule should be read along with Rule 8(7) which states: When the child is released in a case where apprehending of the child is not warranted, the parents or guardians or a fit person in whose custody the child alleged to be in conflict with law is placed in the best interest of the child, shall furnish an undertaking on a non-judicial paper in Form 2 to ensure their presence on the dates during inquiry or proceedings before the Board. Thus, when a case does not warrant exercise of power of apprehension by police, an undertaking on a non-judicial paper in Form-2 should be obtained from the parents or guardians and such undertaking along with Social Background Report of the child in Form-1 and information regarding the nature of offence alleged to have been committed (which means F.I.R. or DD Entry as the case may be), should be forwarded to the JJB. The parents/ guardians of the child should be informed as to when the child is to be produced for hearing before the JJB. Further, the procedure to be adopted by the Board in such cases is provided under Rule 9(4) which states: Where the child alleged to be in conflict with law has not been apprehended and the information in this regard is forwarded by the police or Special Juvenile Police Unit or Child Welfare Police Officer to the Board, the Board shall require the child to appear before it at the earliest so that measures for rehabilitation, where necessary, can be initiated, though the final report may be filed subsequently.

4.19 Age determination

Section 94 of the J.J. Act, 2015 provides the primary legal framework for age determination. However, the law on other ancillary issues is also provided under Section 9. Prior to the enactment of J.J. Act 2015, the law concerning age determination was contained in Section 49 of the J.J. Act, 2000 and under Rule 12 of the Juvenile Justice (Care and Protection) of Children, Model Rules 2007.

Wherever State Governments had made their own State Rules under the J.J. Act, 2000, the rule corresponding to JJ Model Rule 12 would apply.

Prior to the passing of J.J. Act 2015, the J.J. Act, 2000 as amended in 2006, lay down the law on relevant date to reckon the age of juvenility. Prior to August 2006, this used to be an area of confusion because the definition of 'juvenile in conflict with law' did not provide for the relevant date on which juvenility had to be ascertained. The definition under Section 2(l), J.J. Act, 2000, prior to the amendment used to be 'juvenile in conflict with law means a juvenile who is alleged to have committed an offence'. Various Courts interpreted this provision differently, leading to utter confusion regarding the relevant date on which age could be determined. Some High Courts considered the date of commission of offence, some considered the date of registration of the F.I.R. and some even went on to consider the date of arrest or the date of the child's production before the Juvenile Justice Board. This confusion was settled by the Supreme Court in Pratap Singh v. State of Jharkhand, [(2005) 3 SCC 551] and subsequently re-affirmed in Hari Ram v. State of Rajasthan,[(2009) 13 SCC 211]. In these cases, the Supreme Court held that the relevant date for determination of age is the date of commission of offence, so far as it is concerned with a child alleged to have committed an offence. The judgment in Pratap Singh Case led to the amendment on this aspect in year 2006. The Juvenile Justice (Care and Protection of Children) Act, 2000 was therefore amended in 2006, by which the definition of juvenile in conflict with law was amended to reflect the judgment. After this amendment, the definition of juvenile in conflict with law in Section 2(l), was juvenile in conflict with law means a juvenile who is alleged to have committed an offence and has not completed eighteenth year of age as on the date of commission of such offence. This position continues to be the same even under the J.J. Act, 2015 which defines 'child in conflict with law,' under Section 2 (13), as below:

Child in conflict with law means a child who is alleged or found to have committed an offence and who has not completed eighteen year of age on the date of commission of such offence.

Section 5 and Section 6 of the J.J. Act, 2015, are also relevant and need to be taken note of, because they provide for the situations where a child has attained the age of eighteen years and ceases to be a child adult during the pendency of proceedings, or has been apprehended after ceasing to be a child. Even if a person ceases to be a child, the person shall be entitled to the benefits of the J.J. Act, 2015, if on the date of commission of offence such person had not completed the 18th year of age.

(i) Procedure for determination of age

Section 94 of the J.J. Act, 2015 prescribes the procedure for age determination. This Section is placed under Chapter X 'Miscellaneous' of the Act, because it applies for all kind of children under the Act, be they 'children in need of care and protection' or 'child in conflict with law'.

(ii) Section 94 Presumption and determination of age

(1) Where, it is obvious to the Committee or the Board, based on the appearance of the person brought before it under any of the provisions of this Act (other than for the purpose of giving evidence) that the said person is a child, the Committee or the Board shall record such observation stating the age of the child as nearly as may be and proceed with the inquiry under Section 14 or Section 36, as the case may be, without waiting for further confirmation of the age.

(2) In case, the Committee or the Board has reasonable grounds for doubt regarding whether the person brought before it is a child or not, the Committee or the Board, as the case may be, shall undertake the process of age determination, by seeking evidence by obtaining, -(i) the date of birth certificate from the school, or the matriculation or equivalent certificate from the concerned examination Board, if available; and in the absence thereof; (ii) the birth certificate given by a corporation or a municipal authority or a panchayat; (iii) and only in the absence of (i) and (ii) above, age shall be determined by an ossification test or any other latest medical age determination test conducted on the orders of the Committee or the Board:

Provided such age determination test conducted on the order of the Committee or the Board shall be completed within fifteen days from the date of such order. (3) The age recorded by the Committee or the Board to be the age of person so brought before it shall, for the purpose of this Act, be deemed to be the true age of that person.

(iii) Age determination under section 94(1), J.J. Act, 2015

If a JJB is satisfied based on appearance, that the person produced before it is definitely a child, there is no need to look for any other evidence. A mere recording of such observation is sufficient.

Section 94(1) allows a JJB to declare someone to be a child based on 'appearance,' and no further process for determination of age is contemplated in such a scenario. The intention behind this provision is that time should not be wasted in calling for documents of age, in cases where a person looks to be a child, merely on appearance. The only requirement for application of 94(1) is that the person produced is a child must be 'obvious'. In cases where the element of obviousness is not there, due process of age determination as prescribed in Section 94(2) should be followed.

In practice however, it has been observed that this provision is not used and JJBs or CWCs tend to look for a document to declare the age.

(iv) Age determination under section 94(2), J.J. Act, 2015

Only when age cannot be declared under Section 94(1), age should be decided by the JJB under Section 94(2) which provides a detailed scheme of documents that need to be considered. Age determination is not an inquiry under Section 94(2). It is pertinent to take note of the fact that word 'inquiry' does not appear in Section 94. This is crucial because the judgment of Supreme Court in Ashwani Kumar Saxena v. State of M.P. [(2012) 9 SCC 750] is based on interpretation of word 'inquiry'. This judgment was given when J.J. Act, 2000 was in force and therein word 'inquiry' was used.

Section 94(2) uses the phrase "by seeking evidence." Therefore, parties are entitled to lead evidence and be allowed to cross-examine witness as well.

(v) Hierarchy of admissible documents on age under section 94(2)

It is evident from a bare reading of Section 94(2) that only few documentary evidences are admissible for determination of age. Matriculation or equivalent Certificate from the concerned examination Board, (if available) and date of birth certificate from the school are accorded first priority as evidence. Only in the absence of these educational documents, the birth certificate given by a corporation or a municipal authority or a panchayat should be considered. The use of the phrase- 'if available,' implies that if the document of matriculation or equivalent certificate from the concerned examination Board is available, it becomes the first priority document. It is only when these are not available that the JJB should look for any other document. The second priority document is 'the date of birth certificate from the school'. The J.J. Act, 2015 does not specify the type of school. The JJ Model Rules, 2007 had specified 'school certificate from school first attended,' which is not the case anymore under the J.J. Act, 2015. Any certificate of birth from any school, which is authentic and most reliable in view of the JJB, is sufficient for declaration of age.

(vi) Medical age determination

(1) An ossification test or (2) any other latest medical test. What is an Ossification Test? An Ossification test is a test which determines age based on the degree of fusion of bone. X-rays of few bones are taken and then the opinion is given about proximate age in a range i.e., between 17 to 19 years. What is any other latest medical test? An Ossification test is not a very accurate means to determine the age of a person. A more comprehensive assessment entails the assessment by a duly constituted Medical Board, as provided for under the erstwhile JJ Model Rules, 2007, in Rule 12(3)(b), who should arrive at an opinion on age based on (1) ossification test, (2) dental examination and (3) opinion based on examination of physical

features like status of pubic hair and growth of sexual organs like breasts, chest hair, beard, etc. It is a common practice in courts to order for an ossification test, without realising the crucial difference between an ossification test and a duly constituted Medical Board. In Siddu @ Siddeshwar v. State, [Criminal Appeal No. 200465 of 2015, decision dated 23.04.2016] before the Karnataka High Court, there were two medical reports, one of an ossification test done by a radiologist and another by a duly constituted Medical Board, consisting of a physician, dentist and a radiologist. The reports gave divergent opinions on the age of the said person. The Karnataka High Court opted to go for opinion given by the duly constituted Medical Board and gave general directions to the Karnataka Government that duly constituted Medical Boards is set up in all the districts, along with a general direction prohibiting individual doctors from carrying out medical age tests. This judgment was given in the context of Model Rule 12 which required medical age examination by a duly constituted Medical Board. Similar directions were given by the Hon'ble Delhi High Court in *Court on Its Own Motion v. Department of Women and Child Development [Writ Petition (Civil) 8889 of 2011]:*

(2) All the members of medical Board (Physiologist [Later on substituted with Physician], Dental Examiner and Radiologist/ Forensic expert) shall give their individual reports based on their respective examinations and the same shall be mentioned in the report, based on which the Chairperson shall give the final opinion on the age within a margin of one year.

(vii) Where two views are possible, benefit is to go in favour of child

Circumstances and evidence may create a situation where two views are possible. In such a situation, it has been held in Arnit Das v. State of Bihar,(2000) 5 SCC 488 that while dealing with the question of determination of the age of the accused for the purpose of finding out, whether he is a juvenile or not, hyper technical approach should not be adopted while appreciating the evidence adduced on behalf of the accused in support of the plea that he is a juvenile and if two views are possible on the same evidence, the court should lean in favour of holding the accused to be juvenile in borderline cases.

This is based on the criminal law principle that benefit of doubt must go to an accused and this holds good in cases of age determination of accused or of children alleged to be in conflict with law.

4.20 Provision relating to bail

The notion of bail under the J.J. Act, 2015, is very different from that of bail as understood in Criminal Law. Such difference is in tune with the child centric and rehabilitative approach of the J.J. Act. It should be kept in mind that considerations for bail under the J.J. Act, 2015, are not the same as laid down under Chapter XXXIII of Criminal Procedure Code. However, since 'bail' itself is a terminology of Criminal Law, it continues to be understood and applied most often as per that framework.

Section 12(1), J.J. Act, 2015 states:-

Bail to a person who is apparently a child alleged to be in conflict with law. (1) When any person, who is apparently a child and is alleged to have committed a bailable or non-bailable offence, is apprehended or detained by the police or appears or brought before a Board, such person shall, notwithstanding anything contained in the Code of Criminal Procedure, 1973 or in any other law for the time being in force, be released on bail with or without surety or placed under the supervision of a probation officer or under the care of any fit person. Provided that such person shall not be so released if there appears reasonable grounds for believing that the release is likely to bring that person into association with any known criminal or expose the said person to moral, physical or psychological danger or the persons release would defeat the ends of justice, and the Board shall record the reasons for denying the bail and circumstances that led to such a decision.

By stating, notwithstanding anything contained in the Code of Criminal Procedure, 1973 or in any other law for the time being in force, the J.J. Act, 2015 overrules the application of Cr.P.C. or any other law on bail in force, from application of Section 12.

(i) Is it mandatory for a person to be declared a child (below 18 years) before bail is granted

Since the J.J. Act, 2015 is applicable to 'children', most often it is seen that the bail application is kept pending till the inquiry on determination of age is concluded. However, it is imperative to take note that Section 12, J.J. Act, 2015, uses 'person' and 'apparently a juvenile'. While use of the word 'person' indicates that the benefit of Section 12 is available to a person and not necessarily to a 'child', the use of the phrase 'apparently a child' makes it abundantly clear that application of Section 12 does not call for a definitive finding on age to be returned before the bail application is considered. Thus, any person who is 'apparently' a child, can be granted bail. It can be argued that the mere production of a person before the JJB by the police is sufficient for the JJB to form a prima facie view that the applicant is 'apparently a child'.

(ii) Is seriousness of the offence alleged a ground for declining bail?

The nature of the offence is immaterial for consideration of bail under the J.J. Act, 2015. Bail is a right and can only be denied in three exceptional circumstances mentioned in Section 12 (1) of J.J. Act, which are:

1. If there is reasonable grounds for considering that the release is possibly bring that child in association of any known criminal.

2. If there appear reasonable grounds for believing that the release is likely to expose the said person to moral, physical or psychological danger.

3. If there appear reasonable grounds for believing that the persons release would defeat the ends of justice.

(iii) Can the police grant bail?

Though it is not explicitly mentioned in Section 12, J.J. Act, 2015, a reading of Section 12(2) makes it clear that the Officer-in-Charge of the police station is empowered to grant bail in bailable as well as in non-bailable offences. Section 12 (2) reads as below:

> When such person having been apprehended is not released on bail under subsection (1) by the officer-in-charge of the police station, such officer shall cause the person to be kept only in an observation home in such manner as may be prescribed until the person can be brought before a Board.

Out of these three exceptional circumstances for declining bail, the most misunderstood one is – *defeat the ends of Justice*. This term has been interpreted by the Hon'ble Delhi High Court in several cases and it has been held repeatedly that the facts for deciding as to what amounts to frustrate the ends of justice must be seen in the context of the purpose of the Act. The phrase "would defeat the ends of justice" therefore cannot be stretched to bring into its ambit the gravity of the offence or the interest of the victim. Judgments of Hon'ble Delhi High Court in Master Abhishek (minor) Vs State: 2005 VI AD Delhi 18 and subsequently reiterated in Dev Vrat (Minor) Vs The State (Govt. of NCT of Delhi):2006[3]JCC1430 may be referred, to further comprehend the position of law on this specific aspect. Relevant observation made by the Delhi High Court in Master Abhishek Case are reproduced below Petitioner was arrested in an offence u/s 323/302/34 IPC in case FIR No. 338/04 dated 5.7.2004 PS Kalyan Puri. The Juvenile Justice Board rejected the application for bail on the observation that the juvenile was of impulsive nature. Further, it was observed that the manner in which the juvenile committed the crime shows his aggressive behaviour as well as tendencies to harm others and that the fact that the person assaulted only with his fist and arms died shows his brutal mental make-up. The Juvenile Justice Board observed that in these circumstances it would not be in the interest of justice to admit the juvenile to bail. The only thing that remains to be seen is whether his release will defeat the ends of justice. Justice here should be interpreted in the context of the other provisions of the Juvenile Justice (Care and Protection of Children), Act 2000. The aim behind this act is the welfare of children. The very preamble of this act describes the purpose of enacting it... "What can be said to be the factors to determine what will defeat the ends of justice have to be located in the context of the purpose of the Act. The purpose of the Act is to meet the need of care and protection of children and to cater to their development needs. This can be done by adopting a child friendly approach in the adjudication is disposition of matters in the best interest of children and for their ultimate rehabilitation. Therefore if there is a factor which requires the Court to keep the child in custody for meeting the developmental needs of the child or for his rehabilitation, or for his care and protection then only it can be said that his release would defeat the ends of justice. Similarly, in Devvrat Case, the Delhi High Court reiterated similar views while making observations given below - The finding recorded in the impugned order is based on the nature of the offence as well as the release of the petitioner not being in the interest of justice. There is a difference between the expressions in the interest of justice and defeat of the ends of justice.

(iv) Exceptional circumstances must be based on some supporting material

It is often seen that the existence of exceptional circumstances for denial of bail is presented as a matter of routine without there being any material on record to support the claim. Such claims are not tenable. In Girijesh v. State of U.P., the High Court of Allahabad vide its judgment dated 15.04.2015 granted bail to the applicant and made the following observation: Even the report of the District Probation Officer, Gorakhpur is not supported by any material as to how minor will fall in company of bad elements if released on bail. The observation of the District Probation Officer in absence of any supporting material becomes bald and vague. Consequently, the same is to be ignored. Similarly, mere risk of child getting into criminal company is not sufficient. Requirement is that there must be 'known criminal' in order to invoke the exception. In Nand Kishore (in JC) Versus State, (No citation available, copy available on www.indiankanoon.org) the Delhi High Court, in its judgment dated 07.07.2006 held as below As regards the first exception, before it can be invoked to deny bail to a juvenile there must be a reasonable ground for believing that his release is likely to bring him into association with any known criminal. The expression known criminal is not without significance. When the liberty of a juvenile is sought to be curtailed by employing the exception, the exception must be construed strictly. Therefore, before this exception is invoked, the prosecution must identify the known criminal and then the court must have reasonable grounds to believe that the juvenile, if released on bail, would associate with this known criminal. It cannot be generally observed that the release of the juvenile would bring him into association with criminals without identifying the criminals and without returning a, prima facie, finding with regard to the nexus between the juvenile and such criminal.

(v) Denial of bail is an exception and is an option of last resort

A careful perusal of Section 12(1), J.J. Act, 2015 demonstrates that denial of bail under J.J. Act is an exception. While interpreting Section 12, the JJB is duty bound to be directed by the fundamental principle of Principle of institutionalisation as a measure of last resort laid down under Section 3(xii) of the J.J. Act. A child can therefore only be institutionalised as a measure of last resort and that too after making a reasonable inquiry. In this regard, it may also be noted that J.J. Act has made it mandatory for JJBs to record the reasons for denying the bail and circumstances that led to such a decision under the proviso to Section 12(1). Such emphatic prescription for granting bail is further fortified by Section 12(4), which provides that if a child in conflict with law who has been granted bail is unable to fulfill the conditions of bail within seven days of the bail order, such child should be produced before the JJB, so that the bail conditions can be suitably modified by the JJB, in order to ensure actual realisation of bail. The duty to seek modification of bail condition is not on the child, but has been shifted to the JJB under the J.J. Act, 2015. Section 12(4) reads as below When a child in conflict with law is unable to fulfill the conditions of bail order within seven days of the bail order, such child shall be produced before the Board for modification of the conditions of bail.

(vi) Is there always a need to file a bail application?

Ordinarily in criminal law, an accused person should apply for bail before a criminal court. This is not the case before the JJB. Since bail is a matter of right for all children alleged to be in conflict with law, the JJB does not have to wait for the bail application to be filed. Whenever a child, who is alleged to have committed an offence, is brought before a JJB, it should consider the question of bail or release on the date of first production itself, irrespective of whether any bail application has been filed or not. Rule 10(1)(iii), JJ Model Rules, 2016, "can be relied upon in this regard which lists certain orders which can be passed on the date of production itself upon review by the Board of social background report, circumstances of apprehending the child and offence alleged to have been committed by the child as provided by the officers, individuals, agencies producing the child." Rule 10(1)(iii), states as follows–

> "Releasing the child in the supervision or custody of fit persons or fit institutions or Probation Officers as the case may be, through an order in Form 3, with a direction to appear or present a child for an inquiry on the next date."

(vii) Is the offence being bailable or non-bailable of any consideration?

In the Criminal Law approach, the question of bail is dependent on whether the offence is bailable or non-bailable. However, under the J.J. Act, 2015, such consideration is immaterial as Section 12(1) does not discriminate between a bailable and a non-bailable offence. It is no argument that bail be granted because offence alleged in bailable, similarly it is also no argument that bail be denied because offence alleged in a non-bailable offence. Considerations for denial of bail are clear and specific, which are mentioned in the proviso to Section 12(1).

(viii) Is bail of a child over 16 years of age and accused of having committed a heinous offence also covered under section 12 of J.J. Act?

Even though the JJB has been granted power to decide whether such a child may be transferred to be tried as adult, the provision on bail under Section 12 remains unchanged. The reason that a preliminary assessment is pending in respect of a child, is no reason for declining the bail.

(ix) Does section 12 include anticipatory bail?

Section 12 (1), use of the words '...appears or brought before a Board...' is indicative of the fact that a child may very well appear before a Board or may be brought before a Board by his parents and can seek bail. There is no need to apply for anticipatory bail under Criminal Procedure Code, because even though "anticipatory bail" is not used in J.J. Act, 2015, it includes a relief, which is similar to anticipatory bail. Benefit of Section 12 is available to any person, apparently a child and is alleged to have committed a bailable or non-bailable offence, and who (1) is apprehended or detained by the police or, (2) appears or brought before a Board. The latter clause would include the anticipatory nature of bail under Section 12 of the J.J. Act.

(x) Is Social Investigation Report (SIR) mandatory of grant of bail?

Section 12 is an exhaustive provision on bail and it does not mandate the consideration of a Social Investigation Report (SIR) before bail is granted. It is true that the SIR is a good and credible document to ascertain whether exceptional circumstances for denial of bail exist or not, but it cannot be treated as mandatory. It has to be kept in mind that under Section 13(1)(ii), at the time of apprehension of child, the police is mandated to give information to the Probation officer or a Child Welfare Officer who is required to submit a SIR within two weeks and such SIR is to be used for the purpose of inquiry, not for bail. Prevalent insistence on availability of SIR is by way of tradition and not by law. Ordinarily if the SIR is available, the JJB may well use it, but its availability cannot be stretched to the extent that it becomes a pre-condition for consideration of bail.

4.2 Transfer of child in conflict with law

Under the Children Act 1960[69], Children's Courts were set-up for exercising the powers and discharging the duties conferred or imposed on such court in relation to delinquent children under this Act,[70] and were empowered to deal exclusively with all proceedings under this Act relating to...delinquent children.[71] Provisions of the Children Act, 1960 were incorporated under the J.J. Act, 1986. Juvenile Courts were established for exercising the powers and discharging the duties conferred or imposed on such court in relation to juvenile delinquents under this Act,[72] and such Juvenile Courts were given the power to deal exclusively with all proceedings under this Act relating to...delinquent juveniles. Similar powers were given to JJBs under the J.J. Act 2000 - power to deal exclusively with all proceedings under this Act relating to juvenile in conflict with law.[73] Provisions for exclusive dealing of juvenile cases by the Juvenile Justice System was strengthened with the insertion of sub-Section (4) to Section 1 of the J.J. Act, 2000[74] - Notwithstanding anything contained in any other law for the time being in force, the provisions of this Act shall apply to all cases involving detention, prosecution, penalty or sentence of imprisonment of juveniles in conflict with law under such other law.

(i) Who may be shifted out of the juvenile justice system?

Per Section 15(1) of the J.J. Act, 2015, the process for assessing whether a child in conflict with law may be denied protection of juvenile justice legislation is to be initiated only when such child is alleged to have committed a heinous offence and has completed or is above the age of sixteen years.

(ii) Procedure to be followed by JJB prior to shifting a child in conflict with the law into the criminal justice system

(iii) Applicable standards for preliminary assessment

It is significant to mention that any law that deprives a person of personal liberty should be fair, just and reasonable[75], and should be accordingly interpreted. Waiver of a child in conflict with the law amounts to deprivation of personal liberty as such child is incarcerated in a place of safety.

Section 15(1) of the J.J. Act, 2015 lays down the procedure to be followed by the JJB once the requirements of heinous offence and age, are satisfied:

In case of a heinous offence alleged to have been committed by a child, who has completed or is above the age of sixteen years, the Board shall conduct a preliminary assessment with regard to his mental and physical capacity to commit such offence, ability to understand the consequences of the offence and the circumstances in which he allegedly committed the offence, and may pass an order in accordance with the provisions of sub-Section (3) of Section 18.

Transfer of a child into the criminal justice system for treatment as an adult can only be done after preliminary assessment by the JJB. The word 'shall' indicate that it is mandatory for the JJB to conduct preliminary assessment. There are three main reasons for conducting the preliminary assessment -to assess (i) the child's mental and physical capacity to commit the alleged offence; (ii) the child's ability to understand the consequences of the offence; (iii) the circumstances in which the child allegedly committed the offence. All these three factors are to be holistically considered by the JJB when deciding whether a child should be transferred from the juvenile justice system. As the JJB is not equipped to assess the child's mental capacity to commit the offence, the legislature has provided that "the Board may take the assistance of experienced psychologists or psycho-social workers or other experts.[76] Prior to examining what is expected of the JJB when conducting a preliminary assessment, it is necessary to understand the standard to be applied for measuring the mental capacity to commit the alleged offence and the child's understanding of the consequences of the offence. Per Section 82,[77] IPC, a child under seven years of age cannot be held culpable for committing an offence. Per Section 83,[78] IPC, culpability of a child above seven years and under 12 years depends on whether that child has "attained sufficient maturity of understanding to judge of the nature and consequences of his conduct on that occasion" – such gauging of maturity is to be done by the JJB. Reading of Section 82 and 83, IPC indicates that the Indian law assumes that all children above twelve years of age understand the nature and consequences of their conduct; therefore, under IPC a child above 16 years has the required maturity and understanding. The fact that Section 15(1) of the J.J. Act, 2015 seeks such determination for a child above sixteen years in spite of Sections 82 and 83, IPC, denotes that the standard for such assessment under juvenile legislation is different from that under IPC. Other than children, Section 84, IPC,[79] exempts 'a person of unsound mind' from culpability - the degree of unsoundness of mind should be such that the person 'is incapable of knowing the nature of the act, or that he is doing what is wrong or contrary to law.' If a child in conflict with the law is of unsound mind, Section 84, IPC gets invoked, and such child would anyways be exempted from culpability.

4.22 Orders that a JJB may pass on completion of preliminary assessment

Order on preliminary assessment should be passed by JJB after giving equal weightage to all the aforementioned three factors, namely, the child's mental and physical capacity to commit the alleged offence; the child's ability to understand the consequences of the offence; and the circumstances in which the child allegedly committed the offence. The fact that a preliminary assessment should be conducted by the JJB prior to waiver shows that every child in conflict with the law who is above 16 years of age and is alleged to have committed a heinous offence is not to be transferred into the criminal justice system – such decision is to be taken by the JJB after careful assessment. The JJB has the power to retain the child within the juvenile justice system: Where the Board is satisfied on preliminary assessment that the matter should be disposed of by the Board, then the Board shall follow the procedure, as far as may be, for trial in summons case under the Code of Criminal Procedure, 1973 (268 of 1974).[80]

Under Section 18(3), J.J. Act, 2015, the JJB on completion of preliminary assessment, and after giving the child a hearing, may transfer the child in conflict with the law into the criminal justice system: Where the Board after preliminary assessment under Section 15 pass an order that there is need for trial of the said child as an adult, then the Board may order transfer of the case to the Children's Court having jurisdiction to try such offences. An order under Section 18(3) should be passed by at least two members including the Principal Magistrate.[81] An order under Section 18(3) should be a reasoned order: Where the Board, after preliminary assessment under Section 15 of the Act passes an order that there is need for trial of the said child as an adult, shall assign reasons for the same.[82]

4.23 Transfer to children's court

Under Section 18(3), J.J. Act, 2015, the 'trial' of the case is transferred to the Children's Court having jurisdiction to try such offences. Under Section 2(20), J.J. Act, 2015: Children's Court means a court established under the Commissions for Protection of Child Rights Act, 2005 (4 of 2006) or a Special Court under the Protection of Child Rights Act, 2012 (32 of 2012), wherever existing and where such courts have not been designated, the Court of Sessions having jurisdiction to try offences under the Act. The preamble of the Commissions for Protection of Child Rights Act provides for constituting of Children's Courts for providing speedy trial of offences against children or of violation of child rights. It is paradoxical that a court that is established to entertain cases relating to offences against children is also empowered to entertain cases of children in conflict with the law. Is it that the legislature felt that the Children's Court would be best able to balance rights of child victims and child offenders? According to Section 20(2), J.J. Act, 2015, the trial of a case registered under the POCSO Act will be dealt with by the Special Court constituted under that Act[83] hence the same court is empowered to conduct trials of an adult accused or a child in conflict with the law. It is apprehended that a court that conducts trials against adults and children may find it difficult to constantly swing between the punitive approach and the rehabilitative approach, thereby causing detriment to the interests of children in conflict with the law. A Sessions Court is designated as a Children's Court under the Commissions for Protection of Child Rights Act and the Special Court under the POCSO Act, such court is not enabled to provide rehabilitative services, nor social work intervention.

4.24 How should the children's court deal with children in conflict with the law?

Upon the child in conflict with the laws case being transferred, the Children's Court should decide as to whether there is need for trial of the child as an adult[84] or whether there is no need for trial of the child as an adult and may conduct an inquiry as a Board.[85]

If the Children's Court passes an order under Section 19(1)(ii), it shall conduct an inquiry as a JJB and pass appropriate orders under Section 18(1) and (2) of the J.J. Act, 2015. The child's case is not remanded to the JJB for inquiry – under Section 8(2), the Children's Court can exercise the powers of the JJB when the proceedings come before them under Section 19. If the Children's Court passes an order under Section 19(1)(i) of the J.J. Act, 2015, it shall conduct a trial and pass appropriate orders considering the special needs of the child, the tenets of fair trial and maintaining a child friendly atmosphere. A child found guilty by the Children's Court is to be sent to a place of safety.[86]

4.25 Orders that may be passed by a juvenile justice board

(i) What orders is the JJB empowered to pass regarding child found to be in conflict with the law?

Section 18(1) of the J.J. Act, 2015 lists the different dispositional orders that the JJB may pass on completion of inquiry. In addition to such orders, the JJB may also pass orders under Section 18(2) of the J.J. Act, 2015 depending on the circumstances and needs of individual children. Section 18(1) is similar to Section 15(1) of the J.J. Act 2000, but Section 18(2) has been freshly inserted in the 2015 Act.

(ii) When may the JJB pass orders under the proviso under clause (g)?

When the JJB has decided that a child found to be in conflict with the law requires institutionalisation in a Special Home that the proviso to sub-Section (1) to Section 18 of the J.J. Act, 2015 comes into play. Such child may be sent to a place of safety instead of a Special Home if the JJB is of the opinion that (a) the behaviour of the child has been such that it would not be in the child's interest to be sent to a Special Home, or (b) "in the interest of children housed in a special home. The proviso is generally deployed by the JJB as a punitive measure, when the nature of the offence is grave. Putting a child in a place of safety sends a message that such child's stay in a Special Home may spoil the other children and that such child is incorrigible.

(iii) What orders is the JJB not permitted to pass?

Section 21, stipulates Order that may not be passed against a child in conflict with the law: No child in conflict with law shall be sentenced to death or for life imprisonment without the possibility of release, for any such offence, either under the provisions of this Act or under the provisions of the Indian Penal Code or any other law for the time being in force.

4.26 Judicial approach to the determination of the age of criminal responsibility

Age determination is one of the most critical areas of litigation, on matters related to Juvenile Justice. A significant proportion of litigation on juvenile justice in superior courts is on age determination and on the claim of being a child. While examining the cases decided by the Hon'ble Apex Court of India, it can be precisely seen that there is no uniform approach regarding the age of criminal responsibility. On various occasions it is found that the Court has reversed its own verdicts. Sometimes the Court stands in favour of relaxing the age of criminal responsibility and in some other cases overruled its own judgment and ordered against the age relaxation vis a vis juvenile offender. In Umesh Chandra v. State of Rajasthan[87] the date of reckoning was decided. The Hon'ble Supreme Court was precisely clear on the date of reckoning and held that "the relevant date for the applicability of the Act[88] so far as the age of the accused, who claims to be a child, is concerned, is the date of occurrence and not the date of trail." This decision was made with reference to the Children Act, 1960. But in 2000, after enforcement of J.J. Act 2000[89] the view of the Honorable Supreme Court seemed to be taken a U-turn as it observed in the case of Arnit Das v. State of Bihar,[90] that "the crucial date of determining the question, whether a person is Juvenile, is the date when he is brought before the competent authority". In 2005 this imperative was again come in consideration in the case of Pratap Singh v. State of Jharkhand,[91] before the five – judge Bench and it was held as "the reckoning date of for the determination of age of the juvenile is the date of offence and not the date when he is produced before the authority or in the court." The Apex Court appreciated the decision in Umesh Chandra case and held that case as correct law. The legislature by the amendment in the section 2(1)[92] of Juvenile Justice Act[93] in 2006[94] removed this ambiguity once for all.

The observation of the Apex court in case of Pratap Singh's case was fortified by subsequent decisions[95] of the Apex Court and finally, the Hon'ble Supreme Court in Hari Ram v. State of Rajasthan[96], in its judgment delivered on 5-5-2009 conclude this dispute and put a final stamp stating that "the law as now crystallised on a conjoint reading of section 2(k), 2(l), 7A, 20 and 49 read with rules 12 and 98, places beyond all doubts that all person who were below the age of 18 years on the date of commission of the offence even prior to 1st April, 2001would be treated as juveniles, even if the claim of juvenility was raised after they attained the age of 18 years on or before the date of Commencement of the Act and were undergoing sentence upon being convicted."

In Rajinder Chandra vs. State of Chhattisgarh *and* Anr[97], the Apex Court of the land shows a lenient approach while determining the age of accused who is at the border line of the threshold fixed by the legislature. In aforesaid case The Hon'ble Supreme Court observed as follows:-

"It is true that the age of the accused is just on the border of sixteen years and on the date of the offence and his arrest he was less than 16 years by a few months only. This Court has, on a review of judicial opinion, held that while dealing with the question of determination of the age of the accused for the purpose of finding out, whether he is juvenile or not, a hyper-technical approach should not be adopted while appreciating the evidence adduced on behalf of the accused in support of the plea of that he was juvenile and if two views may be possible on the said evidence,the court should lean in favour of holding the accused to be a juvenile in borderline cases. The law, so laid down by this Court squarely applies to the facts of the present case."

Adopting the same line of thinking in Hari Ram v. State of Rajasthan[98], the Apex Court has given the reference of special provision provided under Section 25[99] of J.J. Act 2000[100] and held that "though the documents produced in support of the appellants claim of being juvenile, precisely shows that at the time of commission of offence he was 13 days older than the cut-off limit of 16 years as provided in Section 2(h) of the1986 Act[101] and the learned High Court had only corrected the error of the Additional Sessions Judge, Didwana, in regard to the of calculation of the appellants age." The Hon'ble Court further added that "10 years have passed from the date of occurrence of the said offence and the Juvenile Justice Act has been amended to encompass the children who had not attained the age of 18 years for the definition of juvenile, the High Court should have not taken such a hyper-technical view and should not have interfered with the order of the Additional Session Judge, Didwana, declaring the appellant to be juvenile." The Court authoritatively settles the legal position and further added that "A juvenile who had not completed eighteen years on the date of commission of the offence was also entitled to the benefits of the Juvenile Justice Act, 2000, as if the provision of the Section 2(k) had always been in existence even during the operation of the Act 1986." This welfare approach believes that the best interest of the child should be protected and the same is also shown in highly glaring case (Writ Petition) Salil Bali v Union of India[102] where the Hon'ble Supreme Court held that the said "Juvenile Justice Act 2000[103] has been enacted after a protracted advisement and is in consonance with the Standards laid down in United Nation Convention on the Rights of the Child, 1989, The Beijing Rules, 1985, The Havana Rules and other International Instruments for procuring the best interests of the child, with the Primary object of Social re-integration of the child victims and child in conflict with law, without resorting to the Conventional Judicial proceedings which are meant for adult criminals". The learned ASG also referred to the decision of the case State of Tamil Nadu Vs. K. Shyam Sunder[104], wherein it had been observed as "merely because the law causes hardships or sometimes results in adverse consequences, it cannot be held to be ultra vires and unconstitutional, nor can it be struck down".[105] Finally learned ASG concluded his statement that we do not think that any interference is necessary with the Provisions of the Statute until and unless sufficient data is available to warrant any change in provisions of the aforesaid Act and Rules.[106]

Dr. Subramanian Swami v. Raju through Member, Juvenile Justice Board,[107] The Hon'ble Supreme Court held that "The Act must be interpreted and understood to advance the cause of the Legislation and to confer the benefits of the provisions thereof to the category of person for whom the Legislation has been made. Therefore, we deem it proper to proceed, not to determine the correctness of the decision in *Salil Bali's* case." Referring the case of Pratap Singh v. State of Jarkhand.[108] The Hon'ble Apex Court says "The Act 2000 is a beneficial piece of legislation and must therefore receive its due interpretation as a Legislation belonging to the errant Juveniles." The Supreme Court further added that sections 2(k), 14, 15 and 16[109] do not infringe Article 14 and it is not abhorrent to constitutional values.

In Kulai Ibrahim alias Ibrahim v. State, Rep. by the Inspector of police B-1,Coimbatore,[110] the relevant document mentioned in rules 2(3)(a)(i)[111] to (iii) were available but as per the police investigation the same was manipulated and fabricated. Therefore, as per the observations of the Court "if the fabrication is confirmed, it is necessary to go for medical examination report for age determination of the appellant. The Delay cannot act as an impediment in seeking medical report as section 7A of the J.J. Act, 2000 gives right to an accused to raise the question of juvenility at any point of time even after the disposal of the case". This has been confirmed in Ashwani Kumar Saxena v. State of Madhya Pradesh,[112] The Court further observed that "J.J. Act, 2000 is a beneficial piece of legislation and if two views prevail regarding the age determination, the scales must tilt in favour of the view that support the claim of juvenility". Significantly the Court has expounded how "Age determination inquiry" has to be conducted under section 7A of the J.J. Act read with rule 12 of the JJ Rules. Relevant portion of the same is taken out hereunder:

"Age determination inquiry contemplated under section 7A of the Act read with rule 12 of the 2007 Rules enables the court to seek evidence and in that process, the court can obtained the matriculation or equivalent certificates, if available. Only in the absence of any matriculation or equivalent certificates, the court needs to obtain the date of birth certificate from the school first attend other than a play school. Only in the absence of matriculation or equivalent certificate or the date of birth certificate from the school first attended, the court needs to obtain the birth certificate given by a corporation or a municipal authority or a Panchayat (not an affidavit but certificates or documents). The question of obtaining medical opinion from a duly constituted Medical Board arises only if the abovementioned documents are unavailable. In case exact assessment of the age cannot be done, then the court, for reason to be recorded, may if considered necessary, give the benefit to the child or juvenile by considering his or her age on lower side within the margin of one year."

"Once the court following the above mentioned procedures, passes an order, that order shall be the conclusive proof of the age as regards such child or juvenile in conflict with law. It has been made clear in sub-rule (5) of rule 12 that no further inquiry shall be conducted by the Court or the Board after examining and obtaining the certificate or any other documentary proof after referring to sub-rule (3) of rule 12. Further, section 49 of the J.J. Act also draws a presumption of the age of the juvenility on its determination."

In Pratap Singh v State of Jharkhand,[113], a five Judge Bench of Court considered the scope of section 32, 2(h), 3, 26 and 18 of the Juvenile Justice Act, 1986 and took the view that "reckoning date of the determination of age of the juvenile is the date of commission of the offence and not the date when the offender was produced before the competent court".[114]

As above discussed case of the Hon'ble Supreme Court shows that in India any ambiguity regarding the age of the offender has been resolved in favour of the accused. The benefit of the juvenility has been extended respectively in those cases where the offender is on verge of adulthood (16-18 years).[115] But there are notable exceptions to this principle of youth moulding the sentencing discretion and a court determined to *weed out criminality* may choose to *weed out the criminal* even if arguably a child.[116] Because of the increasing of the number of juvenile crime, in various countries, the juvenile justice system begun to move from traditional welfare-ism to crime control. The focus of orientation of juvenile justice system is shifted from the welfare of the child in conflict with law to the public safety. This line of thought took the view that the persons above the age of 16 years were mature enough to know the consequences of their actions and therefore they should not be given exemption from criminal liability. They should be treated same as adult for the offence committed by them. In Om Prakash v. State of Rajasthan and Other,[117] the court has endeavored to ease the shaking conscience of the public in the institutions of the justice administration. It was held that "When the evidence as to the date is doubtful, the Court should not take a causal view and grant protection of the Act .When the date of birth in certificate is not free from ambiguity, Medical evidence has to be given preference over school record in such cases." In this case the Court has given more emphasis to the confidence of public in the institution of the justice administration and set aside the main objective, for which the J.J. Act has been, enacted, i.e, welfare and best interests of the child. The court has referred the case of Ram Deo Chauhan v. State of Assam,[118] in which the court has observed that when the evidence as to the date is doubtful, the court should not take a casual view and protection of the Act. Contrary to the judgment in *Umesh Chandra case*[119], in Arnit Das v. State of Bihar,[120] the Hon'ble Apex Court of the land observed as "the date of determining whether an accused is a juvenile or not under the J.J. Act 1986, is the date on which the accused first appears in enquiring proceedings before the trial court". The Hon'ble Supreme Court held that "the courts should not adopt the *hyper-technical* approach while dealing with the question of age determination of juvenile".

The Hon'ble Supreme Court held that the decision in *Umesh Chandra's case* is the good law. Same approach can again be seen in case of Abuzar Hossain alias Gulam Hossain vs State of West Bengal[121] where in Justice J M Lodha observed : " *An affidavit of the claimant or any of the parents or a sibling or a relative in support of the claim of juvenility raised for the first time in appeal or revision or before this Court during the pendency of matter or after the disposal of the case shall not be sufficient justifying an inquiry to determine the age of such person unless the circumstances of the case are so glaring that satisfy the judicial conscience of the court to order an enquiry into determination of the age of the delinquent...."*

Mahadeo s/o Kerba Maske vs. State of Maharashtra and Another[122] the Hon'ble Supreme Court held that "under the rule 12(3)(b), it is specifically provided that only in the absence of alternative methods described under Rule 12(3)(a)(i) to (iii)[123], the medical opinion can be sought for. In the light of such a statutory rule prevailing for ascertainment of the age of the juvenile in our considered opinion, the same yardstick can be rightly followed by the courts for the ascertaining the age of a victim as well."

The same approach as in above cases, again seen in the latest judgment passed in Parag Bharti v. State of Uttar Pradesh[124] in which the Hon'ble Apex Court observed: *"....The benefit of the principal of benevolent legislation attached to the J.J. Act would thus apply to only such cases wherein the accused is held to be a juvenile on the basis of a least prima facie evidence regarding his minority as the benefit of the possibilities of two views in regard to the age of the alleged accused who is involved in grave and serious offence which he committed and gave effect to it in a well-planned manner reflecting his maturity of mind rather than innocence indicating that his juvenility is more in the nature of shield to dodge or dupe the arms of law, cannot be allowed to come to his rescue...."*

(i) Judicial approach to the sentencing of child offenders

Sentencing in criminal justice procedure is a complex subject, though the punishment is prescribed by the legislature and the courts have to take these principles into consideration while choosing an appropriate sentence for the offender. The principles of sentencing take into consideration the age, character, past record, the physical and mental conditions of the criminal and the circumstances of crime in choosing the appropriate sentence.[125] The sentencing courts are under sheer obligation to follow a balanced approach towards the competing interests of the offender and the society at large. As discussed above that judges have difference of opinion in determining the age of criminality, they are also not of same mind in matter of sentencing. The modern Penology thoughts prefer reformatory approach over deterrence or retribution as the punishment is not considered an end in itself, rather a means to an end i.e. reformation and reintegration of the offender[126]. The Parliament of India signifying its camaraderie with the International Community and in compliance with its commitment to International Obligations has given the most benevolent piece of legislation to the children of the nation in the form of the Juvenile Justice (Care and Protection of Children) Act, 1986, 2000 and 2015. These enactments are in the conformity of the International Standards and norms and providing for the betterment and up-liftment of both the categories of children in need of care and protection and children in conflict of law[127]. The role of the Supreme Court of India and various High Courts has been in some cases very positive and appreciable. The Hon'ble Supreme Court and the High Courts has interpreted the provisions of the enactments in such a significant manner that advances the cause of the juvenile justice. The beneficial provisions have been interpreted in favour of juveniles and the benefit has been provided to a number of juveniles whose cases had even attained finality and they were undergoing sentences. The judicial trends set by the Supreme and High Courts are guiding factor for the lower judiciary. The Hoble Supreme Court of India in Gaurav Jain v. Union of India,[128] showed its benevolent approach towards the prostitutes or fallen women and their children who are victim of their social unsolicited shame affixed for no fault of his or her. The Hon'ble Supreme Court invoke the Article 32 of the Constitution of India and states as "it is an integral part of the Constitution of India and that the children have the right to equality of opportunity, dignity, and care, protection and rehabilitation by the society with both hands open to bring them into the mainstream of social life without pre-stigma affixed on them for no fault of his or her". In the case of Gopinath Ghosh v. State of West Bengal.[129] The Hon'ble Court set aside the sentencing of imprisonment for life imposed by the Trial Court and confirmed by the High Court against a minor who was tried with other accused for murder and remitted the case to learned Magistrate for disposal according to the provisions of the Juvenile Justice Act.[130] The Hon'ble Supreme Court allowed, the first time raised petition "plea of child status" and, by amending the appeal petition, referred the matter back to the lower Court for the determination of age of the offender. It observed: "Ordinarily the Supreme Court would be reluctant to entertain a contention based on factual averments raised for the first time before it. However, the Court is equally reluctant to ignore, overlook or nullify the beneficial provisions of a very socially progressive statute by taking shield behind the technicality of contention being raised for the first time in the Court." To deal with problem raised in the case section 7A has been inserted in the JJAct[131] in 2006.[132] It is notable issue in this section that the claim of juvenility may be raised at any stage of the case even after the disposal of the case. The case of Munna v. State of Uttar Pradesh,[133] is also a good example of benevolent and prudent interpretation of section 15 of the Act 56 of 2000. In this case many undertrials juvenile were incarcerated in Kanpur Central Jail, where the juveniles were sexually abused by their adult inmates. The Hon'ble Supreme Court observed that "Juvenile delinquency is, generally, a product of social and economic maladjustment. Even if it is found that these juveniles have committed any offence, they are not supposed be maltreated. They do not lose their fundamental rights when they enter into the jail. Nonetheless, the object of the punishment being reformation, we fail to see what social objective can be gained by sending them to jails where they come in contact with hard criminals and loose whatever sensitivity they may have to finer and nobler sentiments."

Time and again it is reiterated that the sentence awarded to the errant juvenile should be in proportion to the gravity of the offence and the quantum of punishment /restrictions on the liberty of offender, should be in proportion to as is justified to deal with the risk of re-offending. Following the mandate of Article 37 (a) of the Convention on the Rights of the Child, J.J. Act 2015 has barred the death penalty or life imprisonment without the possibility of release of the child offender. Considerably, under the J.J. Act 2000, the situation was different, as even the imprisonment of life term of any kind (remissible or non-remissible) was entirely barred.[134] However, in practice it is precisely apparent that the sentencing Courts which are committed to weed out criminality may go for weeding out the criminal even if arguably a child. In cases of Amrutlal Someshwar Joshi v. State of Maharashtra[135] where the offenders precise age could not be determined and there was no evidence that the offender was under the age of eighteen at the time of occurrence, the Hon'ble Supreme Court has upheld death sentence. Amrutlal Someshwar Joshi, was executed despite the possibility that he was under age 18 at the time of the crime. In Ram Deo Chauhan v. State of Assam,[136] the appellant has been denied the benefit of the J.J. Act, 1986 despite raising the plea of young age and was awarded death penalty. The Hon'ble Supreme Court, observed as "though the age of the accused – appellant has not been determined conclusively, yet in such a case awarding of lesser sentence only on the ground of appellant being a juvenile at the time of offence committed cannot be considered as a mitigating circumstance in view of the findings that the murders committed by him were most cruel, heinous and dastardly and gruesome". In Hari Ram v. State of Rajasthan and Anr[137] (supra) the accused was charged under the sections 148, 302, 149, 325/149 and 323/149 of the IPC. As per the medical board the accused was just on the border of sixteen years of age. The High Court held as "on the date of the incident the accused was about 16 years old and he could not take the plea of juvenility under the age of 1986 Act and the therefore the provisions of 2000 Act were, could not be applicable". The Hon'ble Supreme Court set aside the Order of the High Court and observed that "the appellant was below the age of 18 years on the date of commission of the offence, hence he could avail the benefit of juvenility under the J.J. Act, 2000 as if the provision of Section 2(k) thereof had always been in existence even during the operation of the 1986 Act by virtue of Section 20 of the J.J. Act, 2000 as amended by the Amendment Act of 2006". Therefore the case of appellant was resubmitted to the JJB, Ajmer, for disposal in accordance with law.[138] In another latest case Mahendra Singh and Others v. State of Rajasthan,[139] once again the Court has upheld the decision laid down in *Hari Ram v State of Rajasthan and Anr (Supra[140])*. The Hon'ble Supreme Court observed that it is beyond doubt that the appellant was below the age of eighteen years on the date of incident, yet he could not claim the plea of juvenility under the J.J. Act 1986 as he is above 16 years. But he is entitled to the benefit of Section 20 of J.J. Act, 2000 to be dealt with by JJB.

In Lingala Vijay Kumar v. Public Prosecutor,[141] appellants were prosecuted for committing dacoity in bank and were awarded sentence of two and half years imprisonment which was enhanced to 7 years Rigours Imprisonment each, by the Hon'ble High Court. On appeal against the enhancement of the sentence, the Hon'ble Supreme Court upheld the verdict of the Hon'ble High Court with some directions to the prison authorities to treat the juveniles compassionately during their prison term. Justice Krishna Iyer observed in this case as: "Seven dangerously ideological teenagers, politically impatient with the deepening injustice of the economic order and ebulliently infantile in their terrorist tactics, were sentenced to seven years in prison for the offence of having robbed the State Bank of a few thousand rupees with non-violent use of crude pistols, and country bombs which, in the language of the Penal Code, amounts to dacoity-a grave property crime."

In Ajhar Ali v. State of West Bengal,[142] the appellant was accused of outraging the modesty of a female under section 354/323 and was awarded six months imprisonment. Declaring the accused-appellant a "road side Romeo" the Supreme Court observed as follows: "As the appellant has committed a heinous crime and with the social condition prevailing in the society, the modesty of a women has to be strongly guarded and as the appellant behaved like a road side Romeo, we do not think it is fit case where the benefit of the Act 1958[143] should be given to the appellant". In instant case the Supreme Court has by passed the statutory principles of juvenile justice in sentencing in the name of other considerations such as protection of women in the society.[144] This was done even after the clear finding of the Supreme Court in *Hari Ram v. State of Rajasthan*.[145] That the J.J. Act, 2000 shall have overriding effect over any other law applicable to the child who is found to be in conflict with such law.[146] One recent case of Jhabua district (Madhya Pradesh) came into light, where two minors were convicted with life imprisonment by children's Court for committing murder on February 28, 2017. The matter dates back to December 5, 2016 when a 14 year old child was returning from school the child was attacked with a knife by two minors over a fight for money and victim was succumbed to injury. The two accused were arrested next day and murder weapon were recovered from them. The matter brought the Juvenile Justice Board, and a social investigation report was submitted by the probation officer stating that both the juveniles were addicted to drugs and also had a criminal history. Considering the report of the probation officer, the JJB handed over the case to the Children's Court on January 4, 2017 and the two minors were sentenced to life imprisonment on February 28, 2017.

However, an appeal was moved to the Madhya Pradesh High Court by the guardians of the minors against the judgment of the children's Court on the ground that the later had not fully appreciated the report of the social investigation and had not considered the mental capacity of the children to commit the offence. It was also stated in the appeal that the Children's Court had ignored the procedure for the proper care plan and the procedure for their care till they attain the age of 21 years. This case of Jhabua district describes the veracities of the working of the J.J. Act, 2015.

(ii) Overriding effect of juvenile justice legislations over other legislations

The core objective of the juvenile justice legislation is the protection of the best interest of the child and the welfare of the child. The J.J. Act has overriding effect over other legislations irrespective of the nature of the offence committed by the juvenile in conflict with law.[147] In the earlier cases, the applicability of the Acts to the child offenders who have committed offences punishable with death penalty or life imprisonment was questioned in view of the provisions contained in the Code of Criminal Procedure.[148] The Hon'ble Supreme Court in Rohtas v. State of Haryana[149] observed as "The High Court was in error in holding that the Code of 1973[150] over-ruled the Haryana Act and that the appellant should have been tried under the Code 1973. The view taken by the Sessions Judge on this point was correct and the case of the appellant should have been referred to the Magistrate concerned for trial in accordance with the provisions of the Haryana Act. [154G-H] Section 5 carves out a clear exception to the provisions of the trial of an offence under any special or local law for the time being in force or any special jurisdiction or power conferred or any special form of procedure prescribed by any other law for the time being in force. The Haryana Act was in force when the Code of 1973 was passed and therefore the Haryana Act far from being inconsistent with Sec. 5 of the Code of 1973 appears to be fully protected by the provisions of Sec. 5 of the Code of 1973 [154E-G]".

In the case of Raj Singh v. State of Haryana[151] the Hon'ble Supreme Court has emphasised on the best interest of the child whether it is neglected child or child in conflict with law and observed that juvenile legislation shall always give supreme importance and stated that the juvenile legislation shall reign supreme in juvenile cases it is irrespective of what the offence has committed by the juvenile.

This means that irrespective of the fact that even if the case is registered under any other Provision/Act, against a juvenile, the juvenile is to be dealt with only under the J.J. Act and not any other special Act for the purpose of enquiry and any final order thereto.[152] In Madan Singh v. State of Bihar,[153] two children charged with TADA offences were dealt under the JJA.[154] By the insertion of sub-section (4) to 1. the conflict come to an end. It is amply clear that now "children coming into conflict with law for any offence have to be dealt with under the provisions of the JJA 2000 notwithstanding anything contrary contained in any other special legislation."

(iii) The special provision in respect of pending cases

General principle is that no law shall be applied retrospectively yet the Juvenile Justice Act provides privilege to the juvenile come into conflict with law. In case of Lallan Singh v. State of Uttar Pradesh [155]it was held "that if any proceeding is pending on the date of enforcement of the New Act, that proceedings shall be concluded under the provisions old Act". In case of Bijendra Singh v. State of Haryana,[156] the Hon'ble court observed as "section 20 of the Act 2000 would be applicable when a person is below the age of 18 years as on April 1, 2001". Jyoti Prakash Rai v. State of Bihar,[157] was a case under section 302, IPC. The question was whether appellant can claim to be Juvenile on the date of the offence. The First Medical Board shows the age to be between 18 and 19 years. The second Report dated 29-7-2001 also gave a similar opinion. Medical Report was never considered by court of law as not being conclusive. It aws held that a flexibility of 2 years is given to such reports. If a test be applied the age as on 1-4-2001 would be 18 years above and below 18 years. The protection under the New Act can be made available.[158,159] In case of Bharat Bhushan v. State of Himachal Pradesh,[160] the appellant was not a juvenile under the J.J. Act 1986 as he crossed the age of 16 years. The Hon'ble Supreme Court held as: "...coming then to the question of reference to the Juvenile Justice Board, we are of the view that such a reference is unnecessary at this distant point of time. The appellant is nearly 36 years old by now and a father of three children. He has already undergone nearly of imprisonment awarded to him by the High Court. In the circumstances, reference to the Juvenile Justice Board at this stage of his life would, in our opinion, serve no purpose. The only option available is to direct his release from custody." In the case of Mohd. Haris alias Ayen allias Aryan v. State of Uttarakhand,[161] the appellant was found guilty of kidnapping and Rape. It was held, on Criminal Appeal, that the accused being juvenile at the time of incident, his conviction was held proper and confirmed but sentenced awarded set aside.

4.27 Conclusion

In the view of previously mentioned judicial decisions of the Apex Court, in various cases, discussed above, it is amply clear that there is divergence of opinion regarding the judicial interpretation of laws. The author glance through the decisions of Supreme Court in the case of Umesh Chandra v. State of Rajsthan,[162] Arnit Das v. State of Bihar[163] and Pratap Singh v. State of Jharkhand[164] and found that on the same issue that is date of reckoning, the judges have difference of opinion. In first most case it was held that the relevant date for the applicability of the Act so far as the age of the offender who raising the plea of juvenility is the date of occurrence not the date of trial. However, in Arnit Das case the Court has reversed its own judgment and held that the crucial date of reckoning is the date when the accused brought before the competent authority. Again in the case of Pratap Singh the Court observed that the reckoning date for the determination of the juvenile is the date of offence, not the date when he produced before the court and the accused can avail the benefit of the Act (J.J. Act 2000) retrospectively if his case was pending at the time when the 2000 Act came into force. Here it is important to note that in *Pratap Singh* case the accused was not the juvenile as per the J.J. Act 1986.[165] It is significant to note that the aim of juvenile justice legislation, in India, down the years has remained the same, irrespective of the legislation in force at the relevant time. In Bhola Bhagat v. State of Bihar, the Supreme Court states that in enacting the J.J. Act 1986, the effort of the legislature was "to reform the delinquent child and reclaim him as a useful member of the society". In case of *Pratap Singh's* case, the Supreme Court's 5-judge Constitution Bench expounded the J.J. Act, 1986 as "beneficial piece of legislation" and held: "It is settled law that the interpretation of the Statute of beneficial legislation must be to advance the cause of legislation to the benefit for whom it is made and not to frustrate the intendment of the legislation."[166]

The new Juvenile Justice (Care and Protection of Children) Act 2015 precisely shows that Juvenile justice system has shifted its focus from the welfare model of Juvenile Justice introduced in 2000 to crime control model (as introduced in 2015). This Act[167] allowed the juvenile justice board to try the child aged between 16 to 18 years of age who is offender of *heinous offences*[168] as the adult in the adult prisons. This is in complete disdain of the International standards laid to deal with the young offenders. The judicial observation of the Supreme Court now focused on the re-orientation of the Juvenile Justice System by shifting its focus in direction of crime-control rather than the model of welfare of child in conflict with law and they are approaching to adopt more stringent law and order that encompass the juvenile offenders in the ambit of criminalisation. In India, the legislative intent commonly seems to provide child offenders another chance in life therefore the legislature has provided admonition, probation and other reformative sentences in lieu of a prison term.[169]

However, contrary to the legislative intent the conservatives believed that it is the seriousness of crime and not the juvenility of the offender which affects the exercise of judicial discretion in choosing an appropriate punishment. It seems that, this is the reason that the young age of the offender is not considered a relevant component in sentencing decisions, it is not decisive and the Supreme Court has, in the past, not hesitated to award death penalty (Ram Deo Chauhan v. State of Assam)[170] to youth offenders even when it was not conclusively proved that they had completed the age of 18 years on the date of occurrence of crime in order to respond to the "collective conscience of the society" or to meets the ends of justice".[171] Similarly the decision of Children's Court in Jhabua district[172] (supra) case in which two minors were convicted for life imprisonment also depicts the veracity of judicial approach.

Significantly the J.J. Act, 2015 and the intention of the Parliament cannot be faulted and if implemented in letter and spirit, the law will be able to attain the objective of maintaining the balance between the society's need for protection from offences and the need of a child to have another chance. Courts sentencing a child offender should adhere to the spirit of the international conventions which emphasise on the importance of avoiding 'criminalisation' of young people whilst also ensuring that they are held liable for their crimes. In the case of Kakoo v. State of Andhra Pradesh,[173] Justice Sarkaria, while reducing the punishment of a 13 year-old boy who has committed the rape of a girl of two years, observed as "an inordinate long imprisonment term is sure to turn Juvenile delinquent into obdurate criminal and laid an emphasis that in case of child offenders, current penological trends command a more humanitarian approach. It is pertinent to note that the children often come into the conflict with law by force of circumstances and not by choice, by providing good and favourable environment and giving suitable training and counseling, there is possibility to reform their anti-social attitudes and to mould them into a responsible and contributing member of the society"[174]. At the last, it is important to note that the objective of juvenile justice legislation, in India, down the years has remained the same, irrespective of the legislation in force at the relevant time. In Bhola Bhagat v. State of Bihar[175], the Supreme Court states that in enacting the J.J. Act 1986, the effort of the legislature was "to reform the delinquent child and reclaim him as a useful member of the society".

REFERENCES

1. Maharukh Adenwalla, Transfer of Child in Conflict with the Law from the Juvenile Justice System, Handbook for Advocates working with Children in Conflict with Law in India Centre for Child and the Law (CCL) National Law School of India University (NLSIU), 2018, Bangalore.
2. Bombay Children Act, 1948, Section 7. "such court shall try all cases in which a child is charged with the commission of an offence".
3. The Children Act, 1960, extended to all Union Territories.
4. Children Act, 1960, Section 5(1).
5. Children Act, 1960, Section 7(1).
6. J.J. Act, 1986, Section 5(1),
7. J.J. Act, 1986, Section 7(1).

8. J.J. Act, 2000, Section 6(1).
9. By the Juvenile Justice (Care and Protection of Children) Amendment Act, 2006.
10. Article 40 of convention on rights of the child states as:
    1. States Parties recognise the right of every child alleged as, accused of, or recognised as having infringed the penal law to be treated in a manner consistent with the promotion of the child's sense of dignity and worth, which reinforces the child's respect for the human rights and fundamental freedoms of others and which takes into account the child's age and the desirability of promoting the child's reintegration and the child's assuming a constructive role in society.
    2. To this end, and having regard to the relevant provisions of international instruments, States Parties shall, in particular, ensure that:
        a. No child shall be alleged as, be accused of, or recognised as having infringed the penal law by reason of acts or omissions that were not prohibited by national or international law at the time they were committed;
        b. Every child alleged as or accused of having infringed the penal law has at least the following guarantees:
        i. To be presumed innocent until proven guilty according to law;
        ii. To be informed promptly and directly of the charges against him or her, and, if appropriate, through his or her parents or legal guardians, and to have legal or other appropriate assistance in the preparation and presentation of his or her defence;
        iii. To have the matter determined without delay by a competent, independent and impartial authority or judicial body in a fair hearing according to law, in the presence of legal or other appropriate assistance and, unless it is considered not to be in the best interest of the child, in particular, taking into account his or her age or situation, his or her parents or legal guardians;
        iv. Not to be compelled to give testimony or to confess guilt; to examine or have examined adverse witnesses and to obtain the participation and examination of witnesses on his or her behalf under conditions of equality;

v. If considered to have infringed the penal law, to have this decision and any measures imposed in consequence thereof reviewed by a higher competent, independent and impartial authority or judicial body according to law;

vi. To have the free assistance of an interpreter if the child cannot understand or speak the language used;

vii. To have his or her privacy fully respected at all stages of the proceedings.

3. States Parties shall seek to promote the establishment of laws, procedures, authorities and institutions specifically applicable to children alleged as, accused of, or recognised as having infringed the penal law, and, in particular:

   a. The establishment of a minimum age below which children shall be presumed not to have the capacity to infringe the penal law;

   b. Whenever appropriate and desirable, measures for dealing with such children without resorting to judicial proceedings, providing that human rights and legal safeguards are fully respected.

   A variety of dispositions, such as care, guidance and supervision orders; counseling; probation; foster care; education and vocational training programmes and other alternatives to institutional care shall be available to ensure that children are dealt with in a manner appropriate to their well-being and proportionate both to their circumstances and the offence.

11. Clause 37.
12. Maharukh Adenwalla, Swagata Raha *et al.*, Handbook for Advocates working with Child in Conflict with law in India, Centre for Child and the Law (CCL) National Law School of India University (NLSIU), 2018, Bangalore.
13. The Juvenile Justice (Care and Protection of Children) Act, 2015, section 19.
14. Juvenile Justice (Care and Protection of Children) Act 2015.
15. Section 2(45) "petty offences" includes the offences for which the maximum punishment under the Indian Penal Code or any other law for the time being in force is imprisonment up to three years.
16. Section 2(54) "serious offences" includes the offences for which the punishment under the Indian Penal Code or any other law for

the time being in force, is imprisonment between three to seven years.

17. Section 2(33) "heinous offences" includes the offences for which the minimum punishment under the Indian Penal Code or any other law for the time being in force is imprisonment for seven years or more.
18. J.J. Act, 2015, Section 8(1).
19. J.J. Act, 2015, Section 8(1).
20. J.J. Act, 2015, Section 1(4)(i).
21. J.J. Act, 2015, Section 4(2).
22. J.J. Act, 2015, Section 14(5)(d).
23. JJ MR, 2016, Rule 10(6).
24. J.J. Act, 2015, Section 14(5)(e) and (f)(i).
25. J.J. Act, 2015, Section 14(5)(f)(ii).
26. J.J. Act, 2015, Section 14(2).
27. J.J. Act, 2015, Section 14(2).
28. J.J. Act, 2015, Section 14(4) proviso.
29. J.J. Act, 2015, Section 14(4) 30. JJ MR, 2016, Rule 9(7).
31. J.J. Act, 2015, Section 91(1).
32. J.J. Act, 2015, Section 91(1).
33. J.J. Act, 2015, Section 3(iii) and (xvi).
34. J.J. Act, 2015, Section 91(2).
35. J.J. Act, 2015, Section 90. 36. JJ MR, 2016, Rule 6(3).
37. J.J. Act, 2015, Section 23(1).
38. J.J. Act, 2015, Section 23(2).
39. J.J. Act, 2015, Section 2(20).
40. Commissions for Protection of Child Rights Act, 2005, Section 25.
41. J.J. Act, 2015, Section 19(1)(a); JJ MR, 2016, Rule 13(1).
42. J.J. Act, 2015, Section 19(1)(a); JJ MR, 2016, Rule 13(1).
43. JJ MR, 2016, Rule 13(6).
44. JJ MR, 2016, Rule 13(2).
45. JJ MR, 2016, Rule 13(3).
46. JJ MR, 2016, Rule 13(8)(i).

47. J.J. Act, 2015, Section 23.
48. J.J. Act, 2015, Section 19(1)(a).
50. JJ MR, 2016, Rule 13(8)(ii).
51. JJ MR, 2016, Rule 13(8)(iii).
52. J.J. Act, 2015, Section 19(3), proviso.
53. J.J. Act, 2015, Section 19(4 and 5).
54. J.J. Act, 2015, Section 19(4).
55. JJ MR, 2016, Form 13.
56. JJ MR, 2016, Rule 13(8)(v).
57. J.J. Act, 2015, Section 20(1); JJ MR, 2016, Rule 13(8)(vi).
58. JJ MR, 2016, Rule 13(8)(vi).
59. J.J. Act, 2015, Sections 20(1) and 20(2)(ii).
60. JJ MR, 2016, Rule 13(8)(vi)(b).
61. JJ MR, 2016, Rule 13(8)(vii)(a).
62. JJ MR, 2016, Rule 13(8)(vii)(c).
63. JJ MR, 2016, Rule 13(8)(vii)(c).
64. JJ MR, 2016, Rule 13(8)(vii)(g).
65. JJ MR, 2016, Rule 13(8)(vii)(f).
66. J.J. Act, 2015, Section 101(1) and (2).
67. J.J. Act, 2015, Section 101(2).
68. J.J. Act, 2015, Section 101(2).
69. The Children Act, 1960, extended to all Union Territories.
70. Children Act, 1960, Section 5(1).
71. Children Act, 1960, Section 7(1).
72. J.J. Act, 1986, Section 5(1),
73. J.J. Act, 2000, Section 6(1).
74. By The Juvenile Justice (Care and Protection of Children) Amendment Act, 2006.
75. Maneka Gandhi v, Union of India : (1978) 1 SCC 248.
76. J.J. Act, 2015, Section 15(1), proviso.
77. Act of a child under seven years of age.
78. Act of a child above seven and under twelve of immature understanding.

79. Act of a person of unsound mind.
80. J.J. Act, 2015, Section 15(2).
81. J.J. Act, 2015, Section 7(3), proviso.
82. JJ MR, 2016, Rule 10A (4).
83. POCSO Act, 2012, Section 28.
84. J.J. Act, 2015, Section 19(1)(i).
85. J.J. Act, 2015, Section 19(1)(ii).
86. J.J. Act, 2015, Section 19(3).
87. AIR 1982 SC 1057.
88. Juvenile Justice Act 1986.
89. Juvenile Justice (Care and Protection of Children) Act 2000. 90. AIR 2000 SC 2264: (2000)(2) JCC(SC) 545.
91. AIR 2005 SC 2731(2005)3SCC551:2005 SCC(Cri) 742:2005 Cr LJ 3091: 2005 Cri LR 288 (SC).
92. Section 2(1) as follows: -Juvenile in conflict with law means a juvenile who is alleged to have committed an offence and has not completed eighteenth year of age as on the date of commission of such offence.
93. Juvenile Justice (Care and Protection of Children) Act 2000. 94. By Act 33 of 2006 (w.e.f. 22-8-2006).
95. Jameel v. State of Maharashtra, (2007)11SCC 420: (2007) 2 SCALE 32; Vimal Candha v. Vikash Choudhry, (2008) 8 Scale 608, Babloo Passi v. State of Jharkhand, AIR 2009 SC 314: (2008) 13VSCC 133: (2008) 13 SCALE 137: 2009 (1) Chand Cri C170., Ranjit v Singh v. State of Haryana, (2008) 9 SCC 453.
96. Criminal Appeal No. 907 of 2009 (Arising out of S.L.P. (Cri) No. 3336 of 2006).
97. (2002) 2 SCC 287.
98. (2009) 13 SCC 211.
99. Notwithstanding anything contained in this Act, all proceedings in respect of a child alleged or found to be in conflict with law pending before any Board or court the date of commencement of this Act, shall be continued in that Board or court as if this Act had not been enacted.
100. Juvenile Justice Act 2000.
101. Juvenile Justice Act 1986.
102. AIR 2013 SC 3743:2013 AIR SCW 5072 2013 Cr LJ 4597.

103. Juvenile Justice (Care and Protection) Act 2000.
104. (2011) 8 SCC 737.
105. Salil Bali v. Union of India, AIR 2013 SC 3743: 2013AIR SCW 5072 Para 29 106. Suman Nalwa and Hari Dev, Commentary on The Juvenile Justice Act, Universal Publication, Haryana second edition 2016.
107. AIR2014 SC 1649:2014 AIR SCW 2021: (2014) 8SCC 390.
108. AIR 2005 SC2731: 2005 AIR SCW 3088 2005 CrLJ 3091.
109. Juvenile Justice Act 2000.
110. AIR 2014 SC 2726:2014 AIR SCW 4022:2014 CrLJ 3775.
111. Juvenile Justice rule 2007.
112. (2012) 9 SCC 750: AIR 2013 SC 553: 2012 AIR SCW 5377.
113. See also Bhola Bhagat vs. State of Bihar (1997) 8 SCC 720, Gopinath Ghosh vs. State of W.B. 1984 (Supp). SCC 228, Bhoop Ram Vs. State of U.P. (1989) 3 SCC 1 and Pradeep Kuamr vs. State of U.P. 1995 Supp (4) SCC 419.
114. See also Umesh Chandra v. State of Rajasthan, AIR 1982 SC 1057.
115. Dr. K. A. Pandey Available at http://epgp.inflibnet.ac.in/index.php (Visited on Jan 12,2018).
116. Dr. K. A. Pandey Available at http://epgp.inflibnet.ac.in/index.php (Visited on Jan 12, 2018).
117. (2012) 5 SCC 201 para 22.
118. (2000) 7 SCC 455.
119. The relevant date for applicability of the Rajasthan Children Act, 1970 so far as the age of the accused, who claims to be a child, is the date of the occurrence and not the date of the trial as is clear from the provision of ss. 3 and 26 of the Act.
120. (2000) 5 SCC 488.
121. (2012)10 SC488, para 36 (iv).
122. (2013) 14 SCC 637.
123. The Juvenile Justice (Care and Protection of Children) Rules, 2007, Rule 12(3) states: In every case concerning a child or juvenile in conflict with law, the age determining inquiry shall be conducted by the court or the Board or as the case may be, the Committee by seeking evidence by obtaining – (i) the matriculation or equivalent certificates, if available; and in the absence whereof; (ii) the date of

birth certificate from the school (other than a play school) first attended; and in the absence whereof; (iii) birth certificate given by a corporation or a municipal authority or a panchayat

124. Criminal Appeal No.486 of 2016 (arising out of Special Leave Petition (Crl)) No. 5839 of 2013 (Decided on May 12, 2016).

125. Dr. K. A. Pandey Available at http://epgp.inflibnet.ac.in/index.php (Visited on Jan 12, 2018).

126. *Ibid.*

127. Venudhar Routiya, A Critical Study Of Juvenile Justice System in India, Man in India, 97 (11): 49-66.

128. AIR 1993 SC 2178.

129. AIR 1984 SC 237:1984 (Supp) SCC 228: 1984 Cr LJ 168.

130. Suman Nalwa and Hari Dev, Commentary on The Juvenile Justice Act, Universal Publication, Haryana second edition 2016.

131. Juvenile Justice (Care and Protection of Children) Act 2000.

132. Section 7A reads as "Procedure to be followed when claim of juvenility is raised before any court- (1) Whenever a claim of juvenility is raised before any court or a court is one of the opinion that an accused person was a juvenile on the date of commission of the offence, the court shall make an inquiry, take such evidence as may be necessary (but not an affidavit) so as to determine the age of such person, and shall record a finding whether the person is a juvenile or a child or not, stating his age as nearly as may be:

    Provided that a claim of juvenility may be raised before any court and it shall be recognised at any stage, even after final disposal of the case, and such claim shall be determined in terms of the provisions contained in the this Act and the rules made thereunder, even if the juvenile has ceased to be so on or before the commencement of this Act. (2) If the court finds a person to be a juvenile on the date of commission of the offence under sub section (1), it shall forward the juvenile to the Board for passing appropriate order, and the sentence any, passed by a court shall be deemed to have no effect."

133. (1982) 1 SCC 545: AIR 1982 SC 806: 1982 Cr LJ 620.

134. *Ibid.*

135. 1994 AIR 2516, 1994 SCC (6) 186.

136. (2000) 7 SCC 455.

137. (2009) 13 SCC 211.
138. Dr. K. A. Pandey Available at http://epgp.inflibnet.ac.in/index.php (Visited on Jan 12, 2018).
139. 2015(13) SCALE 599.
140. (2009) 13 SCC 211.
141. (1978) 4 SCC 196.
142. (2013) SCC 1623.
143. Probation of offenders ACT 1958.
144. Dr. K. A. Pandey Available at http://epgp.inflibnet.ac.in/index.php (Visited on Jan 12, 2018).
145. (2009) 13 SCC 211.
146. Dr. K. A. Pandey Available at http://epgp.inflibnet.ac.in/index.php (Visited on Jan 12, 2018).
147. Section 1(4) "Notwithstanding anything contained in any other law for the time being in force, the provisions of this Act shall apply to all cases, involving detention, prosecution, penalty or sentence of imprisonment of Juveniles in conflict with law under such other law."
148. For example, s 27 of the Code of Criminal Procedure, 1973 permits that cases of children below the age of 16 years who have committed offences other than those punishable with death penalty or life imprisonment may be transferred to the children court.
149. Rohtas Vs State of Haryana, AIR (1979), SC, 1839.
150. The code of Criminal Procedure 1973 151. (2000) 6 SCC 759.
152. Suman Nalwa and Hari Dev, Commentary on The Juvenile Justice Act, Universal Publication, Haryana second edition 2016.
153. Madan Singh v. State of Bihar, 4622(2000).
154. "Notwithstanding anything contained in any other law for the time being in force, the provisions of this Act shall apply to all cases involving detention, prosecution, penalty or sentence of imprisonment of juvenile in conflict with law under such other law.".
155. 2002 Cr LJ 1242.
156. AIR 2005 SC 2262:2005 AIR SCW 2046.
157. AIR 2008 SC 1696: 2008 (2) JCC 777L 2008) 3 SCALE 348.
158. Suman Nalwa *and* Hari Dev, Commentary on The Juvenile Justice Act, Universal Publication, Haryana second edition 2016.

159. See also:Arnit Das v.State of Bihar, 2000(2)JCC(SC)2731L2005) 488. Vishnu v. State of Maharastra, 2006(1) JCC 78: (2006) 1 SCC 283. Birad Mal Singhvi v. Anand Purohit, AIR 1988 SC 1796: 1988 Supp SCC 604.Sushil Kumar v. Rakesh Kumar, (2003) 8 SCC 673, Jitendrea Ram v. State of Jharkhand, 2006 (2)JCC 994: (2006) 9 SCC 428.

160. AIR 2013 SC2018:CrLJ 2932: 2013 AIR SCW 2911.

161. 2014 CrLJ (NOC) 160(Uttarakhand) 162.AIR 1982 SC 1057.

163. AIR 2000 SC 2264(2000) 5 SCC 488.

164. AIR 2005 SC 2731:2005 AIR SCW 3088: 2005 Cr.LJ 309.

165. Section 2(h) "juvenile" means a boy who has not attained the age of sixteen years or a girl who has not attained the age of eighteen years;

166. Handbook for Advocates working with Children in Conflict with Law in India under The Juvenile Justice (Care and Protection of Children) Act, 2015 *and* Juvenile Justice (Care and Protection of Children) Model Rules 2016.

167. J.J. Act, 2015 section 18.Orders regarding child found to be in conflict with law.-(1) Where a Board is satisfied on inquiry that a child irrespective of age has committed a petty offence, or a serious offence, or a child below the age of sixteen years has committed a heinous offence, then, notwithstanding anything contrary contained in any other law for the time being in force, and based on the nature of offence, specific need for supervision or intervention, circumstances as brought out in the social investigation report and past conduct of the child, the Board may, if it so think fit–

    (a) Allow the child to go home after advice or admonition by following appropriate inquiry and counseling to such child and to his parents or the guardian;

    (b) Direct the child to participate in group counseling and similar activities;

    (c) Order the child to perform community service under the supervision of an organisation or institution, or a specified person, persons or group of persons identified by the Board;

    (d) Order the child or parents or the guardian of the child to pay fine:

    Provided that, in case the child is working, it may be ensured that the provisions of any labour law for the time being in force are not violated;

(e) Direct the child to be released on probation of good conduct and placed under the care of any parent, guardian or fit person, on such parent, guardian or fit person executing a bond, with or without surety, as the Board may require, for the good behaviour and child, s well-being for any period not exceeding three years;

(f) Direct the child to be released on probation of good conduct and placed under the care and supervision of any fit facility for ensuring the good behaviour and child's well-being for any period not exceeding three years;

(g) Direct the child to be sent to a special home, for such period, not exceeding three years, as it thinks fit, for providing reformative service including education, skill development, counseling, behaviour modification therapy, and psychiatric support during the period of stay in the special home :

(h) Provided that if the conduct and behaviour of the child has been such that, it would not be in the child's interest, or in the interest of the other children housed in a special home, the Board may send such child to the place of safety.

(2) If an order is passed under clause (a) to (g) of sub-section (1), the Board may, in addition pass orders to– (i) attend school; or (ii) attend a therapeutic center; or (iv) prohibit the child from visiting, frequent or appearing at a special place; or (v) undergo a de-addiction programme.

(3) Where the Board after preliminary assessment under section 15 pass an order that there is a need for trial of the said child as an adult, then the board may order transfer of the trial of the case to the Children's Court having jurisdiction to try such offences.

168. The Juvenile Justice (Care and Protection of Children) Act 2015 (Act 6 of 2016), Sec. 2(33): "Heinous offences" includes those offence for which minimum punishment provided under Indian Penal Code or any other law for the time in force is imprisonment for seven years or more.

169. E-Pathasala Available at http://epgp.inflibnet.ac.in/index.php (Visited on Jan 12, 2018).

170. (2000) 7 SCC 455.

171. Dr. K. A. Pandey, E-Pathshala Available at http://epgp.inflibnet.ac.in/index.php (Visited on Jan 12, 2018).

172. http://timesofindia.indiatimes/city/indore/hc-juvenile-conviction-appeal/articleshow/58172510.cms
173. AIR 1976 SC 1991.
174. Suman Nalwa *and* Hari Dev, Commentary on The Juvenile Justice Act, Universal Publication, Haryana second edition 2016
175. (1997) 8 SCC 720: 1998CrLJ 390: AIR 1998 SC 236.

5

Heinous Crimes and Culpability of Juveniles

5.1 Introduction

In this chapter the author has tried to analyse and focus on two issues, firstly what is heinous crimes and secondly the question of culpability of children for heinous crimes. Further the author has appraised the trend of juvenile (heinous) crimes before and after Juvenile Justice (Care and Protection of Children) Act, 2015 and illustrated some cases of heinous offence committed by juvenile after the enforcement of Juvenile Justice (Care and Protection of Children) Act, 2015.

5.2 The definition of heinous offences

The Juvenile Justice (Care and Protection of Children) Act, 2015 (here in after refered as J.J Act 2015) defines heinous offences as *heinous offences include the offences for which the minimum punishment under the Indian Penal Code, (45 of 1860) or any other law for the time being in force is imprisonment for seven years or more.*" This definition is provided under section 2(33) which was added as a new provision by the Juvenile Justice (Care and Protection of Children) Bill 2015. In the previous Juvenile Justice (Care and Protection of Children) Act 2000, neither any separate definition was provided nor any distinctions were made between the heinous offences and non-heinous offences, the expression used under section 2(l)[1] child in conflict with law includes, culpability of both heinous and non-heinous offences. However, in the new, juvenile Justice Act 2015[2] the definition of offence is not provided, but it classifies the offences into three types, the petty offence, serious offence and heinous offence.

This classification of offence is based on the quantum of punishment. (1)[3] Petty offence includes that offence for which punishment prescribed is imprisonment up to 3 years. (2)[4] Serious offence includes that offence for which prescribed punishment is imprisonment up to seven years. (3) Heinous offences where the sentence prescribed is imprisonment for 7 years or more but more is limited *vide* section 21 of the Act, 2015. In the new Act[5] this definition of *heinous offences* is inserted to reduce the age or to redefine a juvenile's age in serious offences with a view that children who have completed the age of 16 years but not completed the age of 18 years and have committed a heinous crime should be dealt separately[6]. However, the word heinous is nowhere defined in the Indian Penal Code though it is found in series of interpretations of laws and the judgments delivered by the judges. In an informal definition, heinous offences are those offences, which come under the category of *rarest of rare* that give a blow to collective conscience of society. These crimes tend to create extreme revulsion in the minds of the people. Generally, power to exercise remission is not there for such cases. This informal definition is reverberation of the December 16 gang-rape of 2012 in New Delhi, where group of six persons of which one was juvenile below the age of 18 years have raped a young woman. The public demand, shaken by this dastardly gang-rape, of about 16 to 18 year-olds accused of rape deserving to be tried as adults, has opened the passage of the Juvenile Justice (Care and Protection of Children) Bill, 2015.

(i) Definitions of petty, serious, and heinous offences

The J.J. Act, 2015, has introduced a three-fold classification of offences as petty, serious, and heinous. Apart from the difference in proceedings, the classification serves to determine the offences for which a child above 16 years and below 18 can be potentially tried as an adult.

Petty offences are defined under Section 2(45) as petty offences which includes the offences for which the maximum punishment under the Indian Penal Code or any other law for the time being in force is imprisonment upto three years.

Serious offences are defined under Section 2(54) as serious offences which includes the offences for which the punishment under the Indian Penal Code or any other law for the time being in force is imprisonment between three to seven years.

Heinous offences are defined under Section 2(33) heinous offences which includes the offences for which the minimum punishment under the Indian Penal Code or any other law for the time being in force is imprisonment for seven years or more.

Though the heinous offences as defined in the law doesn't comprise only dreadful offences such as rape and murder. Juveniles who are accused of theft, cheating, kidnapping, causing grievous hurt, dacoity, arson, counterfeiting coins, burglary are all now liable to be tried as adults. CCLNLU,[7] has prepared a compilation of 21 sections under Indian Penal code. It has encapsulated some other laws, under which the juveniles can now be tried. The enumeration are as follows:- Commission of Sati (Prevention) Act, Arms Act, Unlawful Activities (Prevention) Act, Terrorist and Disruptive Activities (Prevention) Act, Narcotic Drugs and Psychotropic Substances (NDPS) Act, Maharashtra Control of Organised Crime Act and Food Safety and Standards Act, Scheduled Castes and the Scheduled Tribes (Prevention of Atrocities) Act.

The definition of serious offences is vaguely worded. Even if it is assumed that the definition implies that serious offences are those for which the maximum punishment is more than three years and less than seven years, this leaves out a considerable number of offences. For instance, those offences, which are punishable with imprisonment not exceeding ten years, (or any other term exceeding seven years), cannot be classified into any category. Similarly, offences, which only prescribe a minimum punishment of any term less than seven years also, cannot be classified as serious offences. Since, serious offences according to the J.J. Act, 2015 are those for which prescribed punishment is imprisonment more than three but less than seven years. For example, for the offence of abetting an offence punishable with death or imprisonment for life, Section 115 of the Indian Penal Code prescribes a punishment which may extend to seven years. This means that the sentence passed may or may not be three years, since no minimum limit is prescribed, and the offence is therefore not strictly serious as per the Act.[8] There are at least 55 such offences under the IPC, which do not fall under the definitions of serious or heinous offences.[9] According to Professor Ved Kumari, the definition of serious offences should be read as including offences punishable with imprisonment of more than three years, to overcome the overlap between petty and serious offences.[10] She advances the following interpretation to overcome the ambiguity in the definitions: ...offences punishable with more than seven years of imprisonment but containing no direction for imposition of minimum seven years of imprisonment, need to be classified as serious offences as these offences cannot be included with the definitions of petty and heinous offences using the definitive words 'maximum' and 'minimum' respectively to set the limit of what cannot be included within those categories. Even though the definition of serious offence refers to offences punishable with imprisonment between three and seven years, it poses problem of classification at both the ends due to use of qualifying words in the other two definitions. No such qualifying word setting the boundaries has been used in the definition of serious offences. It is permissible to expand the boundary set by the definition of a serious offence to include offences punishable with imprisonment for more than seven years as this expansion is favourable to children alleged to have committed such offences.[11]

5.3 List of heinous offences as per the juvenile justice (care and protection of children) act 2015[12]

A. THE INDIAN PENAL CODE 1860

Sr. No.	Law	Description	Punishment
1	S. 121	Waging or attempting or abetting to wage war against Government of India	Death or Imprisonment of life
2	S. 195	Giving or fabricating false evidence with intent to procure conviction of offence with imprisonment for life or imprisonment.	Punishment same as the person convicted for that offense would be liable to be punished-minimum 7 years
3	S. 195 A	Threatening any person to give false evidence – if any innocent person is convicted and sentenced in consequence of such false evidence with death or imprisonment for more than seven years	Punishment same as the sentence received by innocent person
4	S. 302	Punishment for Murder	Death or Imprisonment for Life
5	S. 304 B	Dowry Death	Minimum 7 years and can be extended to life
6	S. 311	Punishment for thugs	Imprisonment for life
7	S. 326 A	Acid attack causing permanent or partial damage/deformity	Minimum 10 years and up to life
8	S. 370(2)	Trafficking	Minimum 7 years and up to 10 years + fine
9	S. 370(3)	Trafficking of more than one person	Minimum 10 years up to life + fine

contd..

contd..

Sr. No.	Law	Description	Punishment
10	S. 370(4)	Trafficking of minor	Minimum 10 years up to life + fine
11	S. 370(5)	Trafficking of more than one minor	Minimum 14 years up to life + fine
12	S. 370(6)	Trafficking of minor on more than one occasion	Minimum 10 years up to life + fine
13	S. 370(7)	Trafficking by public servant or police officer	Imprisonment for life – remainder of that persons natural life + fine
14	S. 376(1)	Punishment for Rape	Life imprisonment
15	S. 376(2)	Custodial Rape, rape on minor or pregnant women, etc.	Life imprisonment and shall also be liable to fine
	S.376AB	Rape of a women under 12 years	Minimum 20 years Rigorous Imprisonment upto life
16	S. 376 A	Rape resulting in death or permanent vegetative state of women	Min 20 years or remainder of persons natural life or death
17	S. 376 D	Gang Rape	Min 20 years or remainder natural life
	S.376DA	Gang Rape of a women under 12 years	Imprisonment for life
	S.376DB	Gang Rape of a women under 16 years	Imprisonment for the remainder of natural life, and with fine

contd..

contd..

Sr. No.	Law	Description	Punishment
18	S. 376 E	Repeat of Sec. 376, 376 A or 377 D	Imprisonment for Remainder of persons natural life or death
19	S. 397	Robbery, or Dacoity, with attempt to cause death or grievous injuries	Min 7 years
20	S. 398	Section 398, Attempted to commit Robbery or Dacoity when armed with deadly weapon	Min 7 years
B. THE COMMISSION OF SATI (PREVENTION) ACT, 1987			
21.	S. 4(1)	Abetment of sati when sati committed	Imprisonment for life or death
22.	S. 4(2)	Abetment of sati when sati attempted	Imprisonment for life
C. THE NARCOTIC DRUGS AND PSYCHOTROPIC SUBSTANCES ACT, 1985			
23.	S. 15(c)	Punishment for contravention in relation to poppy straw involving commercial quantity	Min 10 years and up to 20 years
24.	S. 17(c)	Punishment for contravention in relation to prepared opium involving commercial quantity	Min 10 years and up to 20 years
25.	S. 18(b)	Punishment for contravention in relation to opium, poppy and opium involving commercial quantity	Min 10 years and up to 20 years
26.	S. 19	Punishment for embezzlement of opium by cultivator	Min 10 years and up to 20 years

contd..

contd..

Sr. No.	Law	Description	Punishment
27.	S.20C	Punishment for contravention in relation to cannabis plant and cannabis involving commercial quantity	Min 10 years and up to 20 years
28.	S. 21(c)	Punishment for contravention in relation to manufactured drugs and preparation involving commercial quantity	Min 10 years and up to 20 years
29.	S. 22(c)	Punishment for contravention in relation to psychotropic substances involving commercial quantity	Min 10 years and up to 20 years
30.	S. 23(c)	Punishment for illegal import in to India, export from India or transshipment of narcotic drugs and psychotropic substances involving commercial quantity	Min 10 years and up to 20 years
31.	S. 24	Punishment for external dealings in narcotic drugs and psychotropic substances	Min 10 years and up to 20 years
32.	S. 25	Punishment for allowing premises, etc., to be used for commission of an offence.	As much as punishment for that offence
33.	S. 27 A	Punishment for financing illicit traffic and harbouring offenders.	Rigorous imprisonment for minimum 10 and maximum 20 years and fine of minimum 1 lakh and maximum 2 lakh
34.	S. 29	Punishment for abetment and criminal conspiracy	As much as punishment for that offence

contd..

contd..

Sr. No.	Law	Description	Punishment
35.	S. 31 A	Repetition of person convicted of commission, attempt, abetment and conspiracy of offences under S. 19, 24, 27 A and for offences involving commercial quantity of any narcotic drug or psychotropic substance who are subsequently convicted of the commission, attempt, abetment, criminal conspiracy of an offence in relation to certain ND & PS above specific quantity.	Death
D. THE ARMS ACT, 1959			
36.	S. 27(2)	Use of any prohibited arms or prohibited ammunition in contravention of section 7 (Relation to Prohibition of acquisition or possession, or of manufacture or sale, of prohibited arms or prohibited ammunition)	Minimum 7 years and up to life
38.	S. 27(3)	Use of any prohibited arms or prohibited ammunition or does any act in contravention of section 7 that result in death	Death
E. THE UNLAWFUL ACTIVITIES (PREVENTION) ACT,			
39.	S.10(b)(i)	Use of any prohibited arms or prohibit ammunition or does any act in contravention of section 7 that result in death	Death or imprisonment for life

contd..

contd..

Sr. No.	Law	Description	Punishment
40.	S.16(1)(a)	Punishment for terrorist act if such act has resulted in the death of any person	Imprisonment for life or Death
G. THE SCHEDULED CASTES AND THE SCHEDULED TRIBES (PREVENTION OF ATROCITIES) ACT, 1989			
41.	S. 59 (IV)	Punishment for unsafe food where a contravention or failure results in death of a person	Minimum 7 years and up to life
H. THE MAHARASHTRA CONTROL OF ORGANISED CRIME ACT, 1999			
42.	S. 3(2) (i)	Commission of any IPC offence with imprisonment of more than 10 years against the person or property of a member of SC/ST. If an innocent member of a Scheduled Caste or a Scheduled Tribe be convicted and executed in consequence of such false or fabricated evidence	Imprisonment for Life or death
43.	S.3(2)(iv)	Commission of Mischief by fire or explosive substance intending to cause destruction of a building used by a member of SC/ST	Imprisonment for life
44.	S. 3(2)(v)	Commission of any IPC offence with imprisonment of more than 10 years against the person or property of a member of SC/ST	Imprisonment for life

contd..

contd..

Sr. No.	Law	Description	Punishment
I. PROTECTION OF CHILDREN FROM SEXUAL OFFENCES ACT, 2000			
45.	S. 3(1)(i)	Punishment for organised crime which has result in death of a person	Death or imprisonment for life
46.	S.4	Punishment for penetrative sexual assault	Minimum 7 years which may extend to life imprisonment + fine
47.	S.6	Punishment for aggravated penetrative sexual assault	Rigorous imprisonment for 10 years which may extend to life + fine

5.4 Some heinous offence committed by juvenile after the enforcement of J.J. Act 2015

NEWS CLIPPINGS EXTRACTED FROM VARIOUS ESTEEMED NEWS PAPERS[13]

(i) Ryan school murder case

The 16-year-old juvenile killed a 7-year-old student studying in second standard of his school to have exams postponed. Sixteen years old student of the class 11 of Ryan International School, Bhondsi, has slit the throat of 7-year-old student named Pradhyuman Thakur in the toilet of the school. The accused in Ryan school murder case will face the trial as an adult ruled by the Juvenile Justice Board (JJB). This is noteworthy that as per the Section 2(33) of the new Juvenile Justice Act, heinous offences include those in which the minimum punishment is imprisonment for seven years. The Principal Magistrate Davender Singh while delivering the verdict for the board said:

The offence alleged committed by the accused was heinous. While transferring the case to the special children's court, Gurgaon, the board observed, The circumstances show that the teenager was mature enough' to understand the consequences of his alleged act and to think of ways to escape from lawful punishment. The board set aside the claim of defence that the alleged offence of 302 IPC (murder), which lead to a maximum punishment of 10 years, is not made out against the boy.

(ii) A girl of 12-year-old stabbed a class 1 student of her school in Lucknow

Another similar case as in Ryan School Murder case shook the conscience of the public. A class 1 student allegedly stabbed by senior girl student. The boy had deep wound in chest and stomach but was luckily saved by the doctors. The girl was studying in Brightland Inter College School in Triveninagar, Lucknow. The girl has reportedly stabbed in the chest and abdomen of the boy and locked him inside the toilet. The girl identified by the victim with the help of a photograph and while questioning by the police the victim told, A didi with boy-cut hair called me, saying a teacher had asked for me. She took me to the bathroom and slapped me. Then she attacked me with a sharp object. During the second round of questioning, he told police—When I asked didi why she was beating me, she said:

I want the school to declare an early closure today. As per the preliminary investigation made by the police, the girl allegedly tied the victim with her dupatta and then stabbed him with a knife. She locked the boy inside the toilet before leaving the place.

(iii) A seventeen years boy stabbed by other 5 under aged boys in uniform, in a moving bus

A group of five boys has attacked on a 17 years old boy named Mohammad Anas on a moving bus who succumbed to his injuries. The victim was stabbed to death near Ashram, in New Delhi on Nov 23, 2017 after a scuffle with five boys. Mohammad Anas was attacked and a group of five school students in uniform slit his throat allegedly, when he confronted them on suspicion that they had stolen his mobile phone. Taking the advantage of the fact that the bus was moving slowly because of the traffic the boys ran out from the two doors.

The five students had bunked school that day and were taking casual joyrides in bus. They gathered at a park at Madanpur khadar and took a bus to Ashram Chowk. They again took bus-ride towards Badarpur where they killed Mohammad Anas. Praveen Ranjan Joint Commissioner of Police (Southern Range) said no similar case of the students targeting people have emerged so far. The Investigators said that the boys seemed to be unruly by nature. The description of the boys and their uniform, as well as electronic surveillance on the mobile phone they allegedly stole from Anas helped the police to apprehend them from different parts of South Delhi.

(iv) Seventeen years old released on parole goes on revenge spree, kills 2 with help from friends

A week after being released from juvenile justice home, seventeen-years old boy killed two rivals with the help of his four adult aids. The boy had been booked thrice in the past for various crimes. This was a case of revenge killing. The boy who was allegedly involved in double murder was just a week before the heinous crime of double murder, had been released from a juvenile justice home on parole in a snatching case. On the fateful night, the boy called his friend, Manoj, and three others (all four were adult) and intended to take his revenge. All five of them collectively went to Sunil's (the victim) place in west Delhi's Khayala area and called Sunil out to a park on the pretext of resolving their issues. As soon as Sunil arrived at the park, all five of them allegedly attacked on Sunil and stabbed him with a knife and left to bleed. Before leaving the place, they snatched Sunil's gold chain. The victim succumbed to the injury. All the five after that headed to Nabi Karim for next target that is to kill Rahul. However, Manoj decided not to go with them as he had a call from his home and was asked to be at home. The remaining four forcefully entered into Rahul's home in Nabi Karim at around around 2 A.M. The murderer allegedly hauled Rahul to a lonely place near his house and stabbed him to death. After taking their retaliation, the murderer separated their ways because the police of both districts had formed teams to crack the murder case. Delhi Police nabbed Manoj within an hour. After interrogating Manoj the hideout of the other boy was also traced and was arrested by the police. The gold chain has been recovered which was robbed from Sunil. Yet the other three persons involved in the double murder are still at large.

(v) A boy allegedly rapes his classmate at the age of four and half

This was case of a well -known school of West Delhi where a boy aged only four and half years found accused of raping his classmate of his age. The boy raped his classmate in the classroom and in the washroom of the school. After having pain in her private part, the girl told her mother about the incident. The girl told her mother that the boy used his finger and a sharpened pencil to assault her sexually. A case of rape under the Protection of Children from Sexual Offences (POCSO) Act was registered. School was booked for negligence.

(vi) Six minor boys booked for rape of 8 year old girl

Six boys charged for rape of an eight-year-old girl in Pune. Among the six culprits, five were minors. The victim's family knew all offenders. All six of them sexually assaulted her when she was playing. The incident came into light when the girl complaint for pain in lower abdomen and her mother took her to the doctor where the doctor discovered that she has been sexually abused. All the six culprits were booked for the charge of rape.

(vii) Released after two months committing murder, kills again

A seventeen-years-old boy killed elderly women just after his release from a juvenile home for good behaviour. Before this murder, he was booked for kidnapping and murder of a child. As reported by the local police, the juvenile strangulated 65-year-old Mithilesh Jain, a retired Military Engineering Services officer, and robbed the cash, gold jewelry, an i-Pad and two mobile phones. Five months before this murder, the boy had also kidnapped and killed a child because his father failed to pay ransom of Rs 60,000. The accused, was the son of an electrician, and wanted to pay his entry fee into a popular dance reality show on television. The obsession with the TV show led the juvenile to commit robbery-cum-murder. First, on pretext of looking for a friend he managed to convince the elderly woman to open the door of the house. He asked for a glass of water. While the woman went into the house to get the water, he followed and strangled her with his hands. He had been apprehended in the past, on the charge of kidnapping a 13-year-old boy from Badarpur and murdered him in Uttarakhand. After 3 months, he was released on grounds of good behaviour after signing a bond.

(viii) A 16 year-old boy raped and killed a girl

A 16 year-old boy with his adult friend forcefully entered into a girl's house when she was alone and they sexually abused and killed her. After killing the girl, they again raped her lifeless body.

(ix) Two juvenile raped a two years old girl

Two juveniles allegedly abducted a two-year-old girl from West Delhi's Nihal Vihar and raped her in a public park.

(x) 17 years boy kills two in Delhi in one night for revenge

A 17-year-old boy, who had been stabbed a year ago for standing up to youths harassing his sister, went on a gruesome revenge spree. He allegedly killed his attacker in West Delhi's Khyala, returned to his Central Delhi neighbourhood and stabbed to death another of his sister's teasers. In an orgy of violence, the juvenile first went with a friend to Khyala to extract revenge on Sunil, who was serving a jail term for stabbing the boy and was out on parole. The duo stabbed Sunil four times, in the neck and abdomen, with a button knife. The boy returned alone to his locality, Nabi Karim, and went to his second target, Kuldeep. He allegedly stabbed the youth over 20 times to ensure that he was dead. The juvenile and his friend, Manoj, 22, met at a bus stand in Khyala from where they went to Sunil's house. They called him to a park near his house on the pretext of discussing something. They told the police that they engaged him in a conversation for around five minutes, after which they attacked him with a knife. Leaving him to bleed, the duo snatched the man's gold chain and left for Nabi Karim. On the way, Manoj received a call from his family and was asked to come home. As Manoj left, the juvenile did not change his mind and went straight for his second target, Kuldeep. Knowing that Kuldeep would be alone at home at 11 PM, the boy knocked at the door and barged in as soon as it opened. Police said the juvenile pulled Kuldeep by the collar and took him to a dark spot near his house, where he brutally stabbed him over 20 times with the same knife used in the first murder. Kuldeep raised an alarm but by the time other residents came out the juvenile had fled. A police team took Kuldeep to hospital where doctors declared him brought dead on arrival. After a few hours of both the murders, cops from the west district managed to nab Manoj, who later confessed about his involvement in the crime. Meanwhile, cops from the central district traced the juvenile and apprehended him. The juvenile told the cops that he had known Sunil for the past two years and often fought with him over trivial issues. He claimed to have murdered him so that the fights end finally. The boy said he had planned to kill Kuldeep the moment he came out of the hospital after being treated for stab injuries last year. Since then, he had been looking for an opportunity to attack him. "The accused were arrested and investigations were taken up," said Vijay Kumar, Deputy Commissioner of Police (west). The weapon of offence and the gold chain that they had snatched has been recovered from their possession, he added.

(xi) A boy killed his mother and sister

On December 4, 2017, a boy killed his mother and sister at their apartment in Greater Noida West. The boy was often scolded by his parents over his low grades in school. He had also a fierce enmity with his younger sister as she was outstanding in her studies and parents allegedly used to quote her as an example to demean him. The boy had a feeling of jealousy as he thought that his parents did not love him. On the fateful night, the boy and his mother along with his sister went outside to have pizza for dinner and they took their dinner, thereafter they all went to sleep. On the night of the incident, his businessman father was in Surat for business meeting and his grandparents were in Dehradun to attend a marriage ceremony. The immediate cause for murder was that his mother scolded him on the afternoon of the day of the incident. The boy told the officer that his mother scold him for using sofa to study. His mother had asked him to sit on the dining table for study but he refused, when he refused to move she supposedly beat him up. This provoked him to kill his mother but he hadn't thought about killing his sister but was scared as she saw him killing their mother. Therefore, he killed her with the bat blow to her head. The boy a sixteen-year-old teenager addicted to violent video games killed both his mother and his sister with a cricket bat and then disfigured their faces with the pair of scissor and pizza cutter. After killing both he changed his bloodstained clothes, took 2 lakh in cash kept at his parents' bedroom locker and he also took his mother's mobile phone, locked the house from outside and fled away. He kept travelling aimlessly for five days meanwhile he lost his backpack with the money, somewhere between Ludhiana and Chandigarh. By that time, he felt lonely, he took a phone from a passer-by and called his father, cried and hung up. The boy was nabbed from one of the Ghats along the Ganga.

(xii) Two juveniles apprehended for raping 7-year-old girl

Two juveniles allegedly raped a 7 year-old girl in New Delhi. According to the news report, the incident took place when the victim had gone to a public toilet in outer Delhi's Kanjhawala, along with her elder sister. While the victim's sister entered inside the toilet, the victim was sitting outside and waiting. One of the juvenile accused went to the girl, asked her for a bicycle ride, and took her to a secluded place, where the other juvenile was waiting. The duo then allegedly raped the girl. The police apprehended the boys.

(xiii) A 17 year-old boy allegedly rape a 11 year-old girl

A teenager boy allegedly raped a 11 year old girl. This incident took place in a village in Phephana area of Ballia district. The boy was allegedly apprehended by the local police and booked under section 376 of IPC and 34 of POCSO, Act. According to the news reported by the *Times of India*, the girl had gone to the field for nature's call where a seventeen years old boy of the same locality allegedly raped her and left that place leaving the girl in state of shock. The local residents who spotted the girl informed the family members.

(iv) Juvenile gets 20-year jail for rape, murder of 6-year-old

A girl of 6 years old was brutally raped by a juvenile aged 16 in Hisar. The 6-year-old daughter of a dalit couple, who lived with her family in a roadside tent in Hisar's suburban town of Uklana, was kidnapped by the juvenile on the night of December 7, 2017. Her body was found in the empty quarters of the Bharat Sanchar Nigam Limited. About 24 cm long stick had been forcibly inserted in the private part of the girl, damaging her uterus and intestines. The post-mortem report stated. The victim died due to the torture perpetrated by inserting wooden stick into her private parts and the stick was inserted with force which not only caused serious injuries inside uterus but also in the intestine.

MAJOR CRIMES BY MINORS

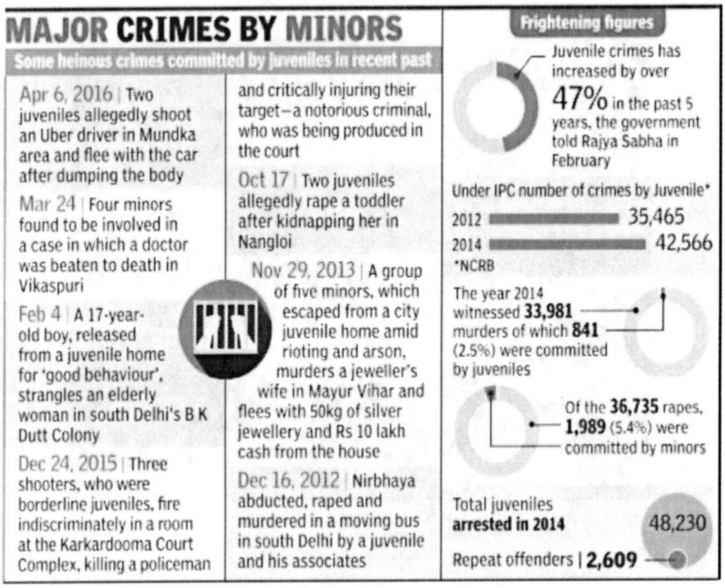

Source: Juvenile delinquency in India • Indpaedia 3.21.2018

5.5 Assessment of the trend of juvenile (heinous) crimes before and after J.J. Act, 2015

THE TREND THAT HAS BEEN AUTHOR OBSERVED THROUGH THE NCRB DATA ANALYSIS

The data provided by the National Crime Record Bureau establishes that crimes by the children between the age group sixteen to eighteen of years have augmented, specifically in particular type of heinous offences.

A cursory look at the data of NCRB on juvenile crimes reveals alarming trend. Since last decades, juvenile, who earlier involved generally in petty offences like theft or trespassing or unlawful assembly have graduated to heinous crimes including rape, murder and kidnapping. The data of last decade shows that, in 2006, 656 rape cases were registered against the children that in 2016 had swelled to 1903.

STATISTICAL DATA (2005-2015) OF RATE OF CRIME BY JUVENILE BEFORE J. J. ACT 2015

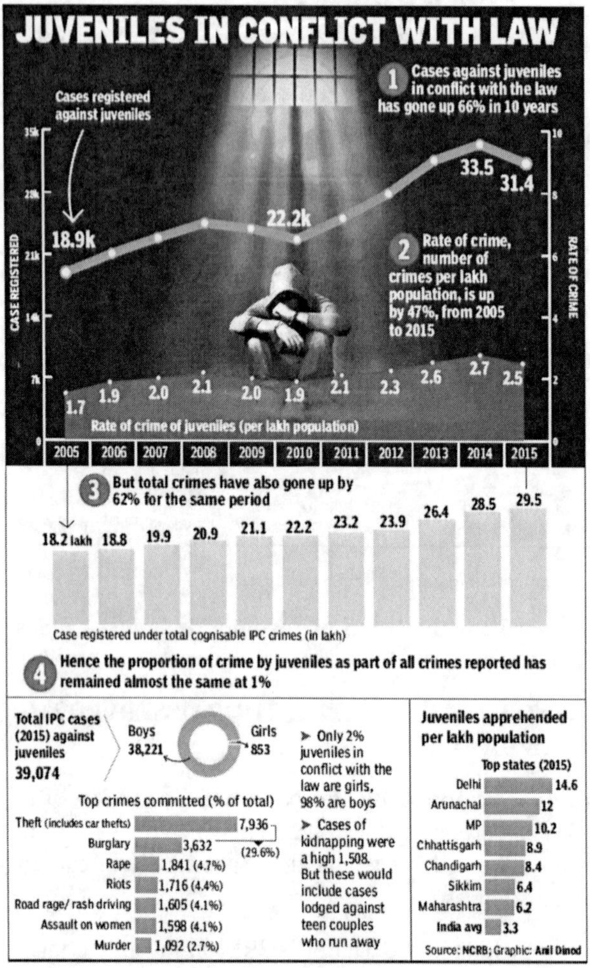

Source: Juvenile delinquency in India • Indpaedia 3.21.2017

STATISTICAL DATA (2005-2015) OF RATE OF CRIME BY JUVENILE AFTER J.J. ACT 2015

Table 5.1: Cases registered against child in conflict with law and Crime Rate under IPC during 2006-2016[28]

Year	Cases Registered		Percentage cases of child in conflict with law to total cognizable Crimes	Rate of crime under cases of child in conflict With law
	Against child in conflict With law	Under cognizable ipc Crimes		
2006	21088	1878293	1.1	1.7
2007	22865	1989673	1.1	2.0
2008	24535	2093379	1.2	2.1
2009	23926	2121345	1.1	2.0
2010	22740	2224831	1.0	1.9
2011	25125	2325575	1.1	2.1
2012	27936	2387188	1.2	2.3
2013	31725	2647722	1.2	2.6
2014	33526	2851563	1.2	2.7
2015	31396	2949499	1.1	2.5
2016	44171	2975711	1.2	2.5

Data appeared in Table 5.1 precisely reflects a staggering increase in the number of cases registered against child in conflict with law. These data swelled from 21088 to 44171 (in categories of child in conflict with law) during the 2006 to 2016 and from 1878293 to 2975711 (Under the total cognizable IPC Crimes). However, the percentages of cases against the child in conflict with law to total cognizable crimes have varied between 1.0 to 1.1 and the rate of crimes under cases child in conflict with law has soared from 1.7 to 2.5.

Table 5.2: Cases registered against child in conflict with law under different crime heads of Indian Penal Code 1860[29]

S.no.	Types of Crime	No. of Cases
1	Murder (Section 302 IPC)	853
2	Attempt to commit murder (Section 307 IPC)	980
3	Culpable Homicide not amounting to murder (Section 304 IPC)	36
4	Attempt to commit Culpable Homicide (Section 308 IPC)	60
5	Rape (Section 376 IPC)	16988
6	Kidnapping and Abduction	1630
7	Dacoity	193
8	Robbery (Section 392 to 394, 397 and 398 IPC)	1358
9	Criminal Trespass/Burglary (Section 457 to 460 IPC) (Total)	2605

Table 5.3: Children apprehended under I.P.C. Crimes by Age Groups and Sex During 2016[30]

S No.	Types of crime	Below 12 years	12-16 years	16-18 years	Total
1	Murder (Section 302 IPC)	13	263	901	1177
2	Attempt to commit murder (Section 307 IPC)	4	239	1035	1278
3	Culpable Homicide not amounting to murder (Section 304)	5	26	38	64
4	Attempt to commit Culpable Homicide (Section 308 IPC)	0	15	65	116
5	Rape (Section 376 IPC)	29	464	1561	2054
6	Kidnapping and Abduction	4	162	1198	1364
7	Dacoity	0	54	273	327
8	Robbery (Section 392 to 394, 397 and 398 IPC)	10	433	1355	1798
9	Criminal Trespass/Burglary (Section 457 to 460 IPC) (Total)	78	1268	2466	3812

Table 5.3 demonstrates the number of cases registered across India against the children for the numerous crimes under various heads of Indian Penal Code during the year 2016. These data are frightening. Table 5.3 establishes the data for children Apprehended under IPC Crimes by Age Groups and Sex during 2016 under different age categories. It is evident that the involvement of children in between the age group of 16 to 18 extremely high. The Table 2 shows that the number of cases of rape charges (that is 16988) is the maximum in all categories of crimes committed by the juvenile in the year 2016.

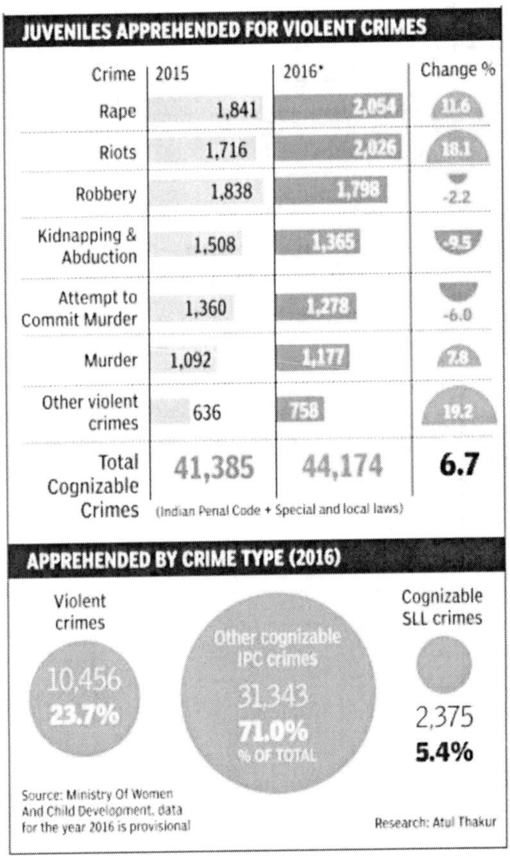

JUVENILE APPREHENDED FOR VIOLENT CRIMES

Source[31] Juvenile delinquency in India • Indpaedia 3.21.2018

INCIDENCE AND RATE OF CHILD DELINQUENCY UNDER IPC CRIMES IN INDIA 2006-2016[32]

Year	Incidence of		% age of child crimes to total crimes	Estimated mid- year population in (in lakh)	Rate of crime by child
	Child crimes	Total crimes			
2006	21088	1878293	1.1	11198	1.9
2007	22865	1989673	1.1	11366	2.0
2008	24535	2093379	1.2	11531	2.1
2009	23926	2121345	1.1	11694	2.0
2010	22740	2224831	1.0	11858	1.9
2011	25125	2325575	1.1	12102	2.1
2012	27936	2387188	1.2	12134	2.3
2013	31725	2647722	1.2	12288	2.6
2014	33526	2851563	1.2	12440	2.7
2015	33433	2949400	1.1	--	2.5
2016	35849	2975711	1.2	--	2.5

CRIME HEAD-WISE NUMBER OF CHILD DELINQUENCY IPC CASES IN (2006-2016)

Crime Head	2006	2007	2008	2009	2010	2011	2012	2013	2014	2015	2016
Murder (Sec. 302 IPC)	605	672	743	844	679	888	990	1007	841	853	892
Attempt to Commit Murder (Sec. 307 IPC)	498	547	563	603	543	-	-	825		980	933
C.H. not Amounting murder to (Sec. 304, 308 IPC)	36	41	23	25	35	51	48	71	52	36	45
Rape (Sec. 376)	656	746	776	798	858	1149	1175	1884		1688	1903
Custodial Rape	0	0	0	0	0	-	-	0		-	0
Other rape	656	746	776	798	858	-	-	1884		-	-
Kidnapping and Abduction (Sec. 363-369, 371-373 IPC)	271	301	354	396	524	760	789	1121		1630	1538
(i) Of Women and Girls	208	205	242	275	391	-	-	969		-	--
(ii) of others	63	06	112	121	133	-	-	152		-	-
Dacoity (Sec. 395-398 IPC)	99	144	161	150	97	134	174	160	193	193	218

contd...

Crime Head	2006	2007	2008	2009	2010	2011	2012	2013	2014	2015	2016
Preparation and Assembly for Dacoity (Sec. 399-402 IPC)	74	87	68	72	51	-	-	87		47	
Robbery (Sec. 392-394, 397, 398 IPC)	230	321	409	500	481	551	767	904	1024	1358	1276
Burglary (Sec. 452, 454, 455, 457-460 IPC)	2270	2675	2603	2702	2431	2271	2609	2625	2605	2605	
Theft (Sec. 379-382 IPC)	4846	531	5606	5615	5253	4930	5320	5528	6717	6046	824
(I) Auto Theft	904	1072	1068	1319	1512	1457	-	-		1977	-
(II) Other Theft	3942	4244	4538	4296	3741	3473	-	-		4069	-
Riots (Sec. 143- 145, 147-151, 153, 153A, 153B, 157, 158, 160 IPC)	988	1440	1574	1422	1081	1347	1690	1486	1092	1017	1315
Criminal Breach of Trust (Sec. 406- 409 IPC)	15	40	53	17	28	24	22	23	47	26	-
Cheating(Sec.419,420 IPC)		111	135	108	134	161	148	136	949	90	162
Counterfeiting (Sec. 231-254,489A-489D IPC)		12	17	11	11	20	33	13	27	12	12
Aroson (Sec. 435, 436, 438 IPC)	36	63	75	79	59	-	-	69		52	78
Hurt (Sec. 323-333, 335-338 IPC)	358	381	425	364	380	-	-	490		1027	1151
Dowry Deaths (Sec. 304 IPC)	60	70	68	87	57	-	-	60		237	-
Molestation (Sec. 354 IPC)	488	476	560	474	546	-	-	142		1439	694
Sexual Harassment (Sec. 509 IPC)	148	129	132	153	174	-	-	312		111	81
Cruelty by Husband and Relatives (Sec.498 IPC)	219	302	239	284	238	-	-	281		97	-
Importation of Girls (Sec. 366B IPC)	0	0	0	0	1	-	--	0		0	-
Death due to Negligence (304A IPC)	163	108	165	165	211	-	-	259		316	319
Other IPC Crimes	4742	5148	5755	6427	5861	12023	13947	7455	17205	15842	10027
Total Cognizable Crimes under IPC	21088	22865	24535	23926	22740	25125	27936	31725	33526	31396	41826

Source: www.indiastat.com

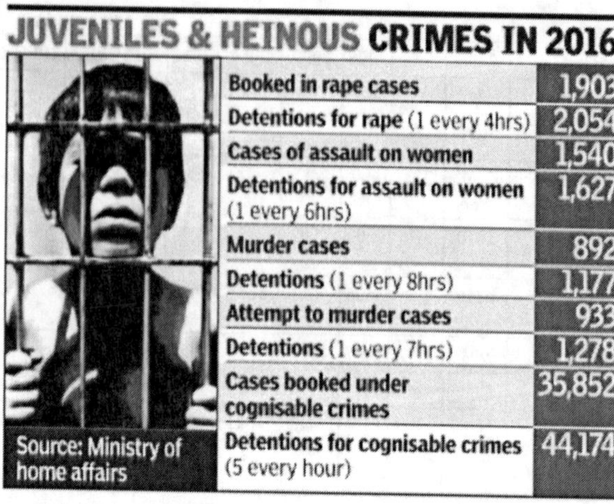

JUVENILES & HEINOUS CRIMES IN 2016

Booked in rape cases	1,903
Detentions for rape (1 every 4hrs)	2,054
Cases of assault on women	1,540
Detentions for assault on women (1 every 6hrs)	1,627
Murder cases	892
Detentions (1 every 8hrs)	1,177
Attempt to murder cases	933
Detentions (1 every 7hrs)	1,278
Cases booked under cognisable crimes	35,852
Detentions for cognisable crimes (5 every hour)	44,174

Source: Ministry of home affairs

JUVENILE AND HEINOUS CRIMES IN 2016[33]

5.6 Culpability of the children for heinous crimes

In case of Gaurav Kumar vs. State of Haryana, the Hon'ble Supreme Court expressed, When we said that we thought that there should be a rethinking by the Legislature, it is apt to note here that there can be a situation where commission of an offence may be totally innocuous or emerging from a circumstance where a young boy is not aware of the consequences but in cases of rape, dacoity, murder which are heinous crimes, it is extremely difficult to conceive that the Juvenile was not aware of the consequences."[34] Many justice systems around the globe hold a perception that children who are serious offenders are beyond the reach of society and are not able to be reformed. It is doubtful that children who have propensity to commit violence or sexual offences will be able to grow out of their behaviour and will continue to commit serious offences as adults. In this way, they allow offence to camouflage the child and provide for deviations within the system from the basic principle, upheld by international standards, of having a separate system for children focused on rehabilitation rather than punishment.

Generally there have been two schools of thoughts with regard to the dealing of the juvenile-in-conflict-with-law (hereafter JICL). First one, is Early Progressivism and second one, is Modern Conservatism.[35] Early Progressivism is oriented to the care and protection of the children by the parents and if the parents are not capable to look after their wards it has to be done by the state to develop these children into better citizens and contributive member of the society. The Early Progressivism believed that the children who came in conflict with legal system are the children in need of care and protection and are not supposed to be punished as adults.[36] The basic postulation of this philosophy was that the children are the most vulnerable, innocent and dependent on the adult section of the society.[37] Their beliefs were that because of environmental conditions like poverty, separation between parents, peer pressure etc., these children have gone astray or wayward children.[38] Instead of punishment, these children are supposed to be cared for and given protection so that they can grow into useful and productive citizen and contributive member of the society. Therefore the Early progressivism believed that the care and protection of children are the first priority of parents or the duty to take care of the children is that of the parents *i.e.* father and mother and if the parents are not able or nor willing to undertake this duty due to poverty or any other reason, then the State has to step in under the principle of *parens Patriae*[39] where the state is clothed with the authority of the parent and nurture the children as a guardian. Therefore the state is obligated to enforce that duty of care and provide protection in form of education, food, shelter and other essential needs.

This thought of Early Progressivism discussed above, could not be sustained longer as the rate of juvenile crime began to increase (particularly in the United State of America) during the 1980s.[40] Now the progressivism took the back seat and steep rise in the rate of juvenile crimes force to think on the line of the crime control rather than the care and protection of *wayward* children. Consequently, the emphasis, which was earlier on child welfare, shifted its lenses towards the public safety /crime prevention and the line of thought, which emerged was known as the *Modern Conservatism.*[41]

The Conservative Reformers of modern era were persistently demanding the re-orientation of the Juvenile Justice System by shifting its focus from the protection and care of the children-in-conflict -with -law to the protection of public safety by criminalising the offenders irrespective of the age of the offenders.[42] The prime focus of the modern conservatives is to weed-out the misfits from the society by punishing and incarcerating, put them out of circulation. The conservative reformist also make difference between the juvenile below 12 years and above 16 years as they took the view that the person above the age of 16 years were having sufficient maturity to know the repercussions and consequences of their acts and they should be treated as an adult the crime committed.[43]

(i) Culpability of juveniles in India for heinous crimes

However, in India the sentencing of death penalty to a child is not allowed. Indian laws prohibit the sentencing to death to child but in practice, this law could not have been followed because of complexities and obscurities in determining the actual age of person. Masses of India were not registered at birth and thus not having birth certificates. In India, about 50 percent of total population has not been registered at birth. In India, many children didn't have the fortune of attending the schools because of the poverty and illiteracy; therefore they can't satisfy the test of age determination. Furthermore, the incompetence and inexperience among defence lawyer aggravate the complexities in bringing the offender's age to the consideration of courts. In case of Someshwar Joshi, Hon'ble Supreme Court has upheld death sentence, where the offender's actual age could not be assessed and there was possibility of that, the offender was below than 18 years at the time of the occurrence of crime. Someshwar Joshi was executed on July 12, 1995[44] irrespective of the possibility that he was below the age of 18 at the time of the crime.

After the enforcement of Juvenile Justice (Care and Protection of Children) Act 2015, the first judge came under the amended juvenile justice law[45] where, a Session's Court in Jhabua district, Madhya Pradesh,[46] sentenced two teenagers to life imprisonment for killing another teenager. A 16 years old boy, was allegedly stabbed in Jhabua, by his two friends. The two accused detained and sent to correction home. They were examined by a board, which found them physically and mentally fit, and aware of the consequences of the offence. A charge sheet was filed within 18 days and they were convicted and awarded life imprisonment under Indian Penal Code,

Section 302 (murder), and Sections 15 and 18 of the Juvenile Justice (Care and Protection of Children) Act, 2015.

In another judgment, Hisar court has sentenced a juvenile to 20 years of rigorous imprisonment for raping and killing a six-year-old girl from Uklana in Hisar idstrict.[47] The court has also imposed a fine of Rs 80,000 on the convict, a 17-year old boy. The case was decided in approximately nine months. The court had convicted the accused. After hearing the appeal, the court pronounced quantum of sentence and awarded 20 years rigorous imprisonment to the convict.

5.7 Conclusion

The burgeoning number of offences caused by the children particularly in between the age group of 16-18 years pave the path of re-enactment of a comprehensive legislation on Juvenile Justice. The J. J. Act, 2015[48] have been enacted with the purposes of creating a fear of punishment by assuming that the trial as an adult, and the consequent transfer out of the juvenile justice system would be a deterrent for possible child offenders.

However, the close scrutiny of NCRB Data reveals that this model have been failed to deter juvenile offenders as was expected with the enforcement of J.J. Act, 2015. Various countries have experienced that the practice of getting tough on child offender like Court Ordered Sanctions, imprisoning etc. has not been effective in solving the problems of child delinquency. The methods of reducing the juvenile crimes by putting the young offenders out of circulation by institutionalising them,[49] will not have a long-term effect and will also defeat the very objective of the Juvenile Justice System.[50]

REFERENCES

1. Juvenile Justice (Care and Protection of Children) Act, 2000.
2. Juvenile Justice (Care and Protection of Children) Act, 2015.
3. Petty offences includes the offence for which the maximum punishment under the Indian Penal Code (45 of 1860) or any other law for the time being in force is imprisonment up-to three years.

4. Serious offence includes the offence for which the punishment under the Indian Penal Code (45 of 1860) or any other law for the time being in force is imprisonment between three years to seven years.
5. Juvenile Justice (Care and Protection of Children) Act 2015.
6. Suman Nalwa and Hari Dev, Commentary on The Juvenile Justice Act, Universal Publication, Haryana second edition 2016.
7. The Centre for Child and the Law, National Law School of India University.
8. Hand book for Advocates working for CCL in India. See at megpolice.gov.in/pdf/child_ protection/Handbook percent 20for percent 20Advocates.visited on Dec. 2017
9. See, following Sections of the IPC: 115, 121A, 122, 123, 130, 132, 194, 232, 238, 240, 251, 255, 304, 305, 306, 307, 313, 314, 315, 316, 326, 327, 328, 329, 331, 333, 363A, 364, 366, 366A, 366B, 367, 372, 373, 377, 382, 386, 388, 389, 394, 395, 396, 399, 400, 412, 413, 436, 449, 450, 454, and 455.
10. Ved Kumari, the Juvenile Justice (Care and Protection of Children) Act 2015 – Critical Analyses, Nexis Publication, Haryana, 2017.
11. *Ibid.*
12. Prepared by the Center for Children for Child and the Laws, National Law School of India University, Bangalore.
13. *The Times of India*, *The Hindustan Times*, The pioneer, The Hindu. etc.
14. *The Times of India*, Published on September 8, 2017, Haryana.
15. *The Times of India*, Published on 16 January 2018, Lucknow.
16. *The Times of India*, Published on Nov 23, 2017.
17. *The Hindustan Times*, Published on May 25, May 2017.
18. *The Times of India*, Published on November 23, 2017.
19. *The Times of India*, Published on December 22, 2017.
20. *The Times of India*, Published on May 2, 2016.
21. *The Times of India*, Published on April 22, 2017.
22. https://timesof india.com/cities/delhi-toddler-s-rape-2.
23. https://timesofindia.iniatimes.com /city/delhi/17-year—old-kills-in-night-for– revenge/article. May 18, 2017.
24. *The Hindustan Times*, Published on December 4, 2017.

25. *The New Indian Express*. Published on 7th November, 2017.
26. *The Times of India*, Published on May 2, 2018.
27. *The Times of India*, Published on Sep 20, 2018,
28. NCRB Data, published on August, 2017.
29. NCRB Data, published on August 2017.
30. NCRB Data, published on August 2017.
31. From October 19, 2017: Times of India (http://epaperbeta.timesof india.com/Article.aspx?eid =STATOISTICS-JUVENILE-CRIMINALS-ARE-BECOMING-MORE-VOILENT-19102017010020)
32. NCRB Data, Published on August, 2017.
33. Juveniles and heinous crimes in 2016

    From: Chethan Kumar, Oct 25 2017: *The Times of India*(http:// epaperbeta.timesofindia.c om/Article.aspx?eid=31808&articlexml= One•juvenile•held•for•rape•every•4hours•25102 017022018)
34. Hon'ble Judges/Coram: Dipak Mishra and Prafulla C. Pant, JJ. IN THE SUPREME COURT OF INDIA S.L.P. (Crl.) Nos. 2366-2368/2015 Decided On: 06.04.2015 Gaurav Kumar Vs. State of Haryana.
35. Richard M. Lerner and Laurence Steinberg (ed), Handbook of Adolescent Psychology 536-545 (John Wiley and Sons.inc. New Jersey, 2004).
36. Muzaffar Husain Mir, Age of Criminal Responsibility and Child Criminal Justice: Imperatives of Developmental Model of Juvenile Justice for India, Vol. 2. Jamia Law Journal, 2017.
37. Anthony M. Platt, The child savers: the invention of delinquency 137-172 (University of Chicago Press, Chicago, 1977).
38. Supra note 2 at 536.
39. Don Cipriani, Children's Rights and the Minimum Age of Criminal Responsibility: A Global perspective 4-8 (Ashagate Publishing Limited, Surrey, 2009).
40. Jhon Dilulio, The Coming of the Super-Predators Weekly Standard, Nov. 27, 1995.
41. Muzaffar Husain Mir, Age of Criminal Responsibility and Child Criminal Justice, Imperatives Of Development Model for Juvenile Justice of India, Jamia Law Journal, Vol. 2, 2017.
42. J. Sprott, Understanding the public Opposition to a Separate Youth Justice System 44 CAD 399 (1998).

43. Kevin Hile, Trail of Juvenile as Adults: Point – Canter point 26-35 (Chelsea House Publishers, Philadelphia, 2003).

44. Amrutlal Someshwar Joshi v. The State of Maharashtra (1994) 6 SCC, 2000.

45. Juvenile Justice (Care and Protection) Act, 2015.

46. http://timesofindia.indiatimes/city/indore/hc-juvenile-conviction-appeal/articleshow/58172510.cms

47. https://indianexpress.com/article/cities/chandigarh/chandigarh-juvenile-gets-20-year-imprisonment-for-rape-murder-of-6-year-old-girl-5365640/

48. Juvenile Justice (Care and Protection of Care) Act, 2015.

49. Elizabeth Scott and Laurence Steinberg, Rethinking Juvenile Justice 270 (Harvard University Press, Cambridge, 2008).

50. Jerome Ballet, Mario Biggeri, *et al.*, Children's Agency and the Capability Approach: A conceptual Framwork in Mario Biggeri Jerome Ballet, *et al.* (eds.), children and the Capability Approach 22-40(Palgrave Macmillian, New York, 2011)

6

Public Perception and Opinion on Crimes Committed by Children

6.1 Introduction

This chapter is based on the empirical study on the burning issue of the child delinquency and its impact on society. To fulfill the objectives of this study the author has prepared an interview schedule containing objective questions based on different aspects of child delinquency problem. Which took two considerations into account firstly, online survey method and secondly, one to one interaction for collecting public opinion on the issue of rising child delinquency. This study took 201 respondents from different and unorganised sector. The respondents were subject to different questions (as annexed)* and the responses derived from them, are represented in the form of tables and graphs. The results drawn from the tables and graphs based on their responses have been analysed and interpreted hereunder for candid understanding. Every head has been discussed in the following pattern, introductory remarks followed by frequency distribution accompanied with tabulation where required and lastly with comments and conclusion.

*At the last of this book

6.2 Age of Respondents

Table 6.1: Age Frequency of the respondents

Sl. No.	Age (in Yrs.)	Frequency	Percentage (%)
1	12-18	10	5
2	19-30	74	36.8
3	31-45	62	30.8
4	45-60	44	21.9
5	Above 60 Years	11	5.5
	Total	**201**	**100**

Responses

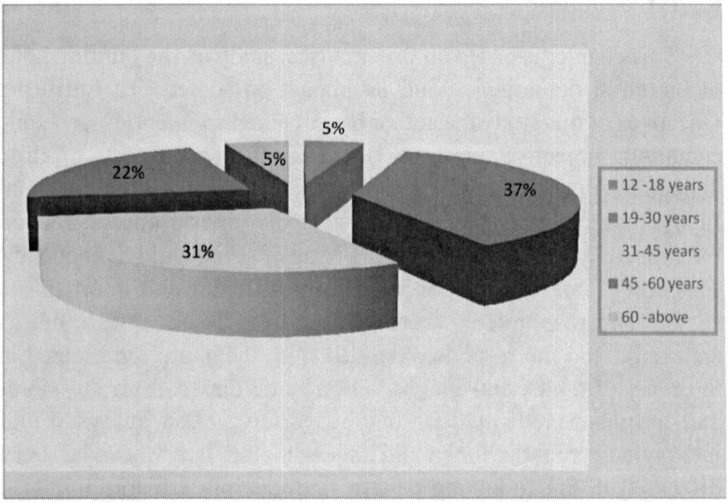

Fig. 6.1: Age frequency of the respondents.

Analysis

This study comprises of the sample size of 220 respondents; 68 percent of whom were between the ages 19-45 years of age. The maximum percentage of respondents falls within the age group of 19-30 years (consisting of 36.8 percent of the sample) and this figure is closely followed by the age-group of 31-45 years (comprising of 30.8 percent). The respondents falling between the age bracket 45-60 years of age also played significant role in sample, comprising of about 21.9 percent of total sample. The pie-chart above reveals that the lowest accountability lied on the shoulders of those respondents who fell within the bracket of 12-18 years and above 60 years.

6.3 Profession of the respondents

Table 6.2: Profession of the respondents

Sl. No.	Category	Frequency	Percentage (%)
1	Student	49	24.4
2	Self Employed	52	25.9
3	Service	70	34.8
4	Retired	9	4.5
5	Home Maker	21	10.4
	Total	**201**	**100**

Responses

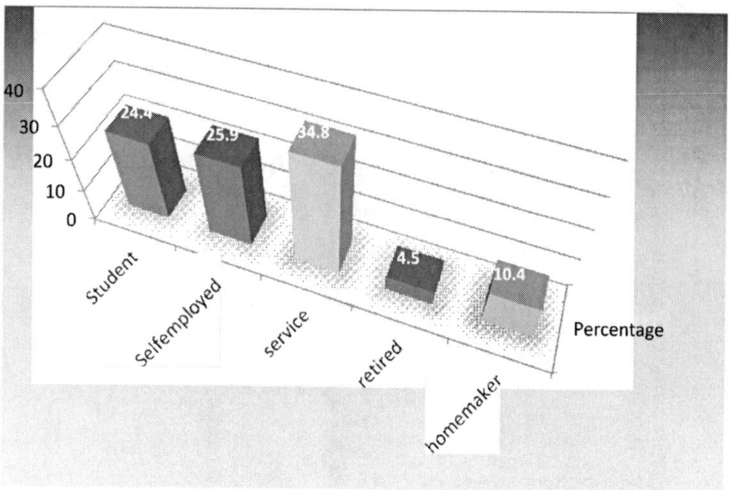

Fig. 6.2: Profession of the respondents.

Analysis

The table above and the pie-chart below shows that the majority of respondents belonged to the service class (comprising of 34.8 percent of the total sample), followed by the self-employed consisting of 25.9 percent. This number is closely chased by respondents who are students that constitute about 24.4 percent. The share of the home makers is 10.4 percent and that of retired persons is 4.5 percent that is very low in figure.

6.4 Education of respondents

Table 6.3: Educational qualification of respondents

Sl. No.	Category	Frequency	Percentage (%)
1	Under High School	4	2
2	High School	9	4.5
3	Graduation	77	38.3
4	Post-Graduation	98	48.8
5	Ph.D.	0	0.5
	Total	**201**	**100**

Responses

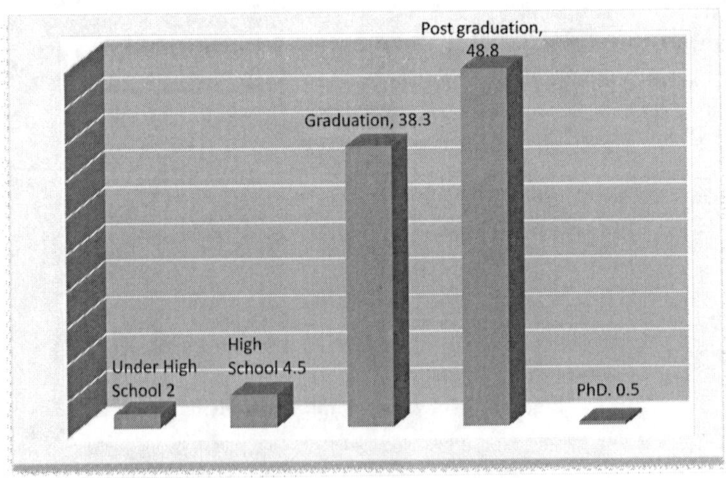

Fig. 6.3: Educational qualification of respondents.

Analysis

This table shows that the majority of respondents, constituting 48.8 percent of the total sample, is highly educated and has completed their post-graduation. This is closely followed by the respondents, who are graduate. The share of those respondents is 38.3 percent .The percentage of sample constitutes respondents who are under high school and high school is quite less, rather negligible in comparison to graduate and post graduates. Major contribution in this survey is of the educated class. Therefore, the responses regarding the knowledge about the child delinquency has come out as more rational.

6.5 Sex/Gender of the respondents

Table 6.4: Sex of the respondents

Sl. No.	Category	Frequency	Percentage (%)
1	Yes	35	17.4
2	No	136	67.7
3	Can't Say	27	13.4
4	Other	3	1.5
	Total	**201**	**100**

Responses

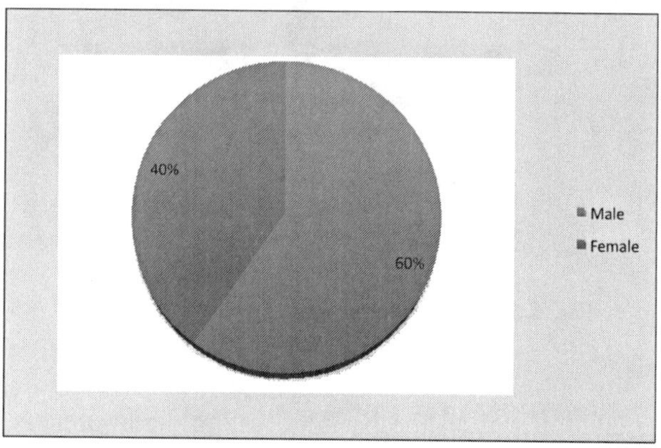

Fig. 6.4: Sex of the respondents.

The above shown table on the basis of gender depicts that the maximum number of respondents are male. The share of male respondent is 59.7 percent of the total sample. About 40.3 percent of the respondents are female. Though the literacy rate and public awareness of female is very low as per the public perception, the ratio of participation of female is not very low either in on line or one to one interaction survey.

6.6 Do you know what juvenile justice is?

Table 6.5: Do you know what juvenile justice is?

Sl. No.	Category	Frequency	Percentage (%)
1	Yes	180	89.6
2	No	17	8.5
3	Can't Say	4	2
4	Other	0	0
	Total	**201**	**100**

Responses

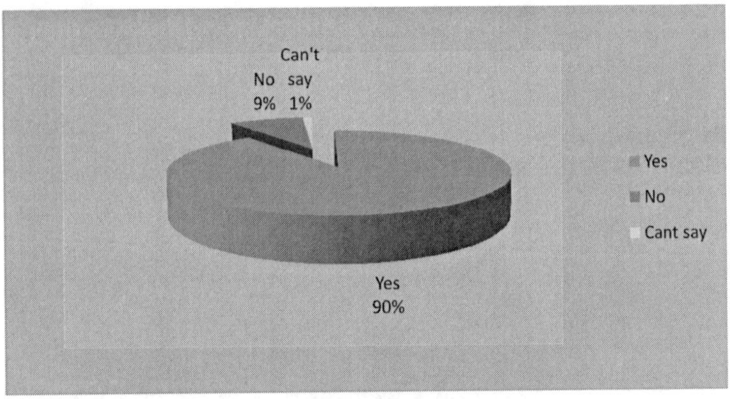

Fig. 6.5: Do you know what juvenile justice is?

Analysis

The table drawn on the basis of testing the awareness of the Juvenile justice system and law reveals that maximum number of respondents comprising of 89.6 percent are quiet aware of the juvenile justice system. Only 8.5 percent says that they have no idea about the juvenile justice. Among the respondents 20 percent of them have told that they have got information about the juvenile justice from the television and newspaper. But 11 percent of the respondents have given very shocking answer where they told that they have no knowledge about any separate justice system for children. To the author it is very interesting to know that 36 percent respondents have good knowledge about the juvenile justice despite not belonging to legal profession.

6.7 Do you think that number of children coming in conflict with law is increasing day by day?

Table 6.6: Do you think that number of children coming in conflict with law is increasing day by day?

Sl. No.	Category	Frequency	Percentage (%)
1	Yes	171	85.1
2	No	14	7
3	Can't Say	15	7.5
4	Other	1	0.5
	Total	**201**	**100**

Responses

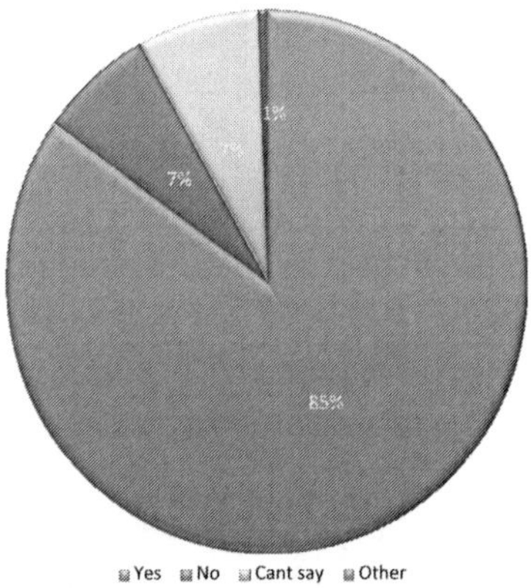

Fig. 6.6: Do you think that number of children coming in conflict with law is increasing day by day?

Analysis

The table and pie-chart above show the responses to the above stated question. Almost 85.1 of the respondents agree with the statement that the number of delinquent juvenile is increasing. Though 7 percent respondents of total sample are not satisfied with the statement. Only 7.5 percent of total sample opted third option i.e. can't say.

6.8. Have you heard about any child in conflict with law (child offender)?

Table 6.7: Have you heard about any child in conflict with law (child offender)?

Sl. No.	Category	Frequency	Percentage (%)
1	Yes	146	72.6
2	No	42	20.9
3	Can't Say	13	6.5
4	Other	0	0
	Total	**201**	**100**

Responses

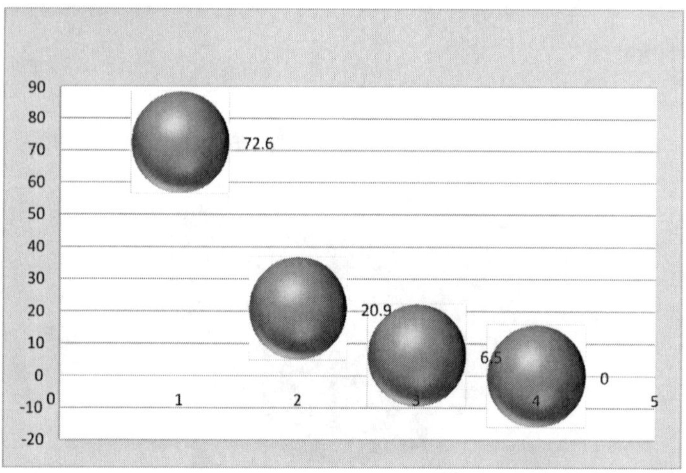

Fig. 6.7: Have you heard about any child in conflict with law (child offender)?

Analysis

The table drawn above shows that the maximum number of respondents, comprising of 72.6 percent of total sample have heard about child offender. Only 20.9 percent of total respondent said that they have no knowledge about any child offender. Yet again very few numbers of respondents can't answer this question.

6.9. Who is child?

Table 6.8: Who is child?

Sl. No.	Category	Frequency	Percentage (%)
1	Person below age of 07 years	33	16.4
2	Person below age of 12 years	43	21.4
3	Person below age of 16 years	67	33.3
4	Person below age of 18 years	58	28.9
	Total	**201**	**100**

Responses

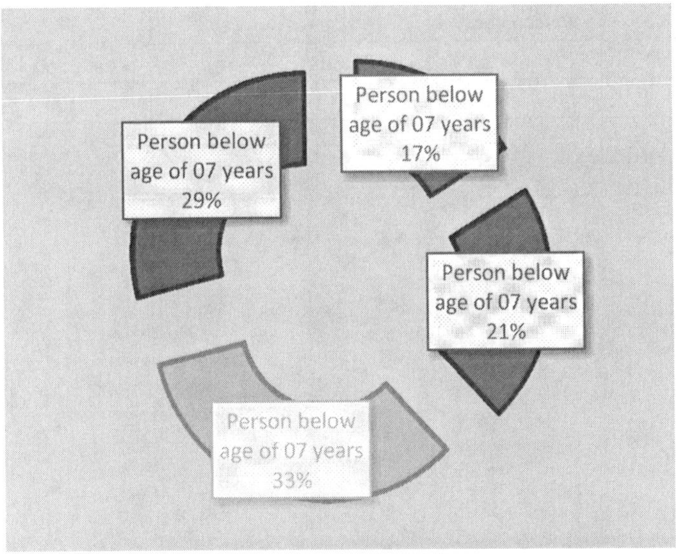

Fig. 6.8: Who is child?

Analysis

The table is drawn on the basis of testing the knowledge regarding the age of the child in legal terms. Almost 16.4 percent of the respondents feel that child is a person below age of 07 years. Around 21.4 percent of the respondents considered the person below the age of 12 years as child. The table shows that the 33.3 percent of total sample of the respondents agree that the person below age of 16 years comes into the definition of child. Majority of people (comprising of 28.9) suggested that 18 years should be the age of majority and below that a person should be treated as child.

6.10. At what age a person should be made criminally liable (age of criminal responsibility)

Table 6.9: At what age a person should be made criminally liable (age of criminal responsibility)

Sl. No.	Category	Frequency	Percentage (%)
1	Person above age of 07 years	8	4
2	Person above age of 12 years	31	15.4
3	Person above age of 16 years	109	54.2
4	Person above age of 18 years	52	25.9
	Total	**201**	**100**

Responses

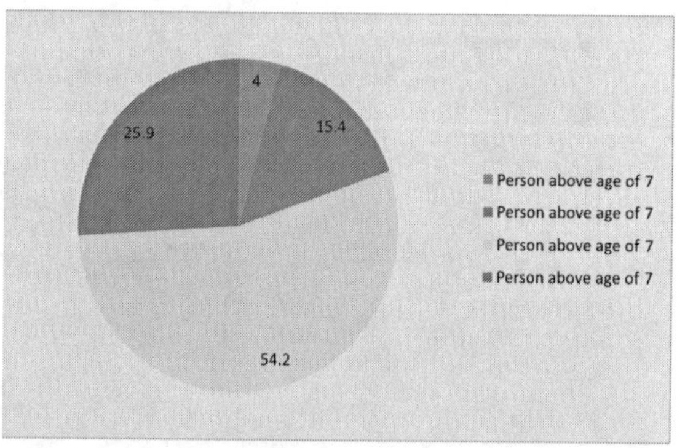

Fig. 6.9: At what age a person should be made criminally liable (age of criminal responsibility).

Analysis

The table shown that the majority of the respondents in the sample (comprising of 54.2 percent) agree that above 16 years should be the age of criminal responsibility. Whereas 25 percent of total respondents feel that at the age of 18 years a person could be make criminally liable. About 15.4 percent of the respondents in the sample say that person above 12 years of age should not get blanket immunity from criminal liability. There are a very few respondents who have opted option number one that is person above 7 years should be make criminally liable.

6.11. What is the cause for child coming into conflict with law (leaned towards criminal activities)?

Table 6.10.What is the cause for child coming into conflict with law (lean towards criminal activities)?

Sl. No.	Category	Frequency	Percentage (%)
1	Parental Neglect	76	37.8
2	Poor Education	56	27.9
3	Poverty	31	15.4
4	Other	38	18.9
	Total	**201**	**100**

Responses

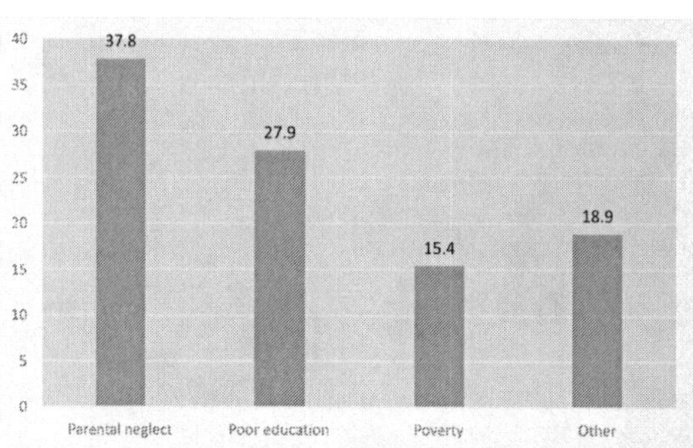

Fig. 6.10: What is the cause for child coming into conflict with law (lean towards criminal activities).

Analysis

In response to the above stated question maximum number of respondents have chosen the option parental neglect as the cause of children leaning towards criminal activity (that constitute 37.8 percent). While 27.9 percent of total respondents agree on second option that is poor education as a cause for child delinquency. The respondents who go for third option i.e. poverty as a reason for children involving in crime have a share in the total sample as low as 15 percent only. The percentage of the respondents who feel that apart from first three options there are some other reason for child delinquency is 18 percent.

6.12. Do you think that children alleged to be in conflict with law become a big problem for societal security?

Table 6.11: Do you think that children alleged to be in conflict with law become a big problem for societal security?

Sl. No.	Category	Frequency	Percentage (%)
1	Yes	145	72.1
2	No	29	14.4
3	Can't Say	25	12.4
4	Other	2	1
	Total	**201**	**100**

Responses

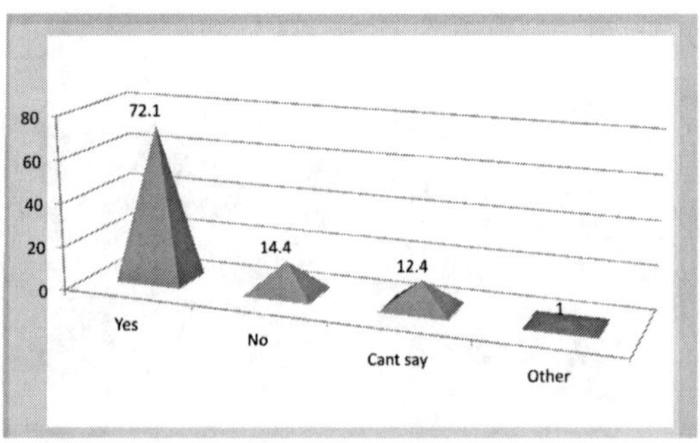

Fig. 6.11: Do you think that children alleged to be in conflict with law become a big problem for societal security?

Analysis

The majority of respondents (comprising of 72.1 percent) strongly supported the statement that the child delinquency become a big problem for the society. Whereas, 14.4 percent of total number do not agree with the statement. Here, the author finds that about 12.4 percent of the people who were not in a position to answer this question.

6.13. Do you think that children to be involved in crime should be punished for their crime in a similar manner as adults?

Table 6.12: Do you think that children to be involved in crime should be punished for their crime in a similar manner as adults?

Sl. No.	Category	Frequency	Percentage (%)
1	Yes	51	25.4
2	No	116	57.7
3	Can't Say	25	12.4
4	Other	9	4.5
	Total	**201**	**100**

Responses

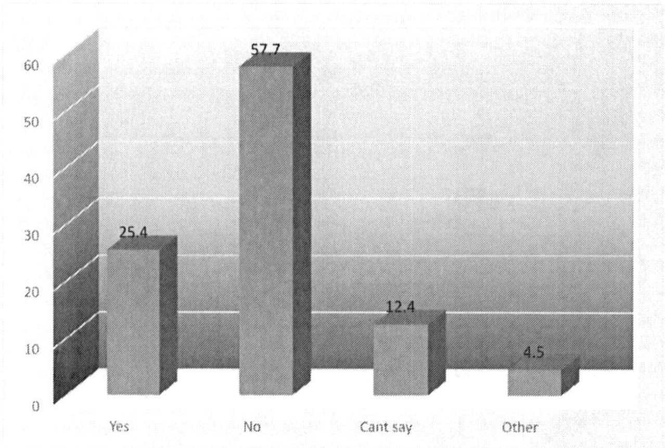

Fig. 6.12: Do you think that children to be involved in crime should be punished for their crime in a similar manner as adults.

Analysis

While answering this question, maximum number of total sample constituting of 57.7 percent believes that a child should not be punished same as adults. They are not in favour to punish juveniles. They think that reformative approach will reduce the possibility of repeat offence. Only 25.4 percent of total number says that delinquent juvenile should be punished. They are of view that the current law does not act as a deterrent for juveniles committing heinous crimes. Yet again 12.4 percent are neutral in their response.

6.14. Do think that a child should be punished for very serious crime in a similar manner as an adult

Table 6.13: Do think that a child should be punished for very serious crime in a similar manner as an adult

Sl. No.	Category	Frequency	Percentage (%)
1	Yes	121	60.2
2	No	55	27.4
3	Can't Say	19	9.5
4	Other	5	2.5
	Total	**201**	**100**

Responses

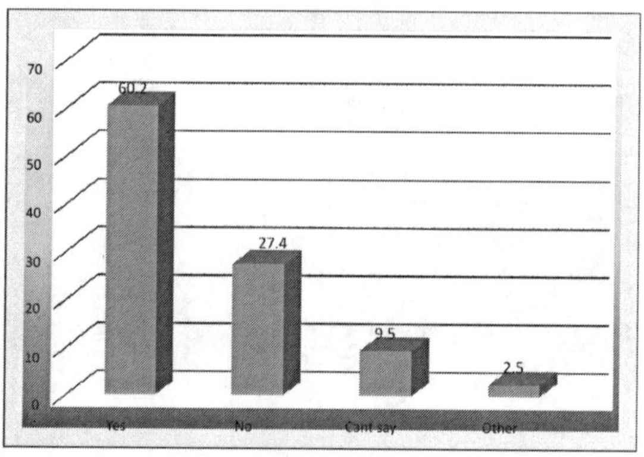

Fig. 6.13: Do think that a child should be punished for very serious crime in a similar manner as an adult.

Analysis

When the author interviewed the respondents on this question, the maximum number of total sample constituting of 60.2 percent responded that a child should be punished in a similar manner as an adult. They believe that punishing the child will act as a deterrent for child offenders committing heinous crimes. Only 27.4 percent of total number are not in favour to punish delinquent juveniles same as adult's. Yet again 9.5 percent are neutral in their response.

6.15. Do you think that a child alleged to be in conflict with law (apprehended for committing a crime) should be placed in police lock up.

Table 6.14: Do you think that a child alleged to be in conflict with law (apprehended for committing a crime) should be placed in police lock up

Sl. No.	Category	Frequency	Percentage (%)
1	Yes	60	29.9
2	No	112	55.7
3	Can't Say	21	10.4
4	Other	8	3.5
	Total	**201**	**100**

Responses

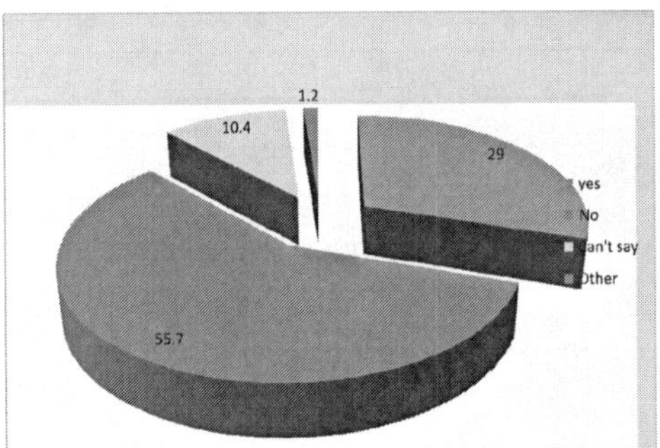

Fig. 6.14: Do you think agree that child alleged to be in conflict with law (apprehended for committing a crime) should be placed in police lock up.

Analysis

Almost 29.9 percent of the respondents included in the sample feel that delinquent juvenile should be put in the police lockup otherwise they might become a nuisance for society. More than half namely 55.7 percent of the total respondents don't agree to put the delinquent child in police lockup. About 10.4 percent of the total respondents did not answer the question.

6.16. Do you agree that there should be a joint proceeding of a child alleged to be in conflict with law with a person who is not a child when the child has committed crime in his association?

Table 6.15: Do you agree that there should be a joint proceeding of a child alleged to be in conflict with law with a person who is not a child when the child has committed crime in his association?

Sl. No.	Category	Frequency	Percentage (%)
1	Yes	105	30.3
2	No	61	52.2
3	Can't Say	32	15.9
4	Other	2	1.7
	Total	**201**	**100**

Responses

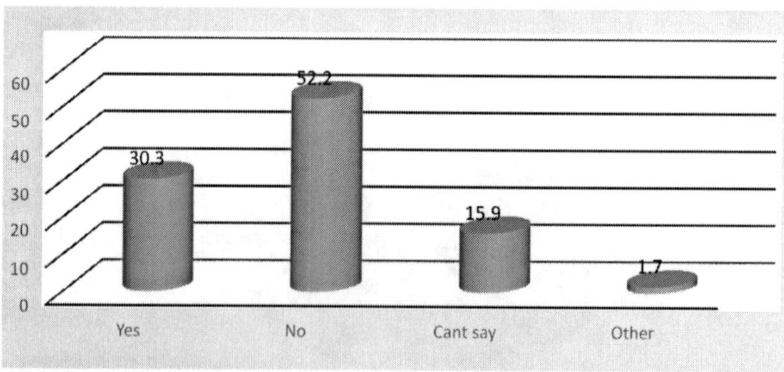

Fig. 6.15: Do you agree that there should be a joint proceeding of a child alleged to be in conflict with law with a person who is not a child when the child has committed crime in his association?

Analysis

The table drawn here shows that 30.3 percent of the total sample believes that there should be a joint proceeding of a child alleged to be in conflict with law along with a person who is not a child, and has committed crime in his association. Joint proceeding could be helpful in saving time and money. Whereas majority of respondents i.e. 52.2 percent did not agree for joint proceeding of a child and adult criminal. Remaining 15.9 percent have shown no interest in answering this question.

6.17. Do you agree that when a child alleged to have committed a non-bailable offence is apprehended or detained by the police, he should be released on bail?

Table 6.16: Do you agree that when a child alleged to have committed a non-bailable offence is apprehended or detained by the police, he should be released on bail?

Sl. No.	Category	Frequency	Percentage (%)
1	Yes	75	37.3
2	No	93	46.3
3	Can't Say	29	14.4
4	Other	10	5
	Total	**201**	**100**

Responses

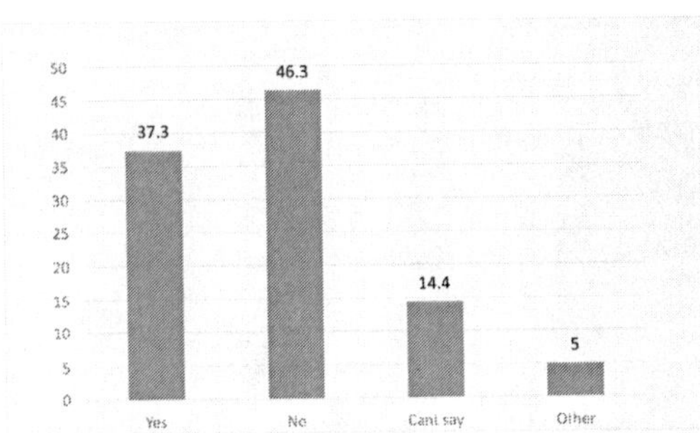

Figure16: Do you agree that when a child alleged to have committed a non-bailable offence is apprehended or detained by the police, he should be released on bail?

Analysis

This table shows that the majority of respondents constituting of 37.3 percent have shown their apprehension in releasing a delinquent juvenile on bail if he has committed a non-bailable offence. They feel that releasing such a delinquent child is not safe for the societal security. While about 46 percent of the total respondent are in support to release the child on bail though he has committed a non-bailable offence. Only 14.4 percent have opted the 3rd option i.e. can't say.

6.1 Do you think that minor should be treated same as adult for criminal responsibility if he completes 18 years of age during pendency of case?

Table 6.17: Do you think that minor should be treated same as adult for criminal responsibility if he completes 18 years of age during pendency of case?

Sl. No.	Category	Frequency	Percentage (%)
1	Yes	91	45.3
2	No	83	41.3
3	Can't Say	23	11.4
4	Other	4	2
	Total	**201**	**100**

Responses

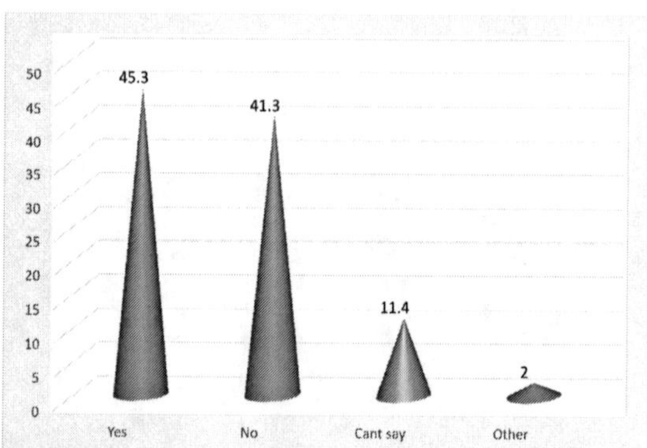

Fig. 6.17: Do you think that minor should be treated same as adult for criminal responsibility if he completes 18 years during pendency of case?

Analysis

The table drawn above clearly shows the sample is split into two half. The majority of about 45.3 percent respondents included in the sample are in support to treat the child as an adult if he / she completes his/her18 years during the trail. They are of view that a delinquent juvenile should not get immunity of being a child after completing his/her 18 years. They even believe that giving blanket immunity to the juvenile after completing 18 years could defeat the purpose of J.J. Act. Nearly about 41.3 percent of respondents in the sample are not in favour to treat the juvenile as an adult after attaining 18 years of age. Another 11.4 percent did not answer the question and opted third reply as their response.

6.19. Do you agree that when a child, who has been found to have committed a heinous offence, attains the age of twenty one years and is yet to complete prescribed term of stay in a place of safety, should be sent to adult prison?

Table 6.18: Do you agree that when a child, who has been found to have committed a heinous offence, attains the age of twenty one years and is yet to complete prescribed term of stay in a place of safety, should be sent to adult prison?

Sl. No.	Category	Frequency	Percentage (%)
1	Yes	115	57.2
2	No	53	26.4
3	Can't Say	31	15.4
4	Other	2	1
	Total	**201**	**100**

Responses

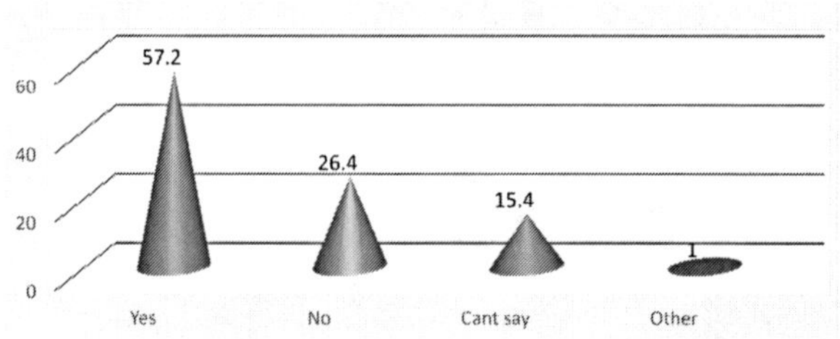

Fig. 6.18: Do you agree that when a child, who has been found to have committed a heinous offence, attains the age of twenty one years and is yet to complete prescribed term of stay in a place of safety, should be sent to adult prison?

Analysis

The study shows that more than half of the respondents constituting 57.2 percent of total sample are in support to send the juveniles to adult prison who has completed the age of 21 years. Yet another segment of nearly 26.4 percent of total sample feels that putting them with adult prisoners may turn them into hardcore criminals. The number of respondents who are not in position to answer this question are very less that is 15.4 percent .

6.20. Do you agree that children should be sentenced to death or for life imprisonment without the possibility of release for very serious offences?

Table 6.19 Do you agree that children should be sentenced to death or for life imprisonment without the possibility of release for very serious offences?

Sl. No.	Category	Frequency	Percentage (%)
1	Yes	35	17.4
2	No	136	67.7
3	Can't Say	27	13.4
4	Other	3	1.5
	Total	**201**	**100**

Responses

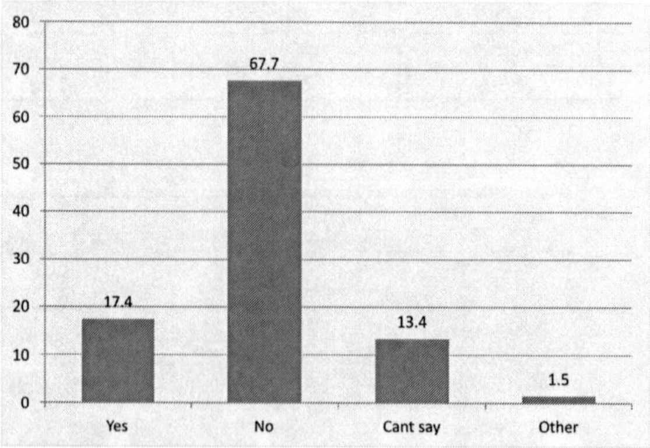

Fig. 6.19: Do you agree that children should be sentenced to death or for life imprisonment without the possibility of release for very serious offences?

Analysis

The table drawn here shows that 17.4 percent respondent of total sample believes that children should be sentenced to death or life imprisonment without the possibility of release. They believe in get tough approach. While another big segment that constitutes more than half i.e. 67.7 percent of total sample shows lenient attitude towards the child offenders. The numbers of respondents who are not interested in making any view to this issue are very low.

6.21. Do you think that children should be given special exemption from criminal responsibility?

Table 6.20: Do you think that children should be given special exemption from criminal responsibility?

Sl. No.	Category	Frequency	Percentage (%)
1	Yes	54	26.9
2	No	117	58.2
3	Can't Say	26	12.9
4	Other	4	2
	Total	**201**	**100**

Responses

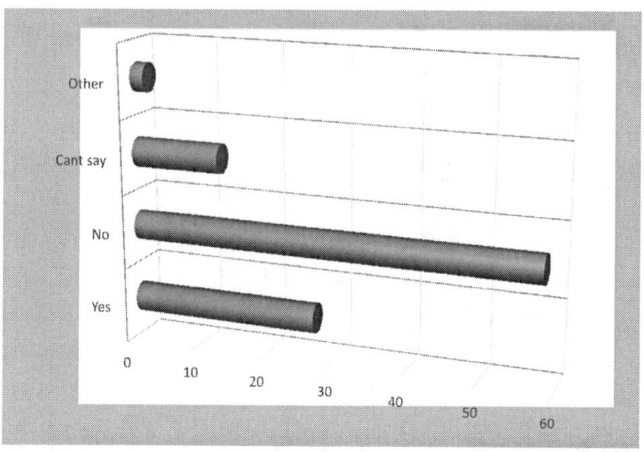

Fig. 6.20: Do you think that children should be given special exemption from criminal responsibility?

Analysis

More than half (comprising of 58.2 percent) of the respondents included in the sample believe that the children should not be given blanket immunity in the name of juvenility. They feel that if a child commits a heinous crime he should be punished same as adults. Only 26.9 percent says that a child should not be punished. Further they added that the children should be given a chance of reformation.

6.22. Do you think that reducing the age of criminal responsibility can help in curing the child delinquency (child coming into conflict with law) problem?

Table 6.21: Do you think that reducing the age of criminal responsibility can help in curing the child delinquency (child coming into conflict with law) problem?

Sl. No.	Category	Frequency	Percentage (%)
1	Yes	54	26.9
2	No	117	58.2
3	Can't Say	26	12.9
4	Other	4	2
	Total	**201**	**100**

Responses

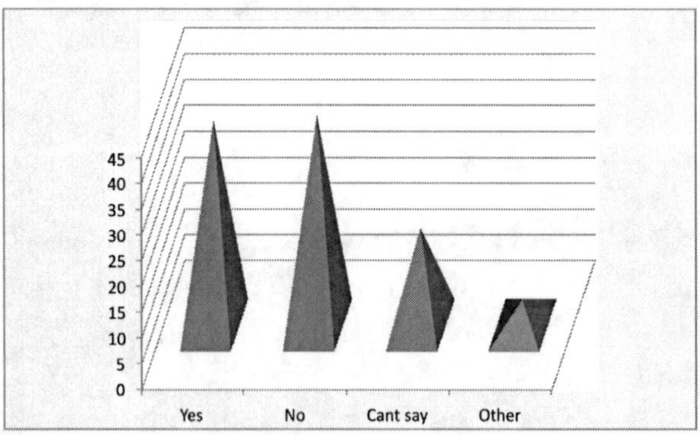

Fig. 6.21: Do you think that reducing the age of criminal responsibility can help in curing the child delinquency (child coming into conflict with law) problem?

Analysis

When the author interviewed the respondents on this question, 58.2 percent of total sample feels that the reduction of the age of criminal responsibility cannot be helpful in curing the child delinquency problem. Only 26.9 percent of the respondent believes that reducing the age of criminal responsibility can be helpful in controlling the number of juvenile crimes.

6.23. What do you think is the major cause that leads children to commit crime?

Table 6.22: What do you think is the major cause that leads children to commit crime?

Sl. No.	Category	Frequency	Percentage (%)
1	Neglected by Parents/Society	73	36.3
2	Poverty	74	11.9
3	Lack of Education	52	25.9
4	Drugs	5	2.5
5	Internet	31	15.4
6	Other	13	6.5
7	Other (Please Specify)	3	1.5
	Total	**251**	**100**

Responses

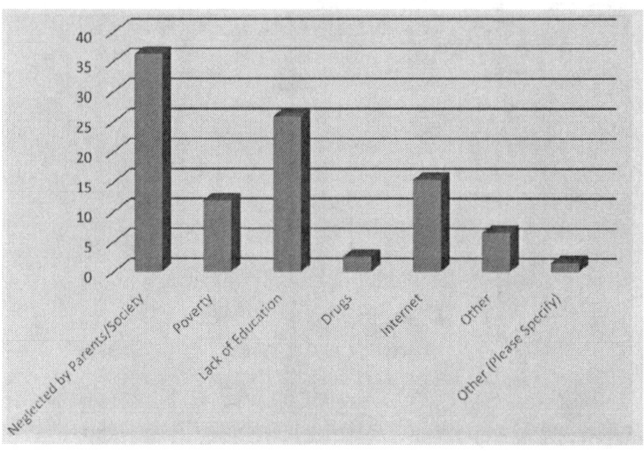

Fig. 6.22: What do you think is the major cause that leads children to commit crime?

Analysis

Almost 36.3 percent of the respondent included in the sample feel that children that come from broken homes are more prone to involve in criminal activities. About 11.9 percent of the respondents believe that poverty is primary issue which leads a child to commit crime. Around 25.9 percent of the people says that the lack of education is the main reason of child delinquency.

6.24. Do you think that children who are involved in criminal activities may be reformed?

Table 6.23: Do you think that children who are involved in criminal activities may be reformed?

Sl. No.	Category	Frequency	Percentage (%)
1	Yes	157	78.1
2	No	12	6
3	Can't Say	31	15.4
4	Other	1	0.5
	Total	**201**	**100**

Responses

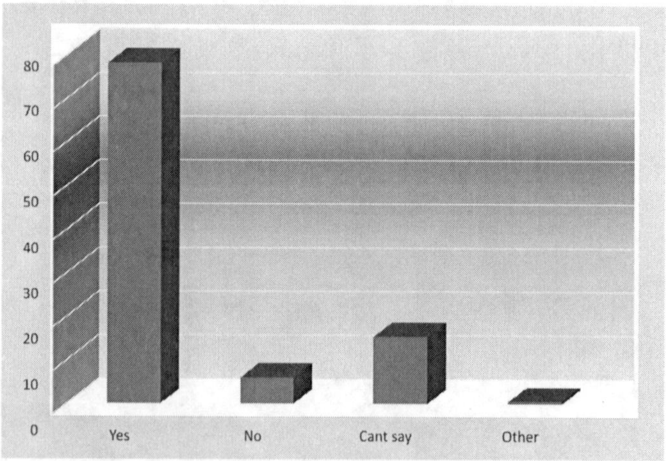

Fig. 6.23: Do you think that children who are involved in criminal activities may be reformed?

Analysis

The maximum percentage of the table consist of the respondents that strongly believe that child who is involved in criminal activities may be reformed. They believe that children often involve in crime by force of circumstances and not by choice and by providing good and favourable environment and giving suitable training and counseling, there is a possibility to reform their anti-social attitudes and to mould them into a responsible and contributing member of the society. 15.4 percent of total sample hold a perception that children who are serious offenders are beyond the reach of society and are not able to be reformed. They doubt that children who have propensity to commit violence or sexual offences will be able to grow out of their behaviour and will continue to commit serious offences as adults.

6.25. Do you think that most children in conflict with law are trapped and used by adult criminals for their own benefit?

Table 6.24: Do you think that most children in conflict with law are trapped and used by adult criminals for their own benefit?

Sl. No.	Category	Frequency	Percentage (%)
1	Yes	143	71.1
2	No	24	11.9
3	Can't Say	33	16.4
4	Other	0	0
	Total	**201**	**100**

Responses

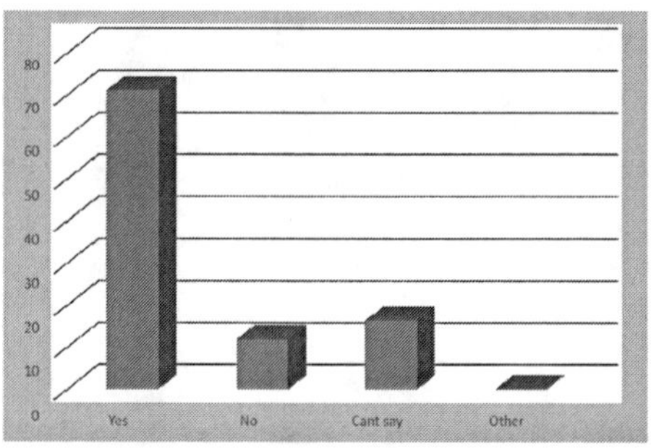

Fig. 6.24: Do you think that most children in conflict with law are trapped and used by adult criminals for their own benefit?

Analysis

The maximum number of respondents (comprising of 71.1 percent) supported the view that juveniles are used by adult criminals for their own benefit. Only 11.9 percent of the total respondents are in not favour of the above mentioned statement.

6.26. As per your opinion what would be the best way to reform children in conflict with law.

Table 6.25: As per your opinion what would be the best way to reform children in conflict with law.

Sl. No.	Category	Frequency	Percentage (%)
1	Rehabilitation and social re-integration	64	31.8
2	Skill development and recreational activities	56	27.9
3	Counseling therapy	56	27.9
4	School program	19	4.5
5	Other	4	2
6	Other (Please Specify)	2	1
	Total	**201**	**100**

Responses

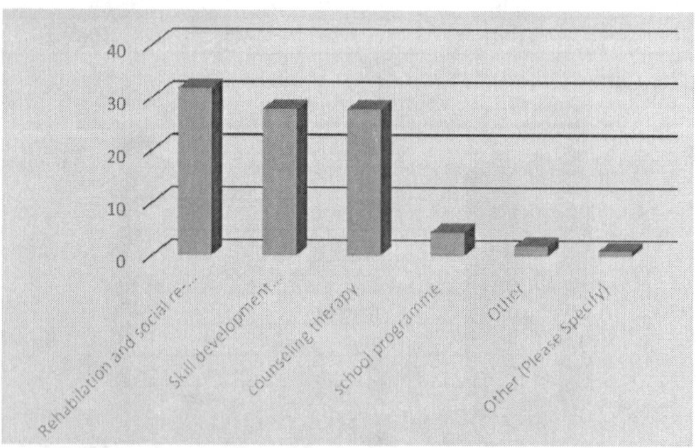

Fig. 6.25: As per your opinion what would be the best way to reform children in conflict with law.

Analysis

The question asked in furtherance of remedy sought for this juvenile delinquency problem, reveals that 31.8 percent people feels that a delinquent child should be given a chance of rehabilitation and social re-integration. Nearly about 27.9 percent of the respondents in the sample feels that skill development and re-creational activities may be helpful in drawing and guiding them back in mainstream of the society and integrating them as part of the contributive member of society. Yet again the same number of respondent (constituting 27.9 percent) are of view that counseling therapy is the best way to reform the children who has propensity of enlisting into the register of delinquent child. It's only 4.5 percent of the respondents, who have advocated for the school programmes as the solution to child delinquency.

6.27 Conclusion

The outcome of public opinion on child delinquency, reveals that maximum number of the respondents are quiet aware of the juvenile justice system and they agree that the juvenile crimes are increasing day by day and become a public concern. Though the respondents are not agree on the point that the reducing the age criminal responsibility may be helpful in reducing the rate of juvenile crime. They are of view that the current law does not act as a deterrent for juveniles committing heinous crimes. Majority of people suggested that 18 years should be the age of majority, below that a person should be treated as child. The maximum number believes that a child should not be punished same as adults but the support to treat the child as an adult if he / she completes 18 years of age during the trial. They are of view that a delinquent juvenile should not get immunity of being child after completing his 18 years. They even believe that giving blanket immunity to the juvenile after completing 18 years could defeat the purpose of J.J. Act. Majority of people are not in favour to punish juveniles. They feel that reformative approach will reduce the possibility of repeat offence. They feel that only a child committing heinous crime, should be punished same as adults. Maximum number of people don't agree to put the delinquent child in police lockup, neither they favour for joint proceeding of a child and adult criminal. On the issue of releasing a child on bail the majority has supported to release the child on bail though he has committed a non-bail able offence and are in support to send the juveniles to adult prison who has completed the age of 21 years. Yet another segment of sample feels that putting them with adult prisoners may turn them into hardcore criminal.

The question asked in furtherance of remedy sought for this juvenile delinquency problem, people feels that a delinquent child should be given a chance of rehabilitation and social re-integration, skill development and re-creational activities may be helpful in drawing and guiding them back in mainstream of the society and integrating them as part of the contributive member of the society.

The results drew from the public responses along with their interpretation leads the author to conclude that the increasing trend of heinous crimes being committed by children in recent times has compelled a re-thinking in handling of child offender's age group of 16-18 years. Further, children involved in heinous crimes such as murder and rape were more amenable to reforms and should be given a chance of fresh start in life. The children between 16-18 years who has committed serious offense, which is well within the existing juvenile system, then no need to push juvenile offenders into adult criminal system.

7

Conclusion and Suggestions

7.1 Conclusion

The new Juvenile Justice (Care and Protection of Children) Act, 2015 precisely shows that Juvenile justice system has moved from the welfare model of Juvenile Justice introduced in 2000 to crime control model (as introduced in 2015), though this Act maintain the definition of child same as earlier. It define child as a person who has not attained the age of 18 years, but it has authorised the courts to treat 16-18 years old children charged with commission of heinous offences as adult and deal with them in adult criminal court. Enforcement of this Act force the juvenile to enter into the criminal regime as transferring to the adult system breeds more criminal activities by young persons in their later lives. The prime two reasons of enforcement of J. J. Act, 2015 were, firstly, the Juvenile Justice Act, 2000 was facing implementation and procedural delays. Secondly, the increasing number of juvenile crime between the age group of 16-18 years as indicated by the National Crime Record Bureau. However, this Act can be criticised on various grounds. First, it "violates the very essence of juvenile justice Act." Secondly, it violates various fundamental rights as guaranteed by the Constitution of India. Third, this Act ignores the social backgrounds and psychological factors while sentencing. Fourth, this Act has given a sword in the hand of angry parents who want to restrain their children from getting into elopement, which increased number of cases of kidnapping and sexual assault against the juvenile. However, this Act is aimed at catering to the basic needs of children through appropriate care, protection, development, treatment and social integration, but apparently, it seems more retributive than reformative. It is retributive as it contains provisions to treat the juvenile between 16-18 years as adult for heinous crimes and after the attainment of the age of 21 years in place of safety, the juvenile will send to adult prison for remaining period of punishment. However, all this decisions will be taken by the Juvenile Justice Board. Therefore, it is clear that once a juvenile is declared guilty of heinous crime, he will not get the benefit of juvenility. Treating the children between the age group of 16-18 differently also violates Article 14, 15(3) and 20 of Indian Constitution. Article 15(3) obligates the Government to make special provision for the benefit of children. United Nation Standard Minimum Rules for the Administration of Juvenile Justice, 1985 also given prime importance to the juvenile in conflict with law and circumstances of both the offenders and the offence whereas in new Act only type of offence is given importance. In *Pratap Singh v. State of Jharkhand,* 3 *SCC 551(2005),* it was observed by Court that "in Rule 4 of United Nations Standard Minimum Rules for the Administration of Juvenile Justice, while defining a juvenile criminality or criminal responsibility, the moral and the psychological components must be given prime importance." However, in the current Act this psychological factor has been ignored. According to Maharukh Adenwala, "the Juvenile Justice (Care and Protection of Children) Act 2015 has reversed the well founded principle of juvenile justice by allowing Juvenile Justice Boards to waive the right of children above the age 16 years who have committed a heinous offence and push them into the criminal justice system, which means that the treatment of a juvenile will depend upon the type of offence committed instead of his situation." Section 15 of the Act directs the Board to conduct the preliminary assessment in case of a 16-18 years old child alleged to have committed a heinous offence to determine, whether, the child should be transferred to the Children's Court to be tried as an adult. The Juvenile Justice Board comprising of a magistrate and two social workers, will decide on the physical and mental capacity of the child; whether the juvenile who has committed such an offence has the ability to understand the consequences of the act and in what circumstances the offence has been committed. There is great chance of uncertainty in the preliminary assessment and age determination inquiry as both are challenging. The individualised assessments of adolescent mental capability are impracticable. The method of so-called introductory assessment by the Juvenile Justice Board may result in procedural arbitrariness and may cause arbitrary transfer of juvenile cases to adult criminal system which may cause violation of very foundation of Constitution. The very spirit of Article 20(1) is also undermined in the existing law as the Article prohibits the infliction of greater punishment than what would have been applicable under the law of land but the provisions of new J.J. Act, 2015 send the juvenile who has completed the age of twenty one but not completed the full term of punishment, to adult prison.

The enforcement of The Juvenile Justice Act, 2015 has also raised controversy regarding the Age of Consent, when read with the Protection of Children from Sexual Offences Act, 2012 (POCSO Act) and the Prohibition of Child Marriage Act (PCM Act). The POCSO Act prescribes the age of Consent is 18 years and if any offence is committed by a Juvenile under the POCSO Act then as per the section 23 of the POCSO Act it will be dealt as per the provision of Juvenile Justice Act, 2000 (Now as per the new amended Act). Precisely the PCM Act states that since the child marriages are voidable but not void[1] in such a situation, the juvenile who are involved in love relation can marry each other and can enter in consensual sexual act. Here it is crucial to note that the consensual sexual act may attract the provision of POCSO Act and as per J.J. Act, 2015 the juvenile may be tried as adult. In a hypothetical situation, when both the boy and girl are involved in a consensual sexual relation, then the male child shall be treated as Child in Conflict with Law and the female will be treated as Child in need of care and protection. This situation may arise because in section 3, penetrative sexual assault starts with he and it excludes the women from its periphery. It deems girls as abettor only and not an active criminal. The same situation was faced in *Court on its own motion v. State,* where the girl and boy had eloped and the parents of the girl filed a complaint of kidnaping and sexual assault against the boy. Here the petitioner Lajja Devi wrote a letter to the court which was taken as a writ petition and held that similar other cases of elopement be dealt with the same. The court found that the girl had eloped with the boy with her own consent and denied staying with her parents. Considering the gravity of the situation, the court protected the nuptial tie of the couple and sent the girl to Nari Niketan while sentencing the boy to stay at juvenile home for three years. This case, however happened before the amendment and now the scenario has changed under the new Juvenile Justice Act when read with POCSO Act, in similar situation there is a doubt whether court can give similar decision or not.

However, the judicial observations of the Courts also seems to be focused on the re-orientation of the Juvenile Justice System by shifting its focus in the direction of crime control rather than the due process model of crime control and they are more and more adopting the law and order that encompasses the juvenile offenders in the ambit of criminalisation. In India, the legislative intent commonly seems to provide child offenders another chance in life therefore the legislature has provided admonition, probation and other reformative sentences in lieu of a prison term. However, contrary to the legislative intent the conservatives believed that it is the seriousness of crime and not the juvenility of the offender which affects the exercise of judicial discretion in choosing an appropriate punishment. It seems that, this is the reason that the young age of the offender is not considered a relevant component in sentencing decisions. It is not decisive, the Supreme Court has, in the past, not hesitated to award death penalty (*Ram Deo Chauhan* v. *State of Assam*)[2] to youth offenders even when it was not conclusively proved that they had completed the age of 18 years on the date of occurrence of crime in order to respond to the "collective conscience of the society" or to meet the ends of justice." Similarly the decision of Children's Court in Jhabua district[3] case in which two minors were convicted for life imprisonment also depicts the veracity of judicial approach. After the enforcement of Juvenile Justice (Care and Protection of Children) Act 2015, the first such case under the amended Juvenile Justice Law[4], come into light i.e Jhabua District case. In this case the sessions court in Jhabua district, Madhya Pradesh, sentenced two teenagers to life imprisonment for killing another teenager. A 16 years old boy, was allegedly stabbed in Jhabua, by his two friends. The two accused detained and sent to correction home. They were examined by a board, which found them physically and mentally fit, and aware of the "consequences of the offence." A charge sheet was filed within 18 days and they were convicted and awarded life imprisonment under Indian Penal Code, Section 302 (murder), and Sections 15 and 18 of the J.J. Act, 2015. In another judgment, where Hisar court has sentenced a juvenile to 20 years of rigorous imprisonment for raping and killing a six-year-old girl from Uklana in Hisar district.

Significantly, the J.J. Act, 2015 and the intention of the Parliament cannot be faulted and if implemented in letter and spirit, the law will be able to attain the objective of maintaining the balance between the society's need for protection from offences and the need of a child to have another chance. Courts sentencing a child offender should adhere to the spirit of the international conventions which emphasise on the importance of avoiding "criminalisation" of young people whilst also ensuring that they are held liable for their crimes. In the case of *Kakoo v. State of Andhra Pradesh,*[5] Justice Sarkaria, while reducing the punishment of a 13 year-old boy who has committed the rape of a girl of two years, observed as "an inordinate long imprisonment term is sure to turn Juvenile delinquent into obdurate criminal and laid an emphasis that in case of child offenders, current penological trends command a more humanitarian approach. It is pertinent to note that the children often come into the conflict with law by force of circumstances and not by choice. By providing good and favourable environment and giving suitable training and counseling, there is a possibility to reform their anti-social attitudes and to mould them into a responsible and contributing member of the society." At the last, it is important to note that the objective of juvenile justice legislation, in India, down the years has remained the same, irrespective of the legislation in force at the relevant time. In *Bhola Bhagat* v. *State of Bihar*[6], the Supreme Court states that in enacting the J.J. Act 1986, the effort of the legislature was "to reform the delinquent child and reclaim him as a useful member of the society."

The crucial issue in periphery of juvenile justice is the determination of age on which a person can be held liable for criminal act. Various Courts interpreted this provision differently, leading to utter confusion regarding the relevant date on which age could be determined. Some High Courts considered the date of commission of offence, some considered the date of registration of the F.I.R.

and some even went on to consider the date of arrest or the date of the child's production before the Juvenile Justice Board. This confusion was settled by the *Supreme Court in Pratap Singh* v. *State of Jharkhan*[7], and subsequently re-affirmed in *Hari Ram* v. *State of Rajasthan.*[8] In these cases, the Supreme Court held that the relevant date for determination of age is the "date of commission of offence", so far as it is concerned with a child alleged to have committed an offence. The judgment in Pratap Singh Case led to the amendment on this aspect in year 2006. The Juvenile Justice (Care and Protection of Children) Act, 2000 was therefore amended in 2006, by which the definition of juvenile in conflict with law was amended to reflect the judgment. After this amendment, the definition of juvenile in conflict with law in Section 2(l), was "juvenile in conflict with law means a juvenile who is alleged to have committed an offence and has not completed eighteenth year of age as on the date of commission of such offence." This position continues to be the same even under the J.J. Act, 2015.

Child offenders should be treated differently from adults, it has been also acknowledged on International platforms. The United States Supreme Court that "teenagers don't have fully development brains and that youths are less mature and not fully developed, and thus are less culpable."[9] It has been observed by the United States Supreme Court that "developments in psychology and brain science continue to show fundamental difference between juvenile and adults minds. In this respect to punish a juvenile, like an adult would result in excess punishment. This is the reason why it is now widely recognised that a child offender requires a different approach from that which would be adopted in relation to an adult criminal and underlines the need to have a differential sentencing policy for person below the age of 18 years whose cognitive faculties do not reach complete state of development even in the early twenties." The principal aim of differential sentencing of child offender is to prevent them from reoffending. Sentencing needs to show that the conduct of the child offender is not acceptable and should also address any other factors that may lead to reoffending in future. At the same time, the dispositional order passed on a child offender should also demonstrate the efficacy of criminal law and must restore the confidence of the society in rule of law.

In the international standards, the underlying premise for treating children and young people differently when they come into conflict with the law is that they are more susceptible to positive influence and more likely to change their behaviour compared to adults. The UN Committee on the Rights of the Child stated authoritatively in General Comment No. 10 as "in order to protect the best interests of the child, traditional objectives of criminal justice, such as repression/retribution, must give way to rehabilitation and restorative justice, and that this can be done in concert with attention to effective public safety." That is why a different parallel legislation has been made, and that resulted in the creation of a separate system, specifically meant for juvenile, namely, the juvenile justice system, to deal with children alleged or found to have committed offences. Children's Courts were set-up "for exercising the powers and discharging the duties conferred or imposed on such court in relation to delinquent children under this Act,"[10] and were empowered "to deal exclusively with all proceedings under this Act relating to...delinquent children."[11] Provisions of the Children Act, 1960 were incorporated under the J.J. Act, 1986. Juvenile Courts were established "for exercising the powers and discharging the duties conferred or imposed on such court in relation to juvenile delinquents under this Act",[12] and such Juvenile Courts were given the "power to deal exclusively with all proceedings under this Act relating to...delinquent juveniles".[13] Similar powers were given to JJBs under the J.J. Act 2000 -"power to deal exclusively with all proceedings under this Act relating to juvenile in conflict with law."[14] Provisions for exclusive dealing of juvenile cases by the Juvenile Justice System was strengthened with the insertion of sub-Section (4) to Section 1 of the J.J. Act, 2000.[15] However the J.J. Act 2000 was enacted for the protection of children this Act was amended twice in 2006 and again in 2011 to address gaps in its implementation and make the law more child friendly. Whereas, the increasing cases of crimes committed by the children between the age group of 16-18 years in recent years make it apparent that the existing provisions and system under the Juvenile Justice (Care and Protection of Children) Act, 2000 are not well equipped to tackle child offenders in this age group. The data provided by the national Crime Records Bureau shows that crimes by children between the age group of 16-18 years been augmented, especially in particular categories of serious and heinous offences. Therefore, numerous changes were required in the J.J. Act, 2000 to tackle the above mentioned issues and as consequence of that a comprehensive legislation came into force that is Juvenile Justice (Care and Protection of children) Act 2015. In all above mentioned Acts there was no categorisation of offences committed by the juveniles. In India as well as on International platform the right of every child is well recognised and advocated as that child offenders should be dealt differently from adults. "The right of the child alleged as, accused of, or recognised as recognised as having infringed the penal law must be treated in accordance with the provisions of article 40 of CRC". Therefore it is apparently clear that every person who is under the age of 18 years at the time of the commission of an offence must be treated as per the provisions of juvenile justice. [16] This well-entrenched practice of child offenders without exception being dealt with under the Juvenile Justice System, has been overturned by the J.J. Act, 2015, which allows the JJB discretion to exclude from the juvenile justice system, children above 16 years who have allegedly committed heinous offences.

The Juvenile Justice Act, 2015 legitimises the transfer of the juveniles who are above the age of 16 to adult courts, if the Juvenile Justice Board inferred that the level of maturity of the juvenile indicates that he committed the heinous offences as an adult and not as a child.[17] Such rationale for differential treatment of child embraces, a child criminal is the outcome of unfavourable environment and is entitled to a fresh chance under healthier surroundings.[18] Prospect of his reformation are fully expected.[19] The new Juvenile Justice system, which establishes a link between the gravity of the offence committed and the maturity of the child, defeats the objectives of juvenile justice law as it lets the crime overshadow the child.[20] The transfer mechanism envisaged by the 2015 Act is not in consonance to principles of constitutional law and international principles governing juvenile policy. Though a child committing a "heinous crimes" would require more intensive scrutiny, and ought not be treated similarly to children committing less serious crimes.

However, the analysis of statistical data available at official sites indicates increasing involvement of the juveniles in heinous crimes.

The closer scrutiny of NCRB Data reveals that this model would fail to deter juvenile offenders as presumed. Children constitute about 41 percent of India s total population[21] over 2462 juveniles, mostly between the age group of 16 to 18; have been arrested for crimes like rape and murder across Indian states in 2016, the highest in last decade. As many as 44171 such cases were recorded in 2016 as compared to 21088 cases in 2006.[22] The experience of various countries [23] has shown that "getting tough" with the young offenders like imprisoning them, the court-ordered sanctions, etc. will solve only short term problems by reducing juvenile crime rate and putting the young offenders "out of circulation" by institutionalising them. But these methods will not have a long-term effect and will defeat the very purpose of the Juvenile Justice System, which is, building capability of the young offender so as make him/ her self-reliant and valuable citizen of society.

Many justice systems around the globe the hold a perception that children who are serious offenders are beyond the reach of society and are not able to be reformed, doubt that children who has propensity to commit violence or sexual offences will be able to grow out of their behaviour and will continue to commit serious offences as adults. Dr Ved Kumari, in her book, *Justice System in India: From Welfare to Rights* (2010) mentioned, "When the nature of the crime is serious, the criminal justice system treats the child as monstrous and incapable of rehabilitation and therefore equates them to adults. This is described as the crime overshadowing the child, as the psychological, social and legal construction of childhood can be lost, understated, ignored or overshadowed by the notion of crime." Around the world, 58 countries practice harsher punishment and even death punishment to juveniles for heinous crimes.[24] This practice is absolutely banned by international human rights law as declared in the International Covenant on Civil and Political Rights (ICCPR), the U.N. Convention on the Rights of the Child, and the American Convention on Human Rights. The ICCPR was adopted by the United Nations General Assembly, and was ratified on March 23, 1976.

Article 6(5) of the treaty states: "Sentence of death shall not be imposed for crimes committed by persons below eighteen years of age." The ICCPR has 172 parties and six more signatories without ratification. As parties to the treaty, including the U.S., which ratified the Covenantion in 1992, but with certain reservations. The U.S. was one of three countries which took substantive reservations to Article 6 the others were Norway and Ireland. However, those reservations became silent, when death penalty was abolished by the Norway and Ireland. Subsequently, the U.S. Supreme Court declared the execution of juvenile offenders to be unconstitutional. In *Roper v. Simmons* in 2005 The United States Supreme Court observed that sentencing the death penalty on offenders who were below the age of 18 years at the time of the murder for which they were charged violates the Eighth Amendment. It is a violation of international law to sentence a person to death for a crime they committed before they turned 18.The acknowledgement of this ban is so universal that it is broadly recognised as a peremptory norm of customary international law. "The death penalty for juvenile offenders appears to have been abandoned by nations everywhere in large part due to the express provisions of the United Nations Convention on the Rights of the Child and of several other international treaties and agreements. Since 1990, juvenile offenders are known to have been executed in only eight countries: China, Democratic Republic of Congo, Iran, Pakistan, Yemen, Nigeria, Saudi Arabia, and the United States."

Significantly, it has been observed that from the global perspective the term juvenile justice includes, civil and political as well as economic, social and cultural justice. By implication, it refers to both, after onset of delinquency and before the onset of delinquency. To be more precise, the first one refers to the administration of juvenile justice by applying internationally accepted standards and norms and second refers to schemes and policies of the government to prevent the first incident of crime. However, the proper functioning of justice administration and welfare administration from one platform at the municipal level appears to be debatable. At the municipal level implementation of the binding international covenant is confronted with the problem of coordination, monitoring etc. apart from the constitutional limitation created by the principles of federalism.

The reports indicate that the juvenile who receive less familial supervision, or who live in dysfunctional family settings or in disadvantaged families have more chances of getting involved in delinquent behaviour. Juvenile delinquency is a problem which despite of different and varied cultural backgrounds is found with common characteristics universally. In a developing country like India, juvenile crimes are steadily rising due to the environment and social context that provokes his actions. The persistent poverty, unemployment, increasing population inequalities and changing values, etc. along with these factors there are some factors which are responsible for rising graph of delinquency, such as crimes shows that are shown on the television, media, adverse effects of peer pressure, family disintegration lavish lifestyle, too much freedom from the parents and social maladjustment. With changing societal trends, children now appear to possess strong likes and dislikes and also show expressions that indicate maturity at a very early age. These qualities also make children more vulnerable to the designs of the criminality such as abusers, peddlers, and traffickers. Moreover, the influence of the media on the psychosocial development of children is profound. With advent of communication technology in recent times, a child's exposure to media including television, radio, music, video games and the internet, has increased manifold. Various other reasons can be suggested for this rising graph of juvenile delinquency.

According to the psychiatrists and women right activists, easy access to pornography and changing food habits can be attributed as a cause for this change in behaviour of juveniles, who show rising involvement in sexual offences. It has been pointed out in the same discussion that the youngsters are not able to control their biological impulses prompted by hormonal changes. The weakening social ties at community, peer and family level in India is also a factor for this rising trend of juvenile crimes. The family as a basic unit of human society is specially getting weaker in urban areas, with lesser family control on children. The community networking and involvement in affairs of individual members has also become slack. Peers groups are becoming less active, with the youth mainly spending time indoors watching television, or playing games on mobiles or computer. The games involve lot of plots of violence, killing others etc, which instills violence as normal in the young minds. The mind of the youth is place where lot of information keeps gathering. There is no way to filter this information and tell the youth what information is correct or what is not. Further, these days children fewer options of venting out their frustration and negativities, leading to pent-up teenage aggression. Children have great potential to be rehabilitated and reintegrated back into their communities and that this can be the key to preventing juvenile offending from escalating into prolific adult offending. Children are at a stage in their development when beliefs, opinions and personalities are evolving and shifting. There is potential for them to be informed and moulded by rehabilitative and educational measures. Punitive measures, on the other hand, do nothing to address the root causes of offending, can arrest children's development, can blow them off course so that their life chances are diminished, and can lead to increased offending. Children should be treated differently from adults not for sentimental reasons, but because of their greater physical and psychological vulnerability and the fact that they are more open to influence and pressure from others. Recognising that children's crimes may stem from immature judgment and youthful vulnerability to error, impulse and influence, the court stated that exacting full moral accountability for a misdeed might be too harsh; the court should instead afford children "some leeway of hope and possibility". Conversely, it is found that a system focused on rehabilitation and social reintegration can help to reduce recidivism by seeking to address the underlying causes of a child's offending.

Children are supposed to symbol of powers, which are in need of double sided protection. On the one hand, they need to be provided with the basic necessities for their development, making them physically strong, mentally alert, academically brilliant by affording them, irrespective of their sex, family atmosphere for proper growing and grooming of the child. On another hand requires prevention and treatment of a child who is termed as delinquent.

7.2. Suggestions on the Basis of Findings

- The increasing number of crimes committed by children in the age group of 16-18 years makes it evident that the current provisions and system under the Juvenile Justice (Care and Protection of Children) Act, 2015, are not well equipped to tackle child offenders in this age-group. The National Crime Records Bureaus establishes that crimes by children in the age-group of 16-18 years have increased especially in particular type of heinous crimes but this data was based on number of FIRs registered and did not provide subsequent information of conviction. This is admitted fact that FIR/Complaint is just an information regarding occurrence of an offence. The increased reporting of crime against children in the specific age-group should not necessarily lead to assumption of increased conviction of juvenile in the crime. The realistic figure of involvement of juvenile in heinous crime needs to be based on completion of investigation, filling of filling report by the police before the court and pronouncement of judgment.

- Under new J.J. Act, 2015, reducing the age of criminal responsibility from 18 to 16 for heinous and embracing, the rape and kidnapping as heinous crimes lead to increase the number of crime of rape and kidnapping also raised a contention regarding the children who involved in consensual relationship with one other. As the young boy who involve into consent love affair would be charged for rape and kidnapping on the complaint by the girl or her angry parents. With the rising of consensual age to 18, it is but natural that there has been a rise in the rape cases registered, since 16-18 is the peak age for exploratory sex acts. So there is need of appropriate inquiry regarding the consent of the girl at the time of preliminary inquiry by board.

- It has been observed that Juvenile Justice System has suffered, due to lack of effective inter and inter-system coordination. Three main and interdependent power centers-the police, the magistracy and personnel involved in managing institutions, in effect pool their resources in ad hoc system of co-operation. They are governed by different agencies and instead of working in co-operation to achieve a common goal-justice to Juvenile-work at cross purpose. Hence, it is suggested that there must be an effective co-ordination among these agencies meant for achieving the goal of Justice to Juveniles.

- The police play a key role in Juvenile Justice System. It is found that the attitude of police towards Juvenile is totally unchanged. It applies the methods in dealing with children which it applies in case of adult offenders. Because these police officers also deal the cases of adults criminals and they are specially trained to handle the adult criminals. It is suggested that independent cadre of special juvenile police unit should be constituted, and normal police should not be included in this cadre. The state governments should be directed to establish a special juvenile police unit in every district and the unit must be specially instructed and trained in child psychology and child welfare.

- The Juvenile Justice (Care and Protection of Children) Act does not make any difference between a male and a female child. Such scheme of the Juvenile Justice Act, however, fails to take a note of the fact that the female juvenile being highly vulnerable is likely to be more comfortably and conveniently exploited and even abused adversely. Such a female juvenile needs special protection even at an observation home or at a place of safety. Notwithstanding the fact that voluntary social organisations may come forward to provide a place of safety. An inbuilt safety mechanism is required to be provided to such a female juvenile in the Act itself.

- There is no provision of providing legal aid under Juvenile Justice (Care and Protection of Children) Act. No assistance is provided by the lawyer to a juvenile facing a criminal charge before the Board. This is a serious loophole in the Act, which requires immediate attention.

- It is found that numbers of pending cases re increasing day by day in Juvenile Courts, which is against the interest of child. Hence, it is suggested that there must be speedy disposal of cases within the earliest possible period from the date of charge framed against the juveniles.

  There must be separate homes for juvenile in conflict with law and children in need of Homes should not be constructed like jails. The homes for children should be video linked to facilitate inspection and supervision by the Board so as to keep a check on anything done against the best interest of the child.

Also, surprise visits should be made at the special homes, and observation homes.

- It is observed that there is little awareness among the people about the Juvenile Justice System. The system lacks public cooperation and support. Hence it is suggested that a mass awareness programme should be carried on because without public cooperation and support no system including Juvenile Justice System be sustained.
- The state governments should be directed to establish a special juvenile police unit in and every district and the unit must be specially instructed and trained in child psychology, child welfare. The public prosecutors handling the cases should be sensitised and given training with the juvenile police.
- As soon as a juvenile in conflict with law is apprehended by the police he/she should be placed under the charge of the special juvenile police unit or the designated police officer.
- A time limit should be fixed for investigation. Juvenile police officers, who investigate the case, must submit the final form within 60 days or 90 days depending upon the nature of the offence from the date of complaint.
- A social worker may be associated in the investigation made by the police officer. In the child cell at least one lady police officer should be posted /appointed.
- The police department also plays a very important role in ensuring child protection. But, practically police officials are not aware about provisions of the J.J. Act. Hence, awareness programmes should be conducted at the police station level wherein Principal Magistrate and members of Juvenile Justice Board, members of child welfare committees and NGOs should also be involved.
- All stakeholders must follow the International Principles on Child Rights and a relevant judicial system. The Principle of the best interest of the child should dominate all other aspects. Children should be allowed to exercise their rights to be heard and their view should be given voltage according to their age

and maturity. There should not be any discrimination of children on the basis of gender, caste, race, nationality, language, age, and status including disability.

- The Juvenile Justice System must be child considerate and it should include: (1) A comprehensive and unambiguous laws which reflect rights of the child, (2) Incorporates procedure for dealing with children in conflict with the law and children in need of care and protection without following the strict procedures. (3) The facilities for access to advice, information, counseling and support (legal and otherwise.

- All set up should endeavour to provide a child friendly environment and should be staffed by personnel having knowledge of legislation and procedure specific to children. The personnel should further be trained and skilled on effective interaction with the children, such an arrangement would meet the specific needs of children.

- All actors of justice including magistrate, prosecutors, police, social welfare officers, probation officers, superintendent of observation homes should be provided joint training so as to ensure co-ordination and co-operation of local government to make the judicial system more sensitive the rights of the child should be incorporated in the training of the justice sector on human rights.

- It is highly desirable that all the actors of justice should have a basic knowledge of law relating to children. Module of law relating to children should be incorporated in the course of LL.B. and B.A.LL.B. Degree professions should be provided with pre-service training having a child specific module as a mandatory course.

- Specialised juvenile prosecutors should be trained for dealing with the cases relating to children and violation of child rights. Juvenile Justice Laws, standards, operating procedures and guidance, social and psychological aspects of delinquent children, child development techniques should be incorporated in the module of training.

- In accordance with the international standards, a separate court system should be established to deal with the cases of child in conflict with the law. Along with the establishment of a separate judicial system, it should also be ensured that children are dealt and tried separately from adults in a child friendly environment.
- Appropriate Scheme for reformation and rehabilitation of convicted children should be formulated and implemented so that after releasing from detention, they can live a meaningful life in society by earning their livelihood.

On the basis of above discussion we can say that we have very good juvenile justice system but there is lack of cooperation among different bodies functioning under juvenile justice system. Fragmentation occurred at the implementation level because these bodies work and regulated under different ministries and departments. Due attention should be given to the need of coordinated and collaborative efforts of all concerned. The person related with juvenile justice system at various levels are unaware of concept, law and philosophy of juvenile justice system and this includes lawyers and judicial officers too. The laws enacted require to be effectively implemented to achieve the desired goal of welfare of the children. The society must encourage children's participation in matters affecting their rights as services to the children are no longer a charity. The judiciary has played an appreciable role and contributed a lot in proper and beneficial implementation of the juvenile justice legislation by interpreting the provisions of Juvenile Justice Acts so as to provide maximum benefit and relief to the maximum number of the juveniles covered under the beneficial and favourable legislation. A good intended legislation, properly and sincerely implemented and visionary interpreted, can significantly reverse the crime trends in the juveniles.

REFERENCES

1. Section 5(iii), Hindu Marriage Act, 1955.
2. (2000) 7 SCC 455.
3. http://timesofindia.indiatimes/city/indore/hc-juvenile-conviction-appeal/articleshow/58172510.cms.

4. Juvenile Justice (Care and Protection) Act, 2015.
5. AIR 1976 SC 1991.
6. (1997) 8 SCC 720: 1998 CrLJ 390: AIR 1998 SC 236.
7. (2005) 3 SCC 551.
8. (2009) 13 SCC 211.
9. Graham v. Florida, 120 S Ct. 2001 (2010); Roper v. Simmons, 543U.S.551 (2005).g41
10. Children Act, 1960, Section 5(1).
11. Children Act, 1960, Section 7(1).
12. J.J. Act, 1986, Section 5(1).
13. J.J. Act, 1986, Section 7(1).
14. J.J. Act, 2000, Section 6(1).
15. By The Juvenile Justice (Care and Protection of Children) Amendment Act, 2006.
16. Clause 37.
17. The Juvenile Justice (Care and Protection of Children) Act, 2015, section 19.
18. Report of the Indian Jail Committee, 1919-20 available at https://archive.org/details/eastindiajailsco01indi.
19. *Ibid.*
20. https://www.firstpost.com/india/latest-census-data.
21. NCRB data 2016 published on August 2017.
22. Supra note 1 at 1-24.

References

BOOKS:

A.K. (1955). The Delinquent Boys Glencoe, The Free Press Crime in India. (2014).

Adenwalla, M., Child Protection and Juvenile Justice System for Juvenile in conflict with the law. Childline India Foundation Mumbai, 2006.

Adenwalla, Maharukh, 2006. Child Protection and Juvenile Justice Sysyem: for Juvenile in Conflict with Law, 13, Childline India Foundation.

Allen Reed, Ben, Fitzpatrick and Peter Seago. Criminal law, 3rd edn. 2006, Sweet and Maxwell, London.

Alok Kumar, A.P The Problem of Child Sexual Abuse in India Laws, Legal Lacuna and the Bill – PCSOB-2011. J Indian Acad Forensic Med, pp. 170, 2012.

Attar, A.D., Juvenile Delinquency -A comparative Study, Bombay, Popular Prakashan,1964.

Babu, S. 2007. Social Justice and Labour Jurisprudence: Justice V.R. Krishna Iyers. Sage Publication Inc. Bainham, A, 1998.

Bajpai, A Child Rights in India-Law, Policy and Practice, Oxford University Press, New Delhi, 2003.

Bandura, A. and Walters, R.H. Adolescent Aggression. New York 1989.

Basu, D.D. Shorter Constitution of India, 12th Edition, Published by Prentice – Hall of India Private Limited, M-97, New Delhi, 2007.

Basu, N. Juvenile delinquency : Social defense through adult education. Social Defense, 1984.

Baxi, U. The Indian Supreme Court and Indian Politics, Eastern Book Company, Lucknow, 1980.

Bernd-Dieter Meier and Abhijit D. Vasmatkar. Juvenile Justice in Different Cultural Contexts: A Comparison of India and Germany. Journal of International Criminal Law Doctrine, 2011.

Bhattacharya, S K. (2000). Juvenile Justice: An Indian Scenario, New Delhi, Regency Publications.

BRANDT, David (2006). Delinquency, Development, and Social Policy. London, Yale University Press.

C. Trinidad and B. Torre. Seeds of Hope: Learning from Programmes for CICL of Cordaid Pertner Organisations (Cordaid, 2011).

Children -The Modern Law, 2nd Edition.

Choudhary, R. N. (2005). Law relating of juvenile justice in India. Allahabad, Orient Publishing Company.

Clayton A. Hartjen, S. Priyadarsini. Delinquency in India: A Comparative Analysis, Rutgers University Press 2009.

Cloward, R. and Ohlin, L. (1960). Delinquency and Opportunity. NY: Free Press Cohen.

Clyde B. Vedder and Dora B. Somerville. The Delinquent Girl, USA, Charles C. Thomas, 154 pp, 1973 and 1975.

David, C. Brody, JD. Criminal Law, Jones and Bartlett Publishers, Canada.

Donna M. Bishop and Scott H. Decker. "Punishment and Control: Juvenile Justice Reform in the USA", in Josine Junger and Scott H. Decker, International Handbook of Juvenile Justice, Springer, 2008.

Elizabeth Scott and Laurence Steinberg, Rethinking Juvenile Justice 270 (Harvard University Press, Cambridge, 2008).

Federico Ferrara and Valentina Ferrara. The Children's Prison: Street Children and Indias Juvenile Justice System 2005.

Frankling E. Zimering. American Juvenile Justice, Oxford University Press, New York, 2005.

Frankling, E. Zimring. American Juvenile Justice, Oxford University Press, New York, 2005.

Grayson, N. Holmbeck. "Adolescenc," in V.S Ramachandran (ed.), I Encyclopedia of Human Behaviour 17 (Academic Press, San Diego, 1994).

Handbook for Advocates working with Child in Conflict with law in India, Centre for Child and the Law (CCL) National Law School of India University (NLSIU), Bangalore, 2018.

Ian Brownlie and Guy S. Goodwin-Gill. Basic Documents on Human Rights, pp. 23-28 Oxford University Press, 5 edn., 2010.

Janet Dine *et al.*, Cases and Materials on Criminal Law; Oxford University Press, New York, 5th edn, 2006.

Jean, Paiget. The Construction of reality in the Child (Basic books New York, 1954).

John, A. Winterdk. Juvenile Justice International Perspectives, Model, and Trends, CRC Press, UK 2015.

Juvenile Delinquency by K. Padmaja.

Kevin Hile. Trail of Juvenile as Adults: Point – Canter point 26-35 (Chelsea House Publishers, Philadelphia, 2003).

Laurence Steinberg. "Adolescent Development and Juvenile Justice," 16(3), The Development of Clinical Psychology, 55 (2008).

Lawrence Steinberg, Deborah Lowe Vandell, *et al.*, Development: Infancy Through Adolescence (Engage Learning, Belmont, CA, 2011) Eva.

Manish Dwivedi 2011. Juvenile Justice System in India, Adhyayan Publisher

McDowell, Gary L., Smith, Jinney (eds). Juvenile Delinquency in the United States and the United Kingdom, 1999.

Michel Burmam. "The End of Era?-Youth Justice In Scotland" in Josine Junger–Tas and Scott. Decker, International Handbook of Juvenile Justice, Springer, 2008.

P. Cane. Responsibility in Law and Morality, 2002, Hart Publishing, Oxford.

Ronald. Bartollas, C. and Millor. The Juvenile Offender Central, Correction and Treatment 1997.

Russel, Heaton. Criminal law, Oxford University Press, New York, 2nd edition, 2006.

Ruth, Shonle Cavan Theodore N. Ferdinand. Juvenile Delinquency (III Edition).

Suman Nalwa and Hari Dev Kohli. Commentary on The Juvenile Justice Act, Second edition, Universal Publication, New Delhi.

The Apprentices Act, New Delhi, Publication Division, 1850.

The Reformatory School, New Delhi, Publication Division, 1876. Hansaria.

Tim, Burn. Youth crime and youth culture in Mike Maguire et.al. (eds.), The Oxford Handbook of Criminology, 4th edition, 2007; Oxford University Press, New York.

V and Jose P. Juvenile Justice System, Delhi. Universal Law Publishing Company Pvt. Ltd. (2011).

Ved Kumari. The Juvenile Justice (Care and Protection) Act 2015: Critical Analyses, 2017, Lexis Nexis Publication, Gurgaon, Haryana.

Ved Kumari, 2004. The Juvenile Justice System in India: From Welfare to Rights (Law in India) Oxford University Press, USA; 1st Edition edition.

William Damon (ed). Handbook of Child Psychology 217-220, John Wiley and Sons, New York, Fifth Edition

Williams, K. S. "Criminology", U.K., Oxford University Press. 2012.

LEGISLATIVE LAWS

Apprentices Act 1850.

Bombay Children Act, 1948.

Code of Criminal Procedure (Amendment) Act 2013(Nirbhaya Act) Indian Penal Code, 1860.

Juvenile Justice Act 1986.

Reformatory School Act, 1897. The Children Act, 1960.

The Juvenile Justice (Care and Protection of Children) Act, 2015. The Juvenile Justice (Care and Protection) Act, 2000.

The Juvenile Justice (Care and Protection) Act, 2016 United Nations Convention on Rights of Child, 1989.

POLICIES, REPORTS AND RESEARCHES

Foundation Research Network on Adolescent Development and juvenile justice, MacArther. (2006, September) Network overview: "A century of change in juvenile justice" (p. 2) Philadelphia.

Hybrid Medical Animation, "Cruel and Unusual Punishment: The Juvenile Death Penalty," American Bar Association 1 (2004).

Justice Verma Committee Report, 2013, http://www.nls.ac.in/ccl/cclpositionpaper.pdf..

Juvenile Delinquency. (2003) World Youth Report.

Legislative Research: Juvenile Justice (Care and Protection of Children) Bill, 2014, available at http://www.prsindia. org/uploads/ media/ Juvenile percent 20Justice/Legislative

National Crime Records Bureau (2014). Crime in India: 2014, available at http://ncrb.nic.in/index.htm

National Crime Records Bureau (2014). Crime in India: 2014, available at http://ncrb.nic.in/index.htm (last accessed February 22, 2016).

National Crime Records Bureau, Ministry of Home Affairs, Government of India, New Delhi. Crimes in India, National Crimes Record Bureau, Ministry of Home Affairs, 2015.

Rajya Sabha Debates (2015, December 22). Debate on Juvenile Justice Bill, available at http://164.100.47.5/ new deb ate/237/ 22122015/

Report of the Indian Jail Committee 1889, April 1889.

The Criminal Law (Amendment) Act, 2013, available at http://india code.nic.in/acts-in-pdf/132013.pdf (last accessed February 13, 2016.

The Gazette of India (2013, April 2).

The Gazette of India (2016, January 1). Juvenile Justice (Care and Protection of Children) Act, 2015, available at http://wcd.nic.in/ sites/default/files/JJ percent 20Act, percent 202015 percent 20_0.

NEWS PAPERS, ARTICLES, JOURNALS AND MAGAZINES

Behavioural Science and Law, Vol.18(2000) Rechard E. Redding. "Adult punishment for juvenile offender, Does it Reduce Crime?" in K. Padmaja (ed.), Juvenile Delinquency, (The ICFAI University, India, 1st edition, 2007).

"Rise of Juvenile Crimes: Time to Recheck Social Moral Fiber". PEOPLE: International Journal of Social Sciences ISSN 2454-5899 © 2018

A.W.G. Kean, "The history of criminal liability of children", Law Quarterly Review 364, 1937.

American Bar Association, Ruban C. Gur, "Declaration of Ruben C. Gur", P.H.D.15(2016).

Amnesty International, "Somalia: Halt execution spree of children in Puntland," April 28, 2017.

Antej Du Bois-Pedai. "Once a sex offender, always a reoffending risk?" Cambridge Law Journal 428, 2010.

Ashok Nigam. "Its time to amend juvenile justice Act", Times of India, Apr. 29, 2013.

B.B. Pandey, "Justice cannot follow a tough act", The Hindu, Sept. 24, 2013.

Catherine Elliott. "Criminal responsibility and children: a new defence required to acknowledge the absence of capacity and choice", Journal of Criminal Law 289, 2011.

Chung, Le Hen and Lawrence Steinberg. "Relations Between Neighborhood Factors, Parenting Behaviour, Peer Deviance and Delinquency Among Juvenile Offenders". Development Psychology. March, 42 (2): (2006). https://doi.org/10.1037/0012-1649.42.2.319.

David S Thanenhaus. "Juvenile Justice in the making", Oxford University Press, New York. 2004.

Devdutta Mukherjee. "Juvenile justice system in India: Do we really care?" available at www.mightylaw.in

Dey, Mousumi. Juvenile Justice in India. International Journal of Interdisciplinary and Multidisciplinary Studies. 1 (6), 2014: Available online at http://www.ijims.com

Douglas Davies, "Introduction: Raising the Issues," in Jean Holm and Jhon Bowker (eds.), Rites of Passage 1-9, printer Publishers, London, 1st edition, 1994.

Dr. K. A. Pandey. "Brain Science, Juvenile Justice (Care and Protection of Children) Act, 2015: A Critique," 7 7 RMLNLU J (2015).

Dr. Mohammed Saheb Hussain and Clement Mashamba, "Protection of the rights of children in conflict with the law; A human right prospective."(2012) 3 SCC 1.

Dr.K. A. Pandey, E-Pathshala Available at http://epgp.inflibnet.ac.in/index.php (Visited on Jan 12, 2018).

Ghosh, Dwaipayan. "100 Juveniles Booked for Murder, 63 Held for Rape", *The Times of India*. June 14, p. 4 (2013).

Haveripet, Rakesh. "Causes and Consequences of Juvenile Delinquency in India". Recent Research in Science and Technology. 5 (3), 2013.

Hirschi, Travis and Michael Gottfredson. "Age and the Explanation of Crime. The American Journal of Sociology", 89 (3), (1983). https://doi.org/10.1086/227905

Human Rights Watch, "The difference between youth and Adults" October, 2005.

J. Sprott, "Understanding the public Opposition to a Separate Youth Justice System" 44 CAD 399, 1998.

Jerome Ballet, Mario Biggeri, *et al.*, Children's Agency and the Capability Approach: A conceptual Framework" in Mario Biggeri Jerome Ballet, *et al.* (eds.), children and the Capability Approach 22-40, Palgrave Macmillan, New York, 2011.

Juvenile Delinquency on the Rise. People: International Journal of Social Sciences ISSN 2454-5899, © The author and GRDS Publishing 2018.

"Juvenile Justice Systems in United States and India: Modern Scenario and Much Needed Modifications", Journal of Law and Criminal Justice Government of India.

Knoester, Chris and Dana L. Haynie. Community Context, Social Integration into Family, and Youth Violence. Journal of Marriage and Family 67 (3): (2005) https://doi.org/10.1111/j.1741-3737.2005.00168.x

Mahrukh Adenwala, "A dislocation of the juvenile justice system," The Wire (The Wire May 23, 2015).

Maruf, Mohammad Muntasir, Farzana Rhaman *et al.* "Socio-Demography, Substance Abuse and Offence Among Inmates with Psychiatric Disorder in Female Juvenile Center, Bangladesh", 2015

Miller, Walter B. Lower Class Sub-culture as a Generating Mileu of Gang Delinquency. Journal of Social Issues, 14, 1958.

Muzaffar Hussain Mir. "Age of Criminal Responsibility and The Child Criminal Justice: Imperatives of Developmental Model of Juvenile Justice For India," Vol. 2. Jamia Law Journal, 2017.

Ombato, John Onyango, Gerald O. Ondick *et al.* (2013). "Factors Influencing Youth Crime". International Journal of Research in Social Sciences. March, 1 (2): 18-21.

Rao, Mohit M. and Vidya Krishnan. "Neuroscience and the Juvenile Legislation" The Hindu, available at http://

www.thehindu.com/ opinion/ neuroscience-and-the-juvenile-legislation/article

Rao, Shakuntala. "Covering Rape in Shame Culture: Studying Journalism Ethics in India's New Television", News Media, 29 (3), (2014).

Ren, Ling, Hangowel Zhang *et al.* "Delinquent Subculture and Juvenile Offenders Attitudes Towards Police in China". Police Quarterly. 19 (1).

Singh, S. Delhi Gang Rape: Case Diary. *The Times of India*, 2013, September 13. available at http://timesofindia. indiatimes. com/india/Delhi-gang-rape-Case-diary/articleshow/ 22455125.cms

Tyagi, Malvika. "Analysis of Juvenile Crime", Economic and Political Weekly, 51 (51): 2016.

Victoria Stachon. "The principle of punishment applied to children with in the juvenile justice system." UCL Jurisprudence Review 53, 2007.

Vincent Tinto. "Stages of Student Departure: Reflections on the longitudinal Character of Student Leaving" 59 THE 438(1988).

Yogesh Snehi. "State and Child Justice: Stories of Delinquent Juveniles" in Economic and Political Weekly, Vol. 39, No. 41, 9 October 2004.

WEBSITES

.ncpcr.gov.in/

http://www.academia.edu/documents/in.juvenile _justice http:// www.childrensright.org/

http://www.home.heinonline.org/

http://www.humanrights.gov.au/publications/what-universal-declaration-human-rights

http://www.justor.com

http://www.manupatra.com http://www.ncrb.gov.in

http://www.nhrc.nic.in http://www.unicef.org

http://wwwoxfordschlor.com/view/ 10.1093/acprof:oso/

https://reprive.org.uk/press/globle-execution-2016

https://www.researchgate.net/publication/299460528_Juvenile_Justice

_Care_and_Protection_of_Children_Act_2015_A_Review: www.org/news/2010/10/08/iran-saudi-arabia

Annexure

Dr. Ram Manohar Lohiya National Law University, Lucknow

Interview Guide / Questionnaire for Stake Holders

(The information shall be kept strictly confidential and shall be used only for the purpose of Ph.D.)

1. Respondent's Age
   a. 12 -18 years
   b. 19-30 years
   c. 31 – 45 years
   d. 46 – 60 years
   e. above 60 years
2. Profession
   a. Student
   b. Self-employed
   c. Service
   d. Home maker
   e. Retired
3. Education
   a. Under high school
   b. High school
   c. Graduate
   d. Post graduate
4. Sex
   a. Male
   b. Female

5. Do you know what juvenile justice is?
   a. yes
   b. no
   c. can't say
   d. other
   e. Please specify, if answer is yes..............

6. Do you think that number of children coming in conflict with law is increasing day by day?
   a. yes
   b. no
   c. can't say
   d. other

7. Have you heard about any child in conflict with law (child offender)?
   a. yes
   b. no
   c. can't say
   d. other

8. Who is a child?
   a. person below age of 07 years
   b. person below age of 12 years
   c. person below age of 16 years
   d. person below age of 18 years

9. At what age a person should make criminally liable (age of criminal responsibility)?
   a. Person above age of 7 years
   b. Person above age of 12 years
   c. Person above age of 16 years
   d. Person above age of 18 years

10. What is the cause for a child coming into conflict with law (leaned towards criminal activities)?
    a. parental neglect
    b. poverty
    c. poor education
    d. other

11. Do you think children alleged to be in conflict with law become a problem of societal security?
    a. yes
    b. no
    c. can't say
    d. other

12. Do you think that children alleged to be involved in crime should be punished for their crime same as adults?
    a. yes
    b. no
    c. can't say
    d. other

13. Do you think that a child should be punished for very serious crime same as adult?
    a. yes
    b. no
    c. can't say
    d. other

14. Do you agree that child alleged to be in conflict with law (apprehended for committing a crime) should be placed in police lock up?
    a. yes
    b. no
    c. can't say
    d. other
    e. Please specify if answer is yes................................

15. Do you agree that there should be a joint proceedings of a child alleged to be in conflict with law with a person who is not a child and the child committeed crime in his association?
    a. yes
    b. no
    c. can't say
    d. other
    e. Please specify if answer is yes.............................

16. Do you agree that when a child alleged to have committed a non-bailable offence is apprehended or detained by the police, he should be release on bail?
    a. yes
    b. no
    c. can't say
    d. other

17. Do you think that minor should be treated same as adult for criminal responsibility if he completes 18 years during pendency of case?
    a. yes
    b. no
    c. can't
    d. other

18. Do you agree that when a child, who has been found to have committed a heinous offence, attains the age of twenty one years and is yet to complete prescribed term of stay in a place of safety, should be sent to adult prison?
    a. yes
    b. no
    c. can't say
    d. other

19 Do you agree that children should be sentenced to death or for life imprisonment without the possibility of release for very serious offences?

a. yes
b. no
c. can't say
d. other (please specify).........

20 Do you think that children should be given special exemption from criminal responsibility?

a. yes
b. no
c. can't say
d. other (please specify).........

21 Do you think that reducing the age of criminal responsibility can help in curing the child delinquency (child coming into conflict with law) problem?

a. yes
b. no
c. can't say
d. other (please specify).........

22 What do you think leads children to commit crime?

a. neglected by parents/society
b. poverty
c. lack of education
d. drugs
e. internet
f. other (please specify).........

23 Do you think that children who are involved in criminal activities may be reformed?

a. yes
b. no

c. can't say

d. other

24 Do you think that most children in conflict with law are trapped and used by adult criminals for their own benefit?

a. yes

b. no

c. can't say

d. other

25 As per your opinion what would be the best way to reform children in conflict with law?

a. Rehabilitation and social re-integration

b. Skill development and recreational activities

c. counseling therapy

d. school programme

e. other

Index

R

S